JOKOWI
AND THE NEW INDONESIA

JOKOWI
AND THE NEW INDONESIA
A Political Biography

Darmawan Prasodjo
Tim Hannigan

TUTTLE Publishing
Tokyo | Rutland, Vermont | Singapore

"Books to Span the East and West"

Tuttle Publishing was founded in 1832 in the small New England town of Rutland, Vermont [USA]. Our core values remain as strong today as they were then—to publish best-in-class books which bring people together one page at a time. In 1948, we established a publishing office in Japan—and Tuttle is now a leader in publishing English-language books about the arts, languages and cultures of Asia. The world has become a much smaller place today and Asia's economic and cultural influence has grown. Yet the need for meaningful dialogue and information about this diverse region has never been greater. Over the past seven decades, Tuttle has published thousands of books on subjects ranging from martial arts and paper crafts to language learning and literature—and our talented authors, illustrators, designers and photographers have won many prestigious awards. We welcome you to explore the wealth of information available on Asia at **www.tuttlepublishing.com**.

Published by Tuttle Publishing, an imprint of Periplus Editions (HK) Ltd.

www.tuttlepublishing.com

Copyright © 2021 Darmawan Prasodjo

Library of Congress Control Number in process

ISBN 978-0-8048-5417-7

24 23 22 21   5 4 3 2 1   2110VP

Printed in Malaysia

Distributed by:

North America, Latin America & Europe
Tuttle Publishing
364 Innovation Drive
North Clarendon
VT 05759 9436, USA
info@tuttlepublishing.com
www.tuttlepublishing.com

Asia Pacific
Berkeley Books Pte Ltd
3 Kallang Sector #04-01
Singapore 349278
inquiries@periplus.com.sg
www.tuttlepublishing.com

Indonesia
PT Java Books Indonesia
Jl. Rawa Gelam IV No. 9
Kawasan Industri Pulogadung
Jakarta 13930, Indonesia
crm@periplus.co.id
www.periplus.com

Contents

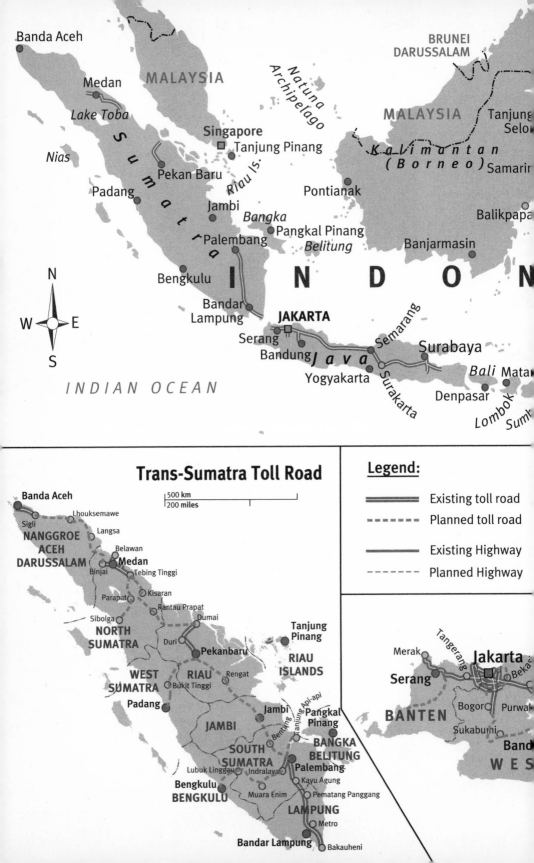

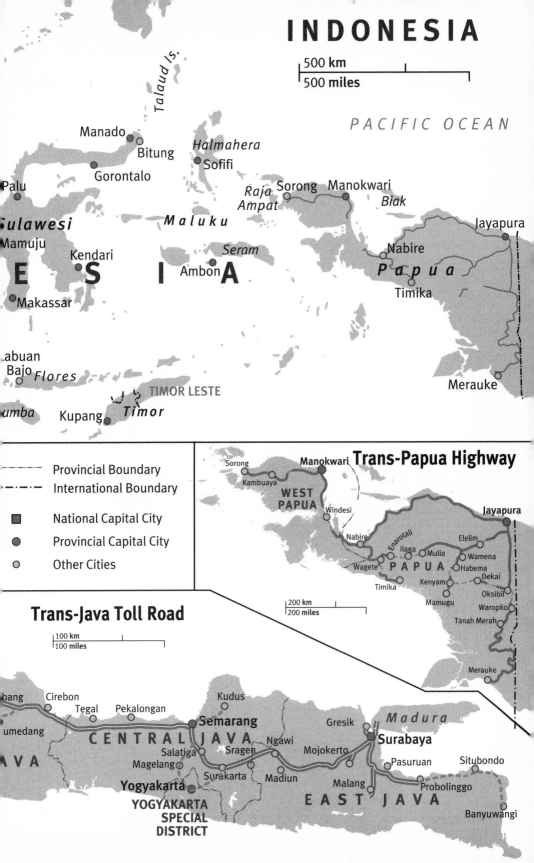

INDONESIA

500 km
500 miles

PACIFIC OCEAN

Talaud Is.

Manado
Bitung
Gorontalo
Palu
Sulawesi
Mamuju
Kendari
Makassar

Halmahera
Sofifi

Maluku

Ambon
Seram

E   S   I   A

Raja Ampat
Sorong
Manokwari
Biak

Jayapura

Nabire

Papua

Timika

Merauke

abuan
Bajo *Flores*
umba
Kupang
Timor
TIMOR LESTE

Trans-Papua Highway

Sorong
Kambuaya
Manokwari
WEST PAPUA
Windesi
Nabire
Wagete
Enarotali
Ilaga
Mulia
Elelim
Wamena
Habema
Dekai
P A P U A
Timika
Kenyam
Mamugu
Oksibil
Waropko
Tanah Merah
Jayapura

Merauke

200 km
200 miles

Provincial Boundary

International Boundary

National Capital City

Provincial Capital City

Other Cities

Trans-Java Toll Road

100 km
100 miles

bang
Cirebon
Tegal
Pekalongan
umedang
C E N T R A L   J A V A
Kudus
Semarang
Salatiga
Magelang
Surakarta
Sragen
Ngawi
Madiun
Mojokerto
Gresik
Madura
Surabaya
Pasuruan
Malang
Probolinggo
Situbondo
Banyuwangi
E A S T   J A V A
Yogyakarta
YOGYAKARTA SPECIAL DISTRICT
AVA

Jokowi (then the Governor of Jakarta and a presidential candidate) and the author, Darmawan Prasodjo, on an aeroplane flying to Manado for one of the campaign rallies for presidency, 2014.

Introduction
The Man for the Moment

On a hot October morning in 2014, Joko Widodo became the seventh president of the world's third largest democracy. As he swore his presidential oath, he was taking the helm of the huge and complex Indonesian nation, a fifty-three-year-old political outsider now in supreme command of one of Asia's largest economies.

Standing in the great space of the Sidang Paripurna I Room in the parliamentary complex in Jakarta, backed by a vast image of the Garuda Pancasila, the emblem of Indonesia, and facing a sea of parliamentarians, state officials, and national and international dignitaries, he appeared a small, almost fragile figure. And to be sure, Jokowi, as he is popularly known, was facing a daunting array of fierce challenges and powerful political contradictions. But when he stepped forward to call for togetherness and an ethos of "work, work, work," he spoke with force and conviction, belying his mild-mannered and easy-going reputation. There were unexecuted plans and unrealized dreams to be addressed. And already his own mind was moving rapidly through the countless items on his very long presidential to-do list.

For the millions watching the live broadcasts of the inauguration around the country, from the northernmost tip of Sumatra to the eastern marches of Papua, this was a moment of renewed optimism on Indonesia's democratic journey. The recent election campaign had been hard-fought, and at times divisive. But the man who had won through in the end felt like something genuinely fresh in an often stale political system. Sixteen years on from the end of the long-running New Order regime and the beginning of Indonesia's period of democratization and reform, here, for the first time, was a president who was not from the established political elite, was not a former general or a scion of a political dynasty, and who had risen, it seemed, entirely on his own merit, from self-made entrepreneur to hometown mayor to governor of Jakarta to the very highest office in the land in the space of a single decade. That meteoric ascent plainly spoke of some very special qualities; but perhaps the most important quality of all for millions upon millions of Indonesians was that this was a leader who seemed to be "just like the rest of us." For some of those watching the inauguration, this was the moment at which Indonesian democracy truly came of age.

But Jokowi himself was not concerned with the symbolism of his own election. He was concerned only with those things around which he had themed his inaugural speech: mutual cooperation, and work, work, work. And there was much of it to be done if he was to lead the process of forging a new Indonesia.

As Indonesia's seventh president, Jokowi inherited a formidable portfolio of problems, many of them deeply entrenched. Perhaps the most obvious was that of infrastructure. Despite years of strong economic growth,

President Jokowi (far right), accompanied by Minister of State Secretary Pratikno and the author, at an event in Bogor Palace, 2019.

Indonesia still lagged badly behind many of its neighbors when it came to hard infrastructure. Expansion of modern toll road networks had been agonizingly sluggish; investment in the railways was severely lacking; and airports, the essential nodes of interisland travel in a vast archipelagic nation, were often inadequate and outdated. The infrastructure deficit contributed, in turn, to a much bigger issue: the severe developmental skew towards Java. In any country, the region that is home to the biggest cities and the largest portion of the population will tend to attract the bulk of the investment. But Indonesia's vast size and island geography has exacerbated the problem over many decades, creating an extreme economic imbalance. While Jakarta and the other urban centers of Java offer all the economic opportunities of twenty-first-century Asia, in other parts of the country progress has at times seemed permanently stalled.

Where well-established pockets of regional prosperity exist, they have often been tied to the exploitation of natural resources. But here, too, there have been persistent failings in the lack of meaningful and equitable local benefits created by resource wealth. There is also the peculiarity, seldom remarked until the Jokowi era, of Indonesia's lack of attention paid to the sea. This is a nation of thousands of islands which nonetheless has traditionally been dominated by an agrarian paradigm which, in turn, has further exacerbated the Java-centric economic imbalance. There were myriad specific issues facing the new president, too: development projects

Jokowi (then the Governor of Jakarta and a presidential candidate), flanked by Ganjar Pranowo (in white; then the Governor of Central Jawa) and the author, at an informal event in Yogyakarta, 2014.

planned by previous administrations which had never been completed; the massive financial burden of an outdated fuel subsidy system which Jokowi's predecessors had baulked at reforming out of political expediency; and much more besides.

All of this fed into the great social conundrum, one especially pressing for a vast developing nation like Indonesia: structural poverty. For all the formidable economic progress and the vast amounts of wealth generated in Jakarta and other big cities, there have always been millions upon millions of Indonesians whose prospects are severely limited, not by any innate internal factors but by inadequate educational provision, limited access to healthcare, and a lack of basic local infrastructure, from irrigation and electricity supplies to decent roads and modern market facilities, or simply by the fact of having been born somewhere other than Java.

These were the challenges facing Indonesia in 2014. Any given moment in a nation's history demands a leader with particular qualities and characteristics, and Jokowi was surely a man amply matched to Indonesia's moment, a decade and a half into the twenty-first century. His business background had made him a natural problem solver. On the factory floor or in the export sector, challenges must be tackled swiftly, deftly, and if the solution is not immediately obvious, creatively. Unlike in the political sphere, if issues are left unaddressed, plans unrealized, projects unfinished from year to year through inertia, lack of will, or absence of imagination, the business will collapse outright. Jokowi had come to politics late, bringing with him the essential agility and problem-solving skills forged during a successful entrepreneurial career. Before becoming president, and before his brief stint governing Jakarta, he had been twice elected mayor of the Central Java city of Surakarta, the town in which he had been born and had lived for most of his life. In that role, he proved to be the absolute antithesis of the cliched image of the corrupt and ineffectual provincial politician. He roundly shook up the city, brought about tangible transformations in infrastructure, and instigated progressive social policies. Moving onto the governorship of Jakarta in 2012, he brought the same approach to bear on the larger and more complex city, fixing things that were broken, creating things that were missing, and picking up unfinished projects that had been neglected for years as too complicated or too costly. And he would take the same approach to the far greater challenges of the presidency.

But beyond the practical drive of the successful local entrepreneur, Jokowi also brought to the presidency a new philosophy of fairness and social justice, forged by his own distinctive life experience, a life experience that had encompassed poverty and prosperity, time spent in contrasting rural and urban environments, personal and professional setbacks and successes. It is this combination of problem solving, creativity, and concern for social justice that has set the tone and the agenda of the Jokowi presidency, and maintained its abiding theme of structural reform in the face of many setbacks and roadblocks. This book tells the story of that presidency, of the man at its heart, and of his unique moment in Indonesian history.

Since Jokowi's first national election victory in 2014 (he went on to win again, against the same rival, in 2019), English-language commentaries on this, the seventh president of the Republic of Indonesia, have often had a curious opacity. This is partly down to Jokowi's own characteristics and political priorities. Unlike his predecessor, Susilo Bambang Yudhoyono, he is not an entirely fluent English speaker. With his talent for engagement at a personal level, he is well able to charm visiting dignitaries and journalists but he is unlikely to be found partaking in cerebral English-language conversation about global issues or the state of the nation. His serious international media interviews, when they take place, are generally done through a translator. Also, unlike his predecessor, he is not particularly enamored of the international summit circuit, and is less directly involved in projecting Indonesia's image abroad. Jokowi is a driven, practically minded man, whose own people are the audience that matters to him most. He came to power with a seriously ambitious domestic agenda, and that, quite naturally, has been his overwhelming priority throughout. What is more, Jokowi as he appears to 270 million Indonesians does not translate particularly effectively for an international audience, either in his language or in his persona. He is not a natural orator in the formidable tradition of Indonesia's first president, Sukarno; but when speaking informally, he has a style that has proven thoroughly engaging to voters: warm and informal, Javanese-accented, often colloquial in his speech, and sometimes gently humorous. None of this, however, is readily transposed into English. A mediated and translated Jokowi, the only Jokowi readily accessible to most non-Indonesians, including some of the foreign journalists reporting on the country, can often seem curiously flat, bland even, in a way that he does not to his primary audience.

As a consequence, and for want of something more meaningful,

The author, Darmawan Prasodjo, with Jokowi
during filming for the Hologram project.

international accounts tend to reach for the handful of well-worn but at times inaccurate or misleading tropes about the president: Jokowi was "born in a shack" and "raised in poverty"; Jokowi is "a heavy metal fan"; Jokowi is a "former carpenter." The first is wholly untrue: he was born in a hospital, and though the homes of his early childhood were certainly modest, they were by no means "shacks." And while he certainly grew up in very close physical and social proximity to real poverty, his own immediate circumstances were rather those of precarity than deprivation, a young family at the start of an upwardly mobile journey. The second certainly is true: Jokowi really does love heavy metal music and has done since his high school days, but that fact does not necessarily best convey his quiet, and in some ways deeply traditional Javanese character. As for the latter, Jokowi is only a "carpenter" in the same sense that Bill Gates is a computer repair guy. With a degree in forestry and a dissertation on the plywood industry to his name, he established a successful furniture manufacturing and export business in his hometown, and by the time he first gained elected office he was wealthy enough to be able to donate his entire mayoral salary back to the Surakarta city coffers, and to provide overseas educations for his children.

What also exacerbates the dissonance between Jokowi as he appears to many Indonesians and Jokowi as he is presented to the wider world, is the inevitable tendency for foreign media narratives to be framed by the specific interests and agendas of those producing them. It is perfectly natural for observers viewing Indonesia from outside to take a particular interest in its government's interactions with the wider world, though this may not be an area particularly high on any domestic list of priorities. But other narratives emerge from publications or organizations concerned with promoting the economic interests of their own home countries, or the demands of a particular political or economic ethos, which may well skew their focus or produce obscure parameters for their critiques.

Finally, there is the legacy of the hyperbolic fervor generated by Jokowi's 2014 election. It was certainly a dramatic moment, with the drama heightened by the obvious contrast, at least in terms of presentation and personal background, between Jokowi and his rival for the presidency, Prabowo Subianto. This contrast, and the general hurly-burly of the campaign, led to an idea in some of the international commentary that the stakes were impossibly high and that Jokowi was some kind of last-gasp savior of Indonesian democracy. With hindsight, the hyperbole is plain to see. Indonesia's democracy has proven very robust in the face of many challenges over the last two decades despite near-constant naysaying from the sidelines; and that democracy itself would unlikely have been seriously imperiled by an alternative 2014 outcome, though the subsequent trajectory of development and structural reform might have been rather different. But the overheated commentary primed an inevitable discourse of disappointment amongst some commentators, just as was the case for Barack Obama in the USA in 2008, a discourse providing little space for a clear-eyed and realistic review of Jokowi's record to date.

None of this particularly helps to frame Jokowi, his government or its policies in their proper domestic perspective. The aim of this book is to address that problem, to put the changes that have come to Indonesia since 2014 in their essential context, and to tell the remarkable story of the Jokowi presidency so far.

A Note about This Book

This biography has its origins in Darmawan Prasodjo's detailed Indonesian-language account, *Jokowi Mewujudkan Mimpi Indonesia* ("Jokowi, Realizing Indonesia's Dream"), published in 2020. A technocrat and sometime parliamentarian, and a personal associate of the president, Darmawan's insider view of the Jokowi government encompasses the day-to-day political practicalities and the hidden human contexts of the presidency, and the nation-shaping processes of development and structural change in both their granular detail and their "big picture" scope. Drawing on these informed perspectives, the original book took a detailed, on-the-ground view of each key area of Jokowi's developmental policies, as well as providing a thoroughgoing account of his family and cultural background, with rich insights into the way this heritage informs his priorities, his philosophy and his political style.

The collaboration on this new, English-language work arose from our observation that a properly detailed and informed biographical account of Jokowi for an international audience was sorely lacking. Also lacking was any single overarching narrative of his presidency to date, or any extended discussion of his developmental priorities and the rationales behind them for a readership beyond Indonesia. There are, of course, myriad short profiles and journalistic accounts, and a smattering of specialist publications; and in time there will doubtless be other detailed accounts of the presidency, carrying the narrative right up to its end-point in 2024. But this is the first full-length political biography of Jokowi. We believe that it will provide an invaluable guide to both the personality of the president and the development of Indonesia since 2014 for international readers, be they professionally engaged in politics, academia or business, or merely curious about the governance and recent history of one of the world's major nations.

In preparing this biography we have sought to preserve the key themes and insights of Darmawan's Indonesian-language book. But we have not simply translated the earlier text. Instead, we have further explored the historical and political contexts for an international readership, and also provided a year-by-year narrative of Jokowi's presidency to date. But the key arguments remain the same: that Jokowi must be understood, first and foremost, as a structural reformer and a problem-solver. Development and structural reform—of infrastructure, of social justice mechanisms, and of national human resources—are not simply important to Jokowi, but absolutely central in his sustained project to transform Indonesia and to put it firmly on the road to developed nation status by the time it celebrates its centenary in 2045. Like so many other things, in Indonesia and around the world, this project has been heavily impacted by the Covid-19 pandemic. But, as we make clear in the pages that follow, what has been done already is of great significance.

As the authors of this book, our hope is that it will provide a complete and detailed portrait, including the necessary historical, cultural and political context, with concrete detail provided by sources within the Jokowi administration. We wish to acknowledge our gratitude to all those who have supported our work, providing information which informed the narrative, feedback and suggestions on the earlier drafts, and sterling efforts in the production of the final version for publication.

Darmawan Prasodjo and Tim Hannigan

The Kali Anyar river, scene of Jokowi's childhood, as it is today.

Prologue
A Child of the Riverbank

The Indonesian city of Surakarta stands halfway between the Merapi and Lawu volcanoes, in the very heart of Java. Also known as Solo, Surakarta was once the capital of the Mataram Kingdom, the last major Javanese polity before the rise of Dutch colonial power in the eighteenth century. It is still the seat of one of Java's enduring royal dynasties today, centered on a *kraton*, the traditional palace compound occupied by the reigning *susuhunan*. It has a reputation as a stronghold of Javanese culture. Surakarta has also had an important political history. It was here, in 1911, that the Sarekat Islam, arguably the single most significant organization in the early development of modern Indonesian politics, was founded.[1]

Beyond the center, Surakarta is a sprawling, low-rise city. The Gilingan neighborhood lies just north of the main railway station. It is a mixed quarter of local commerce and residential streets, strung along the southern banks of the Kali Anyar river. The part of Gilingan immediately alongside the river is still a place of narrow alleyways and densely packed housing. But in the 1960s and 1970s it was markedly more impoverished, with a jumble of bamboo-walled dwellings for which few of the occupants held legal title.

In those days, the river itself, a relatively modest stream reduced to muddy pools and narrow channels in the dry season, functioned as the

---

[1] M. C. Ricklefs, *A History of Modern Indonesia since c.1200*, 3rd edn (Basingstoke: Palgrave, 2012), 210.

main artery for the community that lived on its banks. It was where they bathed, did their laundry, and washed their animals. It was also where local children played and went fishing. The river was a permanent presence and a place of constant activity. Children scampered about while their parents bathed. Alongside them a grandmother might be seen, dressed in a simple cotton wrap, scrubbing dirty clothes on a large rock with a bar of green Sunlight brand soap. In the midst of all this bustle, people talked and gossiped. In the social life of the time, information had a way of spreading like an infection, from mouth to mouth. Interaction between neighbors involved a constant good-natured bartering of information.

"Did you hear last night? Bambang was quarreling with his wife again," says the grandmother to a woman who is busy washing her hair.

"They were at it all day yesterday. What a shame for their little child!" the younger woman replies. The roar of the water means that they have to shout at each other to be heard, though there are only a few meters between them. No matter how sensitive the topic, it is impossible to whisper. Everything must be discussed at full volume.

The chatter of the people washing their clothes and bathing in the river ranges across many topics, trivial and serious. Sometimes they speak admiringly of the kindly matriarchs of the community. Then the conversation suddenly shifts to censorious talk about those local men with a reputation for cheating and fecklessness, or to rumors of a child born out of wedlock. This is the nature of social life for residents of the riverbank: familiar, close, mutual, and complete.

It was in this atmosphere that Joko Widodo, later to be known as Jokowi, and later still to become the seventh president of the Republic of Indonesia, grew up.

....

The Kali Anyar river was central to Jokowi's childhood. He knew every inch of its surroundings. He knew the smell of the air and the taste of the water by heart. For twelve years his family lived in Kampung Cinderejo Lor, a part of the Gilingan neighborhood immediately alongside the river.[2] Jokowi's parents, Wijiatno Notomiharjo and Sujiatmi, did not have enough

---

[2] Domu D. Ambarita, *Jokowi Spirit Bantaran Kali Anyar* (Jakarta: Elex Media Komputindo, 2012), 3–4.

money to take a tenancy on a large residential property, let alone to buy one.[3] Instead, they rented a small house, seven meters by thirty, walled off into sections. The front part of the house was full of simple wooden and bamboo furniture.

The family had lived first in the Srambat area, then moved again to the Dawung Kidul quarter, staying there until Jokowi began attending the Siwi Peni Kindergarten in Balapan,[4] then moving once again to Kampung Cinderejo Lor, all of this within the same general area of Surakarta. If a government official's family often has to move because of new postings, Jokowi's family frequently moved house because of financial imperatives. They were determined to live independently and not to rely on their relatives, even though they came from relatively secure, if by no means wealthy, families. The process of establishing their independence was often a struggle, but for a small boy life on the banks of the river was full of diversion and entertainment.

The Kali Anyar is not a wide, fast-flowing river like the nearby Bengawan Solo,[5] so it made for an ideal children's playground. For the adults, of course, there was always the fear that children might be swept away, particularly when the water was high after the rains. Jokowi's mother was no exception. Her eldest son loved to play in the river, which flowed just twenty meters from the family home, and she was always worried about his safety. Morning, noon and night, the river was his playground.[6] Together with his playmates, Jokowi particularly liked to hunt for eggs laid by ducks along the banks. According to Bandi, one of Jokowi's childhood friends, in those days the Kali Anyar was still relatively clean, unlike today when the river is badly polluted with household waste.

"Usually, after coming home from school, we played in the river, fishing, swimming, and looking for duck eggs along the banks," Bandi recalls.[7]

At that time, according to Bandi, ducks were allowed to roam freely along the banks. He is unsure if they belonged to anyone in particular, but they were certainly not looked after by a duck-herd. The ducks would lay

[3] Yon Thayrun, *Jokowi Pemimpin Rakyat Berjiwa Rocker* (Jakarta: Noura Books, 2012), 2.

[4] Ibid., 2–3.

[5] Kompas Editorial Team, *Ekspedisi Bengawan Solo: Laporan Jurnalistik Kompas* (Jakarta: Penerbit Buku Kompas, 2008), 9.

[6] Alberthiene Endah, *Jokowi Perjalanan Karya bagi Bangsa Menuju Cahaya* (Solo: Tiga Serangkai, 2018), 32.

[7] Irwan Nugroho, "Jokowi Kecil, Pendiam dan Susah Makan," *detikNews*, January 14, 2017, https://news.detik.com/x/detail/investigasi/20170113/Jokowi-Kecil,-Pendiam-dan-Susah-Makan/ [accessed September 19, 2019].

wherever they chose. So, once they had finished swimming in the river, Bandi, Jokowi, and the other children would compete to find eggs. "If you found an egg, you'd boil it there and then, using the river water. You wouldn't use a proper pot to boil it, just an old tin can," Bandi says.[8]

In truth, the Kali Anyar was not just a playground. It was also a school of life for local children. Fishing was another of the young Jokowi's hobbies.[9] Fishing is not just about catching fish, of course; it is an activity that involves self-management, self-motivation, and self-control. Little Jokowi was said to have been a quiet child, but his contemporaries also recall that he was what is called *ngglidhik* in Javanese, always eager test one's own brainpower, to figure out how things work and why. Fishing and thinking go well together.

On the edge of the river, the little boy would sit as still as a statue looking at the ripples and reading the signs in the water. In those moments, he would reflect and think over many things. Unconsciously, these moments were allowing him to form his sense of self. Fishing is a way to practice perseverance, focus, and discipline, and also a way of learning how to achieve a goal through patient process.[10] Of course, at the time, the young Jokowi did not understand that. He simply enjoyed fishing and looking for things to eat. If he caught a fish it was a blessing, and a piece of good luck. If he didn't, it was no great pity for this was just a hobby.

....

Riverbanks in Indonesia are often crowded with informal dwellings, built without proper permission or legal title.[11] Simple houses with walls made of *gedhek* (sheets of woven bamboo) spring up beside the water, and extensive shanty towns sometimes develop where large numbers of people share the ups and downs of life in close proximity. Growing up, Jokowi got

---

[8] Caroline Damanik, "Jokowi Mengenang Masa Kecil di Bantaran Kali Anyar," *Kompas*, October 26, 2016, https://regional.kompas.com/read/2016/10/25/14265431/Jokowi.mengenang. masa.kecil.di.bantaran.kali.anyar [accessed June 21, 2019].

[9] Ambarita, *Jokowi Spirit Bantaran Kali Anyar*, 7.

[10] Dian Kurniawan, "Melatih Kesabaran bersama Pemancing Ramadan Sungai Brantas," *Liputan6*, May 27, 2019, https://www.liputan6.com/ramadan/read/3976800/melatih-kesa-baran-bersama-pemancing-ramadan-sungai-brantas [accessed August 10, 2019].

[11] Hernando de Soto, *Masih Ada Jalan Lain: Revolusi Tersembunyi di Dunia Ketiga* (Jakarta: Yayasan Obor, 1991), 18. This shows how informal settlements emerge in developing countries, including along riverbanks.

used to the prayers and incantations sung by his neighbors, heard clearly through the thin walls. He also grew up listening to their curses and insults as they fought over matters of love and household affairs, or over unpaid rent. Every sentence, even if spoken in a whisper, carried through. There was little privacy in such an environment.

Economically, life was a constant struggle for many on the Kali Anyar riverbank. Pawning one's most valuable possessions was commonplace in Kampung Cinderejo Lor, whether to pay the rent or simply to buy food. And eviction, whether by a landlord looking to make space for higher paying tenants or by the authorities looking to clear the land of squatters, was a permanent threat.

Furthermore, riverbank communities are generally regarded as slums, full of dirt and poverty, and their residents frequently experience discrimination. From a middle-class perspective, and even more so in the eyes of the city authorities, such informal riverbank settlements are typically seen as a sort of urban disease, hotbeds of criminality, places of indolence, drink and gambling, and a source of social problems. Unsurprisingly, such places, particularly when they occupy land earmarked for official control or redevelopment, are often targeted for eviction. This is something that Jokowi experienced during his childhood.

At one point, the house that his father, Wijiatno Notomiharjo, had rented for his family on the banks of the Kali Anyar had to be abandoned because a bus terminal was due to be built in the area.[12] They were evicted and the house was destroyed by government officials. The officials who carried out the eviction and demolition surely could never have imagined that the skinny, crying child in the midst of all the heat and dust and protesting residents would one day become their president.

··

The sort of impoverished or working-class people who lived along the banks of the Kali Anyar are often described in Indonesia as *wong cilik*, a Javanese phrase literally meaning "the little people." The term is regularly deployed in political discourse, frequently with reference to the needs, aspirations, and sensitivities of the *wong cilik*. But Jokowi's claim of a personal

---

[12] This terminal has now been converted into the Pasar Ngudi Rezeki market in Gilingan, which opened in 2015.

connection with this demographic is far more convincing than that of most of his predecessors. Given his Kali Anyar upbringing, he could legitimately claim to come from a *wong cilik* background himself, and to understand what such a background actually means.[13] An upshot of this can be seen in his handling of potentially fraught interactions between the authorities and *wong cilik* communities throughout his political career.

In 2006, during his time as mayor of Surakarta, Jokowi managed to arrange a major relocation of street vendors with minimal conflict. A total of fifty-four public meetings were held with the affected vendors over the course of seven months, a process which successfully dispelled misinformation and mistrust of the sort that has often led to clashes between the authorities and traders elsewhere. Ultimately, around a thousand street vendors moved willingly from Banjarsari Park in the center of Solo to a new, specially constructed location at Pasar Klitikan Notoharjo. Later, when Jokowi became governor of Jakarta, there were echoes of his own childhood experiences during efforts to clean up the informal settlements on the banks of rivers and lakes within the city. His own home on the Kali Anyar had, of course, been targeted for similar clearance many years earlier. But unlike in that instance, Jokowi made extensive efforts to build bridges of communication through official visits and face-to-face discussions with the residents of the Ciliwung River and the Ria Rio and Pluit reservoirs in Jakarta, and to listen to their concerns on a personal level.[14] The approach was successful, and has been seen as a good example of Jokowi's "persuasive and conciliatory approach to dialogue,"[15] one of the key features of his political style.

This dialogical approach is based on a principle of *nguwongke wong cilik*, a Javanese phrase meaning "to humanize the little people"; an attempt to treat those such as street vendors and slum dwellers, people often viewed dismissively by other parts of Indonesian society, with dignity and respect.

....

[13] Alberthiene Endah, *Jokowi Memimpin Kota Menyentuh Jakarta* (Solo: Metagraf, 2012), 21.

[14] Zaenuddin H. M., *Jokowi Dari Jualan Kursi Hingga Dua Kali Mendapatkan Kursi* (Jakarta: Ufuk Press, 2012), 122.

[15] Ahmad Ibrahim Almuttaqi, *Jokowi's Indonesia and the World* (Singapore: World Scientific, 2020), xxvi.

On the banks of the Kali Anyar, the poor and those of modest income lived side by side. But there was also another class of people: the very poorest, often characterized by a lack of direct access to electricity in their homes. Jokowi's family did not suffer such privations, but having extremely poor neighbors was a part of his childhood experience, and the fear of slipping into extreme poverty was a reality for the entire community.

Jokowi described this aspect of his childhood during a speech in Bogor in February 2019: "I was born into a family of modest circumstances. My father used to sell bamboo and wood in the market. My father also worked on the side as a driver. We lived on the banks of the Kali Anyar river, but were evicted and forced to find another rented house.

"Although of modest circumstances, my family was happy. However, we were haunted by the fear of not being able to seek medical treatment when sick and of being unable to attend school. For that reason, I am determined that the Indonesian people will be free from such fears," he said.[16]

Some manifestation of this desire could be identified in his Smart Indonesia Card (KIP; Kartu Indonesia Pintar) and Healthy Indonesia Card (KIS; Kartu Indonesia Sehat) programs, which were designed to provide educational subsidies and healthcare to the poorest families.

....

Growing up in an economically and socially harsh environment did not mean that Jokowi was surrounded only by gloomy, desperate faces. On the banks of the river, he also often met people smiling cheerfully as they brought home gifts for their wives and children, simple things such as fried snacks, toy boats, or fruit from the market. Something of this informs his current public persona, which is commonly characterized as dominated by positivity and optimism.[17]

Living on the riverbank, Jokowi took on the resilience that he found amongst his neighbors. The friendships formed and the games played on the banks of the Kali Anyar shaped his personality. The stories and experiences of his playmates, neighbors, and family laid the foundations of the values he would carry into adulthood.

---

[16] "Pidato Jokowi yang Menggetarkan di Konvensi Rakyat Optimis Indonesia Maju," YouTube, https://www.YouTube.com/watch?v=VnCRtErmwqo [accessed June 23, 2019].
[17] Alois Wisnuhardana, *Anak Muda dan Medsos* (Jakarta: Gramedia Pustaka Utama, 2018), 146.

The riverbank taught Jokowi much that he needed to know: about communicating with neighbors and the public, about appropriate behavior, and about tactics for dealing with the complexities of life. The riverbank also gave him the spirit to overcome limitations. Rather than symbolizing chaos, the murky, fast-flowing waters of the Kali Anyar could be said to represent the drive to keep moving forward. Indeed, Jokowi's entire approach as Indonesian president, both in terms of his priorities and policy decisions and in terms of his political style and mode of operation, can only be properly understood with reference to his background. Everything, ultimately, can be traced back to the beginning and to the image of a small boy playing on the banks of the Kali Anyar.

....

This book traces Jokowi's story, from his riverbank childhood and family heritage through his first career in the timber industry and as a successful furniture entrepreneur, to his unlikely sideways step into politics. He was already in his forties when he first joined a political party and ran for public office, but the career that followed was surely one of the most meteoric in Indonesian history. After a widely praised spell as mayor of his hometown, he leapt into the country's highest-profile regional post: the governorship of Jakarta. Though hugely popular amongst the residents of Indonesia's vast and complex capital city, his term as governor was cut short, but only because he had moved onwards and upwards to the highest office in the land. In 2014, Jokowi, the boy from the Kali Anyar riverbank, was elected president of the Republic of Indonesia.

His election was widely interpreted as a transformational moment for Indonesia and a crucial watershed in the long process of Reformasi that has continued since the fall of Suharto's New Order regime in the late 1990s and Indonesia's emergence as the world's third largest democracy. Jokowi is the first Indonesian president since the end of Suharto's three-decades reign to have risen entirely on his own merit, to have emerged from outside the country's traditional political and military elites, and to possess no personal connections to the power structures of the old regime. He has frequently been portrayed as the ultimate political outsider, though any informed examination of his own political ethos shows that it is firmly rooted in the ideology of Indonesian nationalism as forged by Sukarno and the other leaders of the country's revolutionary struggle against Dutch colonialism. Like his American counterpart Barack Obama, Jokowi entered the presidential palace on a surge of popular optimism, which at times brought with it unrealistic expectations, just as it did for Obama. Nonetheless, his first term was marked by dramatic achievements, not least in terms of infrastructure development.

Having followed the story of his rise to the presidency, this book then examines Jokowi's first term, with a special focus on his development and social justice policies. These were the priorities which he had identified at the outset and towards which much of his administration's energy has been directed. The way Jokowi chooses and approaches these priorities, this book argues, has been determined by his background and his formative experiences as a child in the tight-knit Kali Anyar community with an ancestry in the villages of Central Java, and as a businessman in the Surakarta timber industry.

In 2019, Jokowi was elected for a second term after a hard-fought campaign. He returned to power with a renewed emphasis on the development priorities of his first five years. And like any president entering a final term (as in the US, an Indonesian president is limited to two terms in office), Jokowi and those around him were beginning to consider the question of legacy. No one, however, could have foreseen the shock that was coming, not only to Indonesia but to the entire world in the form of the Covid-19 pandemic. In its final chapters, this book examines Indonesia's response to that unprecedented crisis and considers how it might impact on and intersect with Jokowi's other achievements so far.

But the story begins with the historical contexts. The chapter that follows this prologue goes back to the years before Jokowi's birth, to Indonesia's emergence as an independent state. It covers the development of the presidency itself and of Indonesia's modern political culture. And it examines the careers and personalities of the five men and one woman who led the country in the decades before a stick-thin former furniture salesman from Surakarta came to power.

President Sukarno declaring Indonesia's independence on August 17, 1945.

Chapter One

Nation and Leader: The Indonesian Presidency

A t 10 a.m. on August 17, 1945, sixteen years before Joko Widodo was born, a small group gathered outside a modest bungalow in Jakarta, a few kilometers southeast of the vast public space at the heart of the city known today as Medan Merdeka, "Freedom Square." A few members of the group were in military uniform but most wore civilian dress. The foremost member of the group, Sukarno, stepped forward to a microphone and read a short proclamation:

> We the people of Indonesia hereby declare the independence of Indonesia.
>
> Matters concerning the transfer of power, etc., will be carried out by careful means and in the shortest possible time.

With that, in one understated symbolic moment, Indonesia had brought itself into being as an independent nation, though it would take some time for the outside world to become aware of the declaration, and it would be several years before the erstwhile colonial power recognized the change in status. In reading the words, Sukarno himself had moved to become the first Indonesian president, the same role occupied by Jokowi three-quarters of a century later.

History, Colonialism, Independence

Indonesia, the nation which came into independent being in August 1945, is the world's fourth most populous country and its third largest democracy. A vast and culturally diverse archipelago, it nonetheless has certain broad commonalities and shared experiences in its precolonial heritage.

Spanning the gap between the Indian and Pacific oceans and the South China Sea, and between Australia and the Southeast Asian mainland, Indonesia has been bonded internally and connected externally by complex networks of trade since prehistory. Maritime commerce brought the region in contact with the Indian subcontinent, and from the early centuries of the current era, Indian religious, cultural, and linguistic traditions began to spread through the western parts of the archipelago. A thousand years later, Islam would arrive and spread in similar fashion.

During this precolonial period, a number of states arose in Indonesia with extensive economic, cultural, and at times political and military influence, most notably the fourteenth-century East Java-based Majapahit kingdom. But the specific territorial limits of the modern nation which Sukarno called into being on August 17, 1945 were determined by a later process: European colonialism.

Indonesia has always possessed a wealth of valuable tropical resources, and from the sixteenth century one particular product category began to attract the attention of newly globally mobile Europeans: spice. For several decades the Dutch, British, and Portuguese vied for control of the lucrative Indonesian spice trade, with the Dutch eventually gaining supremacy. Over the course of three centuries, they built a huge Southeast Asian empire. Like the British elsewhere in Asia, the Dutch established an essentially extractive colonial economy with a particular focus on agricultural commodities and natural resources for export. And through a mix of military conquest and coercive treaty arrangements, they expanded their footprint until it reached the borders of the Indonesian state as it exists today, borders originally defined in relation to the other European colonial occupiers beyond: British, Spanish, German, and Portuguese.

There was much local resistance to Dutch expansion in Indonesia down the centuries, most famously in the protracted Java War of the early nineteenth century led by the mercurial Yogyakarta prince Diponegoro. By the early twentieth century, this had segued into a modern anticolonial nationalist movement. Sukarno was one of the foremost figures of that movement.

Born in 1901 to a Javanese father and a Balinese mother, Sukarno belonged to an emergent Indonesian middle class. He began to engage with politics at an early age. As a student of engineering in Bandung in the 1920s, he set up a study club with a pro-independence ethos, which gave rise in 1927 to a political organization, Perserikatan Nasional Indonesia, renamed the following year as Partai Nasional Indonesia (PNI; the Indonesian National Party).

Indonesia's political awakening had begun in the first two decades of the twentieth century with the establishment of various mass organizations. At the outset, these organizations tended not to have a directly political focus, being aimed instead at educational reform, cultural revival, or commercial interests. And the Dutch authorities were generally tolerant of their activities. But they were laying the groundwork for a modern political culture through their membership and organizational structures. Arguably the most significant of these early organizations was the Sarekat Islam, the "Islamic Union" or SI, which was formed in Jokowi's hometown, Surakarta, in 1911. Despite its name, it was not a religious organization, and various streams of political thought were able to develop within its burgeoning ranks (SI claimed a membership of two million by the start of the 1920s). Another major organization founded in this period was Muhammadiyah, which still exists today. Started in Yogyakarta in 1912, unlike SI, Muhammadiyah did have an explicitly Islamic identity, with an initial focus on educational reform.

During this period, both Islam and socialism appeared as possible potential drivers of the independence movement. But by the 1920s a second generation of young Indonesian activists, with Sukarno at the forefront, had recognized the limits of these competing ideologies in a culturally diverse country that was in many ways preindustrial, thanks to the exploitative colonial economy. They argued instead for a blended ideological approach that placed nationalism at the forefront. Through all the turbulent decades that followed, this nationalism has remained the basic underpinning of Indonesian political culture.

By the 1920s, the idea of Indonesia itself was beginning to solidify. A key moment came in 1928 with the signing of a "Youth Pledge" during a congress of activists in Jakarta:

Firstly: We the sons and daughters of Indonesia acknowledge one motherland, Indonesia.
Secondly: We the sons and daughters of Indonesia acknowledge one nation, the nation of Indonesia.

Thirdly: We the sons and daughters of Indonesia uphold the language of unity, Indonesian.

The "language of unity" was a renamed modern version of Malay, the long-established regional lingua franca which, unlike Javanese, did not have any particular ethnic associations. As Indonesian, or Bahasa Indonesia, it would be spoken across a unified territory by a single people bonded under a single nationality. As for the territory itself, though the idea that an independent Indonesia might take in British possessions in northern Borneo and the Malay Peninsula was occasionally mooted, there was a general understanding that, in essence, "Indonesia" would be the direct postcolonial replacement of the Dutch East Indies.

As the 1930s got under way and the global economy contracted, the Dutch authorities became increasingly intolerant of the independence movement and Sukarno and other key leaders spent periods in jail or in exile. The Dutch empire itself came to an abrupt end in 1942 with the arrival of the invading Japanese, who managed to seize control of the entire archipelago in just two months. The Japanese were initially welcomed as liberators by many Indonesians, and though their rule was exceedingly brutal they mobilized huge numbers of young Indonesians and provided them with military training, and they allowed Sukarno and his key collaborator, Mohammad Hatta, a vital political platform. As World War II progressed and the likelihood of an eventual Japanese defeat increased, Sukarno and Hatta pushed for independence. The Japanese authorities were cautiously supportive. But before any decisive moves had been made, the dropping of atomic bombs on Hiroshima and Nagasaki prompted an abrupt unconditional Japanese surrender. Two days later, under pressure from young revolutionaries who argued that unilateral action was needed ahead of any Dutch return, Sukarno read the proclamation of Independence.

Despite its brief and perfunctory nature, with the famous "etc." to cover all manner of hugely complex details, the proclamation was, in fact, backed by lengthy discussions and negotiations over the nature of the future Indonesian state. Earlier in 1945, two key elements had been put in place. The first was an official national doctrine which Sukarno called Pancasila, a Sanskrit-derived term meaning "five principles," namely, belief in one god; humanitarianism; national unity; democracy; and social justice. The second crucial element was a draft constitution, which called for a unitary republic governed by a president with strong executive powers.

A few weeks after the proclamation of independence, Allied troops arrived in Indonesia to receive the Japanese surrender, with Dutch officials following in their wake. Indonesia's bloody revolutionary struggle quickly got underway. It was not until late 1949 that the Dutch, under considerable international pressure, finally agreed to cede sovereignty, with certain conditions. Rather than the unitary state envisaged in 1945, the Dutch had pressed for the creation of a "Republic of the United States of Indonesia" with a new federal constitution. They had also unilaterally decided, very late in the day, to separate their territory in western New Guinea from the rest of the Dutch East Indies and to retain it as a standalone colonial possession. None of this was palatable to Indonesian nationalists, but pragmatism won over and the arrangements were accepted, temporarily. The following year, with the Dutch out of the picture, the federation was dissolved and a third constitution unveiled. On August 17, 1950, five years after the original proclamation, the unitary Republic of Indonesia came properly into being. Sukarno was president and Mohammad Hatta was vice president.

Sukarno: Electoral Experiments and Guided Democracy

The 1950 Constitution mandated a parliamentary system and a president whose role was largely symbolic. The parliament had been established during the ad hoc maneuvring necessary to get the fledgling state through the turbulent revolutionary period, as had the new post of prime minister to head a governing cabinet. But there were still decisions to be made about how Indonesia should be run.

The key legislative structure involved the Dewan Perwakilan Rakyat, the People's Representative Council or DPR, which, in theory, would be democratically representative. In 1950, this parliament had 236 members, divided among sixteen political parties. The original 1945 Constitution had also called for an upper house which would appoint the president. But the exact configuration of the two-tier legislature, and the final status of the constitution, remained a matter of deadlocked consultation throughout the 1950s. Indonesia did, however, manage one ambitious and organizationally, at least, highly successful experiment with direct democracy during this period.

In 1955, the country went to the polls to elect a new parliament. Across the country more than 39 million people, over 90 percent of all registered voters, turned out in an election which was judged by international observers to be well run and largely free and fair. Unfortunately, it did not produce a particularly decisive outcome. No party came close to achieving an absolute majority, and only a series of shaky and short-lived cabinets and prime ministerships ensued. Eying all of this, Sukarno began to make moves to "bury all the parties," as he put it in 1956, and to come up with a new political system. In 1957, he unveiled his concept of "guided democracy." Sukarno had long argued that Western political ideologies could not be imported wholesale to Indonesia, and he now argued that Western political systems were also ill-suited to Indonesian society. He called for a consensus-based approach instead of the brutal absolutism of "50 percent + 1." Career politicians were to be replaced by representatives of "functional groups" from across society, and formerly competing ideologies, including Islam, socialism, and nationalism, were to be held in a benign and productive balance.

In 1957, martial law was declared and Sukarno began to put his Guided Democracy theory into practice. In 1959, the 1945 Constitution was revived, and Sukarno, already president, also made himself prime minister, a move which effectively abolished that role and which brought the symbolic and executive leadership of Indonesia back together in the office of president.

Sukarno was a leader of astonishing charisma, and one of the twentieth century's great political orators. He was extremely well-read and flamboy-antly multilingual, with a ready stock of literary and philosophical quota-tions in French, Russian, and Italian to bolster his stylish and expressive Indonesian, Dutch, and English. However, his grasp of economics and commitment to the practicalities of day-to-day governance was shaky, and the young Indonesian nation was in a parlous state. Centuries of colonial rule had bequeathed patchy infrastructure, a deeply unbalanced economy, and woefully inadequate apparatus for social justice; and what did exist had been badly battered by the years of war, occupation, and revolution. Sukarno attempted to overcome all of this through endless action and sheer force of personality. He pushed for a state of continual revolution, manifest through frequent confrontation with the outside world. He remained an enormously popular leader, beloved even to the very end. But without the influence of the calmer and more pragmatic collaborators of the early days, not least Mohammad Hatta who had resigned the vice presidency in 1956, Indonesia was moving towards political chaos and economic collapse. The rival forces that Sukarno's system was supposed to neutralize, including the military, religious groups, the nationalist constituency, and the large

Indonesian Communist Party (PKI, Partai Komunis Indonesia), became increasingly antagonistic. By 1961 when a baby boy, initially named Mulyono and later to be called Joko Widodo, was born in Surakarta, Indonesia was riven by deep and dangerous tensions.

The final conflagration came in late 1965. On the night of September 30, a cabal of relatively junior Indonesian Army officers, whose precise motivations and allegiances remain unclear to this day but who were in some way connected to the PKI, organized a putsch of the military's top brass. Six of Indonesia's most senior generals were murdered, but the movement, typically portrayed as an attempted coup, then rapidly fell apart. Within twenty-four hours, Major-General Suharto, head of the army's Strategic Reserve, had taken control, seized the putsch ringleaders, and gained the political initiative. A nationwide bout of violence ensued in which the Indonesian Communist Party was annihilated and many thousands of people associated with it were killed. Meanwhile, in Jakarta, Suharto carefully maneuvered Sukarno out of power. First, in early 1966, he assumed a provisional role allowing him to "take all measures considered necessary to guarantee the security, calm and stability of the government." Then, in March 1967, he became acting president; and finally, in 1968, he took on the full title, becoming the second president of Indonesia. The "New Order" era had begun.

Suharto: The "Father of Development"

Suharto's New Order regime presented itself as a clean break with the past. There was a swift rapprochement with Western powers and an instant pivot from continuous revolution to sensible economics. Suharto turned to the expertise of technocrats and American-educated economists, and with their guidance managed to transform Indonesia's basket case economy into a powerhouse of sustained growth within a few short years. "Developmentalism" became the key New Order approach, and Suharto himself liked to be known as "the father of development."

But in terms of ideology and state organization, there was actually considerable continuity between Sukarno and Suharto. The New Order remained firmly committed to the 1945 Constitution. In 1969, it finalized and formalized the legislative structures it mandated: the People's Representative Council or DPR as the main parliament made of elected and appointed members, which in turn would make up part of an upper house, the Majelis Permusyawaratan Rakyat, the MPR or People's Consultative

Assembly, which would appoint a strong executive president who would in turn appoint a cabinet to oversee the day-to-day running of the country.[1] The role of vice president, unfilled since Hatta's resignation, was revived in 1973, and filled in the first instance by the then sultan of Yogyakarta, who had already had a long political career, having previously served as a minister under Sukarno.

Suharto has often been described as a "dictator," but this requires some nuance. In fact, unlike Sukarno, his regime was committed to regular general elections. The first of these took place in 1971, and they followed like clockwork every five years for the next three decades (the well-oiled practical mechanism of democracy was actually a valuable legacy of the New Order regime for the subsequent Reformasi period). The regime created a vehicle for itself in the form of the Sekretariat Bersama Golongan Karya, the Joint Secretariat of Functional Groups, known as Golkar for short. This was a leftover from Sukarno's Guided Democracy period, an umbrella group for trades unions, social bodies, and workers' organizations which brought with it an enormous de facto membership with automatic allegiance. The New Order transformed Golkar into a highly effective electoral machine, albeit one without a discernible party ideology. The various Islamic political parties, meanwhile, were corralled into a single organization: the Partai Persatuan Pembangunan, the PPP or United Development Party. And the various old nationalist and minority parties were blocked together as the Partai Demokrasi Indonesia, PDI or the Indonesian Democratic Party. Independent parties and candidates were not allowed, and Golkar won a solid majority in every election without really needing to cheat at the ballot box, simply because of its sheer scale and organizational capacity. This, coupled with the fact that a large chunk of the MPR was directly appointed by the president, meant that Suharto's own position was always secure. The electoral situation during the New Order could, arguably, be viewed as the final perfection of Sukarno's dream of Guided Democracy.

A key feature of the New Order era was the Indonesian Army's *dwifungsi* or "dual function" role, in which it was considered a duty of the military to be directly involved in the affairs of the civilian state, with serving soldiers in parliament, heading regional governments and ministries, and running state-owned enterprises. But once again, this was not a Suharto

---

[1] M. C. Ricklefs, *A History of Modern Indonesia since c.1200*, 3rd edn (London: Palgrave, 2001), 359.

innovation. The military had been very much involved in government as part of Sukarno's Guided Democracy project.[2] A further continuity came in the form of Pancasila, Sukarno's five philosophical principles. During the 1950s, Pancasila had received relatively little attention, but Suharto made it the central Indonesian ideology, and every organization in the country had to take Pancasila as its sole guiding ethos.

Because of the lack of proper democracy during the New Order era, because of the rampant corruption and cronyism of its later years, because of its ignominious end, and because of its association with mass violence at the outset, Suharto is often viewed entirely critically today, particularly by non-Indonesians. But it important to acknowledge the achievements of the New Order. As well as rescuing the Indonesian economy, it did much to establish the physical and organizational infrastructure of a functioning state, including the school and healthcare network that would later provide the foundation for Jokowi's own social justice programs. In the early years, Golkar's enormous electoral success was, in part, a genuine expression of public approval for the regime. During Jokowi's later childhood and teens, life for many Indonesians, particularly in the cities, was improving year by year, with better access to services, better infrastructure, and rising incomes.

One area in which Suharto indisputably did represent an absolute break with Sukarno was personality and political style. He was born in 1921 in an impoverished hamlet called Kemusuk near Yogyakarta. During his presidency, he made much of his humble origins.[3] But although his own family was poor, he had received an unusually comprehensive education for a village boy at the time, staying in school until he was seventeen. He was then recruited into the Dutch military on the eve of World War II, and later served in the Japanese-run militia before taking a role in the new republican army during the Indonesian revolution. He rose through the ranks in the years following independence, but did not attract a great deal of attention until the dramatic events of 1965 propelled him to the very top.

Suharto was steeped in traditional Javanese cultural values and Javanese was very much his first language. He had none of Sukarno's verbal dexterity in Indonesian and his spoken English was hesitant and heavily accented. Where Sukarno was a magnetic demagogue, Suharto projected

---

[2] Robert Cribb and Colin Brown, *Modern Indonesia: A History Since 1945* (London: Longman, 1995), 140.

[3] R. E. Elson, *Suharto: A Political Biography* (Cambridge: Cambridge University Press, 2001), 3.

an aura of coolness and restraint. He was unquestionably an autocrat but one without rhetoric and bluster.

Indonesia continued to experience dramatic economic growth throughout the 1980s. But by the 1990s there were signs of popular discontent, particularly over high-level corruption, high-profile cronyism, and a lack of free speech. The economy, meanwhile, was developing the characteristics of an unstable bubble. Throughout this period, the basic mechanism of democracy continued to function, with five-yearly general elections in which the loaded system continued to return Golkar majorities and in which the MPR continued to reappoint the aging Suharto to the presidency. But when the tiger economies of Southeast Asia were hit by a severe financial crisis in 1997, deep resentments erupted on the streets of Jakarta and other Indonesian cities. Faced with huge student protests, riots, and a collapsing economy, Suharto eventually stepped down on May 21, 1998.

After five decades dominated by just two men, Indonesia was at last embarking on the path towards democracy.

Presidents of the Reformasi Era

The 1945 Constitution stated that should a president leave office before the end of a five-year term, he would be replaced by his deputy. Thus, in 1998, Suharto's final vice president, B. J. Habibie, found himself shunted into the top job as Indonesia's third president.

Habibie is a somewhat unusual figure in the history of the Indonesian presidency. Born in South Sulawesi in 1936, he was academically brilliant. He studied aerospace engineering in Europe and completed doctoral research in Germany, going on to become vice president of the German aircraft company Messerschmitt. In 1974, Habibie was recruited by Suharto to join the ranks of his technocratic administration. For most of his subsequent political career, he had roles directly related to his professional and academic expertise, and he only became vice president in 1998, shortly before Suharto's resignation.

As a long-standing Suharto protégé and every inch a member of the New Order establishment, Habibie's presidency was initially viewed with skepticism by those campaigning for reform. However, Habibie recognized the nature of the political zeitgeist and pushed forward swiftly, freeing political prisoners and lifting all restrictions on the press and on political organization. He also committed the country to a truly democratic parliamentary election in 1999, the first since 1955.

As had been the case forty-four years earlier, the 1999 election saw a huge turnout voting for a vast array of different parties, forty-eight in total though only six of those parties gained more than two percent of the vote.[4] And just as in 1955, the end result demonstrated that whenever Indonesian democracy was given full rein, it was unlikely to produce a parliamentary majority for any one party. The biggest share of the 1999 vote (34 percent) went to PDI-P, Partai Demokrasi Indonesia Perjuangan, the Indonesia Democratic Party of Struggle. This party had its origins in a split in the original PDI, one of the two New Order-sanctioned party groupings that had been engineered by the Suharto regime a few years earlier. In 1993, PDI had elected as its chair Megawati Sukarnoputri, the second child of Indonesia's first president. Though Sukarno had been thoroughly discredited after 1965, he had been posthumously rehabilitated (having died in 1970) as the ultimate national hero. At a time of growing public discontent, Suharto's regime had been nervous of allowing a party leader enjoying some of that reflected glory to contest an election. Through heavy-handed manipulation, they managed to have Megawati unseated in 1996, which created an acrimonious split in the PDI membership. After the fall of Suharto, the more legitimate Megawati faction became the new PDI-P.

Many observers had expected Megawati to end up taking the presidency following the 1999 election, but after much post-election maneuvring and coalition building, the MPR instead appointed Abdurrahman Wahid. This led to street protests by PDI-P supporters, whose complaints were somewhat assuaged when Megawati was appointed vice president.

Wahid, popularly known as Gus Dur, was the leader of the Nahdlatul Ulama (NU), a traditionalist Muslim organization founded in the 1920s. With a huge membership, NU had at times functioned as a political party as well as a religious body. It had not taken part in elections in the later New Order years, but in 1998 Wahid had launched a new party, Partai Kebangkitan Bangsa, National Awakening Party or PKB, which was able to connect with the loyal NU base.

Despite his religious background, Abdurrahman Wahid was socially progressive and firmly committed to religious pluralism. And with his warm and informal style, he was personally very popular with the public. But his government was chaotic and hampered by scandal in a period during which Indonesia had barely emerged from the economic near melt-down of 1997–98. In July 2001, with tensions rising within the government

---

[4]Ricklefs, *A History of Modern Indonesia*, 417.

and the legislature, the MPR in Special Session voted to impeach Wahid, replacing him with Megawati.

Indonesia's first female president has been routinely underestimated by observers. The standard critique is that she appears to have inherited none of her father's famous charisma and mastery of political rhetoric, and little of his imagination. However, as a veteran of the early party-based opposition to Suharto, she is a skilled operator and a major player. And though she has never achieved much direct personal success at the polls, she remains one of the most important figures in Indonesian politics as the long-serving chair of PDI-P

The period which followed the fall of Suharto is known to Indonesians as Reformasi, the Reform era. So far, Reformasi has reached no obvious end point, though there have been a series of obvious milestones along the way. The first was the 1999 election. In the years that followed, a number of amendments were made to the 1945 Constitution to further enhance democracy, removing unelected appointees from both the DPR and the MPR, and placing certain constraints on the presidency itself. Elsewhere, the *dwifungsi* role of the Indonesian Army has been revoked and the police force made entirely independent of the military. The next major Reformasi milestone came in 2004 when Indonesians directly elected a president for the first time.

A further constitutional amendment was required for this dramatic new step. It created a system in which presidential candidates, accompanied by running mates, stand for a five-year term. To be elected, a simple majority is required, with an additional requirement of a minimum 20 percent vote share in over half of all the country's provinces. This article was inserted in an effort to avoid any sense of regional dominance in a vast but demographically unbalanced nation (well over half of Indonesia's population lives in the four provinces and two special regions of Java). Failure to meet those conditions in the first round results in a run-off. As in the US, any elected president is eligible to stand for only one further term. In 2004, the incumbent Megawati lost out to her challenger from the Partai Demokrat (PD), the Democratic Party, Susilo Bambang Yudhoyono, popularly known by his initials, SBY.

Born in East Java in 1949, Yudhoyono had had a stellar and multi-faceted military career, with stints lecturing in the Staff College and working in the Army Information Department, and much overseas training. He also served as a military observer under the UN in Bosnia. He was prominent in the pro-reform contingent of the military at the end of the

Suharto era. In the Reformasi period, he retired from the army and moved into civilian politics, serving as a minister under Abdurrahman Wahid.

Highly educated, a slick communicator in English as much as in Indonesian, and with a wealth of international experience, Yudhoyono was expected to do a good job of representing Indonesia on the world stage. In this he certainly succeeded. He took a "million friends and zero enemies" approach to foreign policy, was active in the UN and ASEAN, and was widely lauded internationally.[5] But at home he was hampered by a certain political inertia, brought about by stifling bureaucracy and the challenges of the transactional Indonesian political system. Although he was elected for a second term in 2009, a degree of popular disillusionment with the general state of Indonesian politics had begun to set in. And the fact that Yudhoyono had emerged from the ranks of the Suharto-era military was seen by some as evidence that there had never been a proper break with the old and undemocratic regime. It was for this reason, in particular, that the arrival of Yudhoyono's successor, a bone fide political outsider, would be greeted with such excitement and optimism.

Legislature and Government Structure

Indonesia's system of government is firmly underpinned by the 1945 Constitution, which has undergone a series of amendments in the Reformasi era. The executive consists of the directly elected president and vice president. The president appoints a cabinet of coordinating ministers, ministers, and deputy ministers. As appointees, there is no requirement for cabinet members to be elected parliamentarians. Typically, a cabinet is made up of a mix of politicians from the parties backing the president and technocratic appointees from industry, media, academia, and civil society.

The heart of the legislature is the parliament, the DPR, which, as of 2019, consists of 575 members, all directly elected from regions across the country, headed by a speaker and four deputies. The DPR also makes up the greater part of the MPR, along with the 136 directly elected non-party members of the Dewan Perwakilan Daerah, the DPD or Regional Representative Council. Originally tasked with appointing the president, today the MPR is mainly responsible for handling any amendments to the constitution. It also has the authority to impeach the president and vice

---

[5] Ahmad Ibrahim Almuttaqi, *Jokowi's Indonesia and the World* (Singapore: World Scientific Publishing, 2020), 1.

president, and to make necessary interim arrangements should they fail to complete their terms. It also handles the presidential inauguration.

The DPR has sole authority to pass laws. However, the constitution allows the president to issue new "regulations in lieu of law," known by the Indonesian acronym Perppu, "should exigencies compel." This mechanism is designed to allow for rapid responses to crises and also to enable rapid policy implementation without recourse to the sluggish parliamentary process. However, any such new regulations must be approved, and may be revoked, by the DPR in its next session, a requirement which tends to rein in their excessive or inappropriate use.

Although Indonesia remains a unitary republic, its administration is broken down into a cascading series of regional divisions. The country is divided into 34 provinces, some bigger than a typical European country, both demographically and geographically. These are further subdivided into 514 *kabupaten* (regencies) and municipalities. These regional divisions are structured in much the same way as the national government. Each has its own directly elected head and deputy and its own Regional People's House of Representatives (DPRD). There has been decentralization in recent decades, and regional governments now have considerable powers, making it possible for governors, regents, and mayors to pursue ambitious programs. It was as mayor of a municipality that Jokowi began his political career. He then moved up to the province level as governor of Jakarta before rising to the head of the national government.

The Parties

After the stifling control of the New Order years, Indonesia embraced boisterous multiparty democracy with a vengeance. But for observers from countries where the major parties can be readily positioned on a simple left–right spectrum, the Indonesian political ecosystem can appear bafflingly amorphous. Party distinctions typically appear to be a matter of nuance, style, and personality rather than hard ideology. This often results in arrangements that would be unthinkable in other countries. Candidates and running mates at the regency, province, or national level may well come from completely different parties and may carry the endorsement of still other parties. And the bitter rivals of one election may well end up on the same ticket, or at least in the same coalition, in the next. Some parties, for example, Gerindra and Partai Demokrat, are initially created as vehicles for ambitious individual politicians but go on to become significant presences in the DPR. Parties which fail to win any parliamentary seats, meanwhile, often dissolve and then resurface in new configurations.

At first glance, the most obviously ideological parties might be seen as those with a Muslim ethos. The most significant of these include PAN, the Partai Amanat Nasional or National Mandate Party; PKB, the Partai Kebangkitan Bangsa or National Awakening Party; PKS, the Partai Keadilan Sejahtera or Prosperous Justice Party; and PPP, the Partai Persatuan Pembangunan or United Development Party (which originated as the New Order-sanctioned Muslim party grouping). There are certain distinctions between these Islam-based parties. For example, PAN is associated with modernist Islam, while PKB is strongly connected to the traditionalist Nahdlatul Ulama base.

Given that Indonesia is, by a significant margin, the world's largest Muslim-majority country, it might be assumed that Islam would be the major political driver. However, this has never really been the case. This is partly down to the significant diversity within the Muslim population, and partly down to Indonesia's twentieth-century history. Although political Islam was an element of the independence movement, Sukarno and the other key leaders saw it as potentially divisive and politically limiting, and tended to sideline specifically Muslim agendas, for example, in the formulation of Pancasila. Suharto was similarly disinclined to indulge the interests of political Islam for most of his rule. With the post-Suharto move to democracy, Islam-based parties initially made significant electoral gains, but this was not an ongoing trend, and the cumulative bulk of the popular vote invariably goes to non-religious parties. Consequently, the main Muslim parties have tended to reduce the centrality of Islam to their ideology over the years. They typically campaign on general social, economic, and developmental issues, and may attract non-Muslim voters and even non-Muslim members and candidates.

The rest of Indonesia's major political parties, that is, those that account for the greatest share of the vote, can be broadly categorized as "secular nationalist," with firm commitments to Pancasila and the 1945 Constitution. The lack of obvious distinction between them is sometimes deemed to be a product of Suharto's long stifling of ideological politics. But more positively it can also be viewed as rooted in Sukarno's ideal of a blended approach, tailored specifically to Indonesian conditions and without direct conflict between incompatible ideologies.

Nonetheless, there are certain distinctions between the nationalist parties. Gerindra, for example, could be said to have an element of right-wing populism in its presentation, while Partai Demokrat, the Democratic Party, is solidly centrist. Amongst the largest of the parties, with a significant membership and formidable national infrastructure, is Golkar. The erstwhile electoral vehicle of the New Order, post-Suharto Golkar transformed itself into a democratic nationalist party, with a somewhat right-of-center economic approach. The other party which rivals Golkar for its venerable heritage, comprehensive national organization, and long-established base, and which has taken the single largest share of the vote in recent general elections, is PDI-P, the Indonesian Democratic Party of Struggle, chaired by Megawati and symbolized by the iconic image of a stern black bull on a red background.

Although PDI-P in its current form was only founded in 1999, it can reasonably claim to be the legitimate successor of the original PDI, put together in 1973, which in turn links it to Sukarno's PNI and the other nationalist parties of the 1950s and the revolutionary period. Given this heritage, PDI-P is able to make a strong claim to best represent Indonesia's nationalist tradition, with a particularly firm commitment to Pancasila. It favors economic nationalism, and its rhetoric tends to have a distinct *pro-rakyat*, "pro-the people" bent.

PDI-P was the party that Joko Widodo decided to join in 2004. He was already in his forties, with a successful business career behind him, and he had had no previous experience of politics. He was about to embark on a remarkably rapid rise. But before examining that ascent, we need to go back, back to Surakarta and back to the Kali Anyar riverbank in the late years of the turbulent Sukarno era.

Jokowi (second from right) on a hiking expedition as a student.

Chapter Two

From the Heart of Java: Jokowi before Politics

I n 1961, Indonesia was entering the final stages of the Sukarno era. More than a decade had passed since the revolution, which ended the long centuries of Dutch rule. But for Sukarno, and many thousands of other Indonesians, the struggle was not yet complete: the Dutch had retained the western half of New Guinea, previously an undifferentiated part of their Indonesian territories. This region, known to Indonesians at the time as Irian, remained under colonial rule, and in 1961 Sukarno was preparing to step up the long-running campaign for its return. Also on the international stage that year, he had cofounded the Non-Aligned Movement, an important grouping of mostly postcolonial nations that rejected formal alignment with the world's major competing power blocs. Domestically, meanwhile, the Indonesian economy was in a bad way and political tension was rising rapidly.

However, all that context must have seemed very distant to one young couple in Surakarta, who were preparing for the birth of their first child. The woman, whose name was Sujiatmi, was just eighteen years old. Her husband, Wijiatno Notomiharjo, was twenty-one.

The baby, a boy, was born on June 21, 1961 in the Brayat Minulyo Hospital,[1] not far from the Kali Anyar river. The couple had already been married for two years and the new arrival filled their lives with happiness. They named their son Mulyono, from *mulyo*, meaning "noble."[2]

---

[1] Yon Thayrun, *Jokowi Pemimpin Rakyat Berjiwa Rocker* (Jakarta: Noura Books, 2012), 2.
[2] Alberthiene Endah, *Jokowi Perjalanan Karya bagi Bangsa Menuju Cahaya* (Solo: Tiga Serangkai, 2018), 32.

There are no inherited family names in Javanese culture and there is a considerable degree of fluidity when it comes to given names. People may change or take on additional names at important points in their lives. The baby's father had added the second part of his own name, Notomiharjo, to mark his marriage, and from then on he was generally known as Noto. Names are also sometimes changed during childhood, particularly after persistent sickness or other misfortune, with a new name seen as a means of making a fresh start.[3] This was the case with Mulyono. Early in his life, his parents changed his name to Joko Widodo. "Joko" is a very common Javanese boy's name; "Widodo" indicates health and prosperity.

In 1961, Noto and Sujiatmi were settled in the busy environment of Surakarta. But they were not originally city folk. They had grown up in the Javanese countryside, and each had a distinctive family background that would inform the values and attitudes of their son, and would help prepare him for his future career.

The Village Headman: Jokowi's Paternal Grandfather

The village of Kragan lies in Gondangrejo District, Karanganyar Regency, northeast of Surakarta. Today, this is a busy and increasingly built-up area, just a few kilometers from the outer suburbs of the city. A section of the Trans-Java toll road, opened in 2018, passes nearby. But in the early decades of Indonesia's independence Kragan was isolated and poor, as were most villages in Java at that time. It was the childhood home of Jokowi's father, Wijiatno Notomiharjo, whose own father, Lamidi Wiryo Miharjo,[4] was *lurah*, or headman.

The role of *lurah* was a traditional aspect of local society that had been carried over into the modern state as the highest rank in village governance.[5] It was technically a bureaucratic appointment but it sometimes retained an element of heredity and also of rule by community assent. In the deeply traditional village society of the time, the *lurah* had a cultural standing connected to the lowest ranks of the colonial and precolonial *priyayi* class, or nobility. None of this necessarily implied great power or material wealth, and a *lurah* in a small and impoverished community like

---

[3] Wawan Mas'udi and Akhmad Ramdhon, *Jokowi: dari Bantaran Kalianyar ke Istana* (Jakarta: Gramedia Pustaka Utama, 2018), 31.

[4] Ibid., 58.

[5] "Kedudukan pemerintahan desa," https://guruppkn.com/strukturorganisasi-pemerinta-han-desa [accessed August 15, 2019].

Kragan lived a lifestyle much the same as that of the other villagers. It did, however, imply a great deal of local respect. Lamidi Wiryo Miharjo was generally known as Mbah Wiryo, or simply Mbah Lurah, using a Javanese honorific for a respected elder. He had begun his career as *carik*, or village secretary,[6] before assuming the post of *lurah* in the early 1950s, just a few years after Indonesia gained its independence. He held the position until 1983.[7] Although the *lurah* position is a nonpartisan civil service role, early in his career Mbah Wiryo was also involved in party politics and was active at the village level in the Partai Nasional Indonesia (Indonesian Nationalist Party; PNI),[8] the postindependence successor to Sukarno's original PNI and one of the nationalist precursors of PDI-P.

Amongst the residents of Kragan, Mbah Wiryo was known as an official who was approachable and light-hearted, who took part in communal activities as an equal, and whose home was always open to visitors, especially the village children who were always welcome to play around his house and who were often provided food by Mbah Wiryo and his wife Painem. There was a strong emphasis on nation-building idealism in the early Sukarno years, and as *lurah* Mbah Wiryo was responsible for encouraging positive attitudes amongst his community. The fact that he retained his position through the turbulent transition from Sukarno's rule to Suharto's New Order era is some indication of his skill. The political turmoil of 1965–66 also had an impact at village level, drastically changing the face of Indonesian society.[9] Rural Central Java was certainly affected, and as headman Mbah Wiryo sought to protect all his citizens.[10] As a political party figure at the village level, he had to act deftly to avoid being caught up in the political violence himself. He approached party officials from his own party, the PNI, and Masyumi (Indonesian Muslim Council) to be actively involved in protecting the security of the village, including protecting those villagers who could have become victims of the political upheaval.[11]

According to local reminiscences, this was not the first time Mbah Wiryo had defended the people of Kragan during a time of instability and political violence. During the revolutionary period 1945–49, Dutch

[6] The Javanese government model is discussed in Niels Mulder, *Ruang Batin Masyarakat Indonesia* (Yogyakarta: LKiS, 2000), 75.

[7] The workings of democracy in Javanese villages is discussed in Prijono Tjiptoherijanto and Yumiko M. Prijono, *Demokrasi di Perdesaan Jawa* (Jakarta: Pustaka Sinar Harapan, 1983).

[8] Budhi Wuryanto, *Sukarno Muda* (Yogyakarta: Lokomotif, 2010), 126.

[9] Mas'udi and Ramdhon, *Jokowi: dari Bantaran Kalianyar ke Istana*, 37.

[10] Ibid., 72.

[11] Ibid., 75.

military offensives had an impact on many villages, including Kragan.[12] At the time, Wiryo was serving as village secretary. He learned that Dutch troops had entered the area and he met with their commander at the gate to the village. The older generations who witnessed the incident recall how Wiryo spoke to the commander of the Dutch troops. "In Kragan village there are none of the guerrilla soldiers that are being sought by the Dutch forces. If you do not believe this, please search. If even one fighter is found, just shoot me," he said.[13]

His ability to protect the village was repeatedly tested and proven in other episodes of turmoil during Indonesia's subsequent history. Mbah Wiryo held his position in Kragan for three decades, until his retirement, having passed his entire career in the governance of one small village. Like many village officials, he also combined his civil service position with other customary roles. He is understood to have been the *juru kunci*, the guardian, of the tomb of a historical noble, said to have been an ancestor of Siti Hartinah, wife of Suharto.

Although the point is often made that Jokowi's own origins lie completely outside politics, that he has no hereditary connections to the ruling elite of previous generations and did not grow up in a political environment, his grandfather, Mbah Wiryo, is a significant figure. Growing up, Jokowi's first point of reference and only direct personal connection with governance and public service came via the well-loved and long-serving *lurah*, a man entirely embedded in the village of Kragan in a role where governance and leadership were entirely intertwined with his own daily life amongst neighbors, and where dialogue and community assent were essential.

Wiryo Miharjo and his wife Painem had five children, all male.[14] Their oldest son was Wijiatno. Although his parents lived in Kragan, Wijiatno also spent much time in another village community, Giriroto, around fifteen kilometers to the west in Boyolali Regency, where his grandmother lived in a hamlet called Kelelesan.[15] It was there that he first met a girl a few years his junior from the neighboring Giriroto hamlet of Gumuk Rejo. Her name was Sujiatmi. They played together as children, and then developed a

---

[12] Ibid., 72.

[13] Ibid, 73.

[14] Domu D. Ambarita, *Jokowi Spirit Bantaran Kali Anyar* (Jakarta: Elex Media Komputindo, 2012), 67.

[15] Deden Gunawan and Ibad Durohman, "Kisah Mulyono Menjadi Joko Widodo," *detikNews*, January 14, 2017, https://news.detik.com/x/detail/investigasi/20170113 Kisah-Mulyono-Menjadi-Joko-Widodo/ [accessed September 11, 2020].

romantic attachment as teenagers. Wijiatno would often give Sujiatmi a lift to school on his motorbike.[16] The couple married on August 23, 1959. The bride was sixteen, the groom nineteen. This may seem very young today, but it was entirely normal in rural Javanese communities at that time.[17]

A Family Business: The Maternal Inheritance

Sujiatmi was the middle child of three, *sendhang kapit pancuran* as the Javanese idiom has it, "a lake surrounded by waterspouts," that is, an only girl with both an older and a younger brother.[18] Her home place, Gumuk Rejo, was a hamlet like the other hamlets scattered throughout Java in those days, isolated and with little access to other villages or to the nearest town. Even though it was not far from the city of Surakarta, Gumuk Rejo was a village whose citizens were deeply impoverished despite the fact that the name of the place meant "prosperous hill." The vast majority of the residents were farmers or agricultural laborers.[19] There were, in fact, virtually no other options for employment. Those who owned large tracts of land became farmers and those whose plots were small supplemented their income by laboring for the bigger landowners. It was an undynamic, economically stagnant environment. But Sujiatmi's father, Wiroredjo, commonly known as Wiro, had taken a different path. Instead of becoming a farmer or laborer like his neighbors, he had set himself up as a trader selling timber, bamboo, and charcoal.[20]

The timber trade, contrary to initial appearances, requires extensive practical skill and close knowledge of the entire supply chain, as well as the ability to "read" the various opportunities available in the market. For example, when it came to bamboo, Wiro had to know the best sources and which types of bamboo were available in each place. He also had to find out which types of bamboo were in greatest demand at any one time. *Petung* bamboo is different from *apus* bamboo, which is different again

---

[16] Ibid.

[17] In the 1950s and 1960s, teenage marriages were the norm in Java, with many marriages arranged by the parents. For more on this, see Bramantio et al. eds., *Urban dalam Wacana: Kesehatan, Budaya, dan Masyarakat* (Surabaya: Fakultas Ilmu Budaya Universitas Airlangga, 2013).

[18] In Javanese tradition, boys are symbolized by waterspouts while girls are symbolized by lakes. These terms are usually used to describe families with three children, where the middle child is flanked by siblings of the opposite gender.

[19] Mas'udi and Ramdhon, *Jokowi: dari Bantaran Kalianyar ke Istana*, 104.

[20] Ibid., 103.

from *wulung* bamboo. Buyers also had different demands. A bamboo seller must also know when is the right time to cut down old bamboo trees. Bamboo felled in the dry season will be more resistant to insect attacks. Bamboo should also be felled in the afternoon because water levels have decreased and the plants have stopped photosynthesis. In short, the wood and bamboo trade requires complex knowledge of ever-shifting supplies and markets.[21]

It was in this business environment that Sujiatmi and, in turn, her own son, Jokowi, grew up. Before her marriage, she helped her parents selling wood, bamboo, and charcoal. At the time, her father was expanding their trade in the Srambat area of northern Surakarta,[22] and there was much coming and going between the village and the town. Wiro was also guiding his first son Miyono, Sujiatmi's older brother, to develop his own business in Surakarta, a business which later grew into a relatively large furniture company.

Wijiatno Notomiharjo: Taking a Different Path

In the mid-twentieth century, the oldest son of a village head had a good chance of taking up his father's office.[23] The role of *lurah* in rural Java at the time was, by unofficial convention, often hereditary. However, Mbah Wiryo's oldest son did not choose this path. It would have meant relative security and an assured lifelong civil service position, but it would also have meant a permanent commitment to an isolated and undynamic village environment. He chose instead to take a risk on a new life, leaving the quiet countryside for a busy urban world.

Having married Sujiatmi and taken on a new name, Notomiharjo, to mark the transition, he moved to Surakarta and began working in his wife's family trade: bamboo and wood.[24] To begin with, the young couple helped in the business of Sujiatmi's father.[25] In this new life and new career Notomiharjo was also greatly influenced and supported by his brother-in-law, Miyono. In time, the timber business founded by Sujiatmi's father was developed by the two younger men, who each had their own separate

---

[21] Mas'udi and Ramdhon, *Jokowi: dari Bantaran Kalianyar ke Istana*, 111.

[22] Asita D. K. Anton Nugrahanto, *Sekelumit Kisah Si Tukang Blusukan* (Yogyakarta: Kana Media, 2014), 81–82.

[23] Mas'udi and Ramdhon, *Jokowi: dari Bantaran Kalianyar ke Istana*, 58.

[24] Keen Achroni, *Jokowi Memimpin dengan Hati* (Yogyakarta: Ar-Ruzz Media, 2018), 33.

[25] Mas'udi and Ramdhon, *Jokowi: dari Bantaran Kalianyar ke Istana*, 29.

but mutually supportive businesses, a common enough practice in extended Javanese families working in a single sector. At the outset, Miyono benefited from the greater expertise he had learnt from his father, Wiro, and his company, CV Roda Jati, grew faster than that pioneered by the Notomiharjo-Sujiatmi family.[26] But Miyono was ever-supportive and he would later give great aid to Jokowi on his own journey in the timber trade. But it was from his father, Notomiharjo, that Jokowi developed the courage to take risks, to step aside from an easy though unexciting inheritance, and to have the confidence to break new ground.

Jokowi today remembers his father as a tough fighter for the survival of his family, someone willing to suffer privations rather than run back to his own father's feet. He also recalls Notomiharjo as someone who convinced him that education was the route to changing one's life.[27] "You have to stay in school! Study so you'll be smart. Your destiny will surely change; it won't be difficult as it was for your parents," his father told Jokowi one day during his childhood.[28]

Sujiatmi: Work and Prayer

Jokowi remained close to his mother throughout her life, and until her death in 2020 she was a major influence. He turned to her for advice ahead of every major decision;[29] Jokowi's father, Notomiharjo, died in 2000 at the age of 60.[30]

On one occasion, before the start of his political career, Jokowi wanted to expand his business abroad, specifically to Dubai.[31] He asked for Sujiatmi's advice. She did not give him the green light, but at that moment Jokowi felt that he needed to expand the business so he persisted anyway. The attempt did not succeed.

"I tried it twice, and twice it failed, because my mother had not given her blessing," he says. Jokowi's decision making process throughout both his business and political careers has often been dominated by mechanical mathematical considerations, but his mother complemented this with

---

[26] Ibid., 101.

[27] See also Hasanudin Abdurakhman, *Melawan Miskin Pikiran* (Bandung: Penerbit Nuansa, 2016), 14–16.

[28] Endah, *Jokowi Perjalanan Karya bagi Bangsa Menuju Cahaya*, 31.

[29] Arif Hidayat, *Keajaiban Doa Ibu* (Jakarta: Penerbit Al-Maghfirah, 2013).

[30] "Jokowi Ziarah ke Makan Ayahnya," *Republika*, June 14, 2014, https://republika.co.id/berita/n75og3/jokowi-ziarah-ke-makan-ayahnya [accessed September 11, 2020].

[31] Ambarita, *Jokowi Spirit Bantaran Kali Anyar*, 21.

emotional insights. She was a deeply spiritual woman, who spent much time in prayer, and her family felt that her judgements carried the weight of premonition.

As a young woman, Sujiatmi was closely involved in her husband's timber business. Every morning after cooking and tidying up, she went to their place of business to help tying up the bundles of bamboo and wood and doing odd jobs.[32] When her husband took on extra work as a public transport driver, it was Sujiatmi who took over the responsibility of selling wood and bamboo.[33] Jokowi recalls that as well as dedicating much time to the business, Sujiatmi was very strict in educating her children. But although they were strictly disciplined, the children were never beaten by their parents. "I was never hit with a brush," Jokowi recalls.[34]

In terms of this discipline, Notomiharjo and Sujiatmi seem to have believed that it was the only way to impart their children with good character. Moreover, Jokowi was their only boy and was expected to become the mainstay of the family in the next generation. He was reportedly a *ngglidhik* child, naughty but not truly naughty, tending to silences, but with obvious natural intelligence. As the only boy in the family, he was particularly close to his mother. His three younger sisters were closer to their father.

A Cheerful Child

Sujiatmi was a first-time mother and still a teenager when Jokowi was born, so for the first forty days of his life she returned to her home hamlet, Gumuk Rejo in Giriroto village, where her own mother could help her take care of the baby.[35] Once mother and baby had settled, they returned to the city. In time, Sujiatmi and Notomiharjo had three other children, all girls.

The young family rented a house in an area officially called Kampung Cinderejo Lor, but more popularly known as Randu Alas, after a large *randu alas* (cotton tree) that grew there, right on the edge of the Kali Anyar. However, when the Surakarta City Government converted the land into an intercity public transport terminal the residents were evicted and had to find new places to live. Notomiharjo and Sujiatmi were among the displaced residents, and like their neighbors they received no compensation because neither they nor the landlord held legal title to the land on the

---

[32] Alberthiene Endah, *Jokowi Memimpin Kota Menyentuh Jakarta* (Solo: Metagraf, 2012), 21.
[33] Ibid., 25.
[34] Ibid., 18.
[35] Gunawan and Durohman, "Kisah Mulyono Menjadi Joko Widodo."

riverbank, which was officially state property.[36] The site of their former home became a terminal where local minibuses sought passengers heading to other Central Java towns such as Purwodadi, Semarang, Madiun, and Yogyakarta, as well as the more distant big cities of Surabaya and Jakarta.

As a small child, Jokowi did not understand that the house he lived in did not belong to his parents. So the experience of eviction had a powerful impact in terms of both immediate emotion and a new awareness of the realities and complexities of life.[37] It gave him his first insight into legal issues, from the talk of the adults around him, and a first insight into the way authorities could at times be in conflict with the public.

In the immediate aftermath, the family moved temporarily into the house of Miyono, Sujiatmi's older brother. Miyono was Jokowi's *pakdhe*, his senior uncle.[38] In Javanese culture, the oldest man or woman in a group of siblings generally takes the role of head of the extended family in adulthood, a role acknowledged by the honorifics *pakdhe* for a man and *budhe* for a woman. As well as general social seniority, the *pakdhe* or *budhe* of a particular family will often take on certain financial responsibilities when other, more junior family members are in need. Jokowi's parents' temporary residence with Pakdhe Miyono reflected this. Eventually, Notomiharjo and Sujiatmi were able to earn enough money to find another rental property of their own, and Notomiharjo found temporary work as an intercity public transport driver to supplement the income from his embryonic timber business and to support his young family.[39]

Although they remained in the same neighborhood, these moves required an adjustment, familiarity with new neighbors, and the making of new friends and acquaintances. Other moves followed during Jokowi's childhood and youth. Each time he moved he had to familiarize himself with a new set of neighbors, becoming ever more flexible and used to dealing with different people with different origins and ways of life. There was, however, always a tight sense of community in the close-knit urban *kampung*, as much as there was in the rural villages of his grandparents. On feast days and during important family events such as weddings or circumcision ceremonies, people would practice a sort of open house, and there would be snacks and entertainment for the local children. Even a neighbor the young Jokowi had previously only briefly passed in the street

---

[36] Thayrun, *Jokowi Pemimpin Rakyat Berjiwa Rocker*, 6.

[37] Endah, *Jokowi Memimpin Kota Menyentuh Jakarta*, 22.

[38] Achroni, *Jokowi Memimpin dengan Hati*, 25.

[39] Thayrun, *Jokowi Pemimpin Rakyat Berjiwa Rocker*, 7.

would welcome him into their home on a feast day. Inside the houses he would learn intimate details of neighbors' lives, see the aged members of the family who no longer went outside, and the chronically ill who were kept away from the world.[40]

The local grapevine always hummed with gossip and news, and even a young child like little Jokowi would pick up word of serious or negative matters, learning of a misfortune that had befallen a neighbor: a theft, a sickness, a death. There were also superstitions and magical stories. He took it all in, but as he grew towards adulthood he came to understand that not everything he heard was strictly true.

Although he was forbidden to do so, as a child Jokowi loved to swim in the river with his best friend, Bandi.[41] He called the older boy "Mas," a common Javanese term of address, while Bandi called him "Le," short for *thole*, which means "boy." They are said to have been as close as brothers. It was Bandi who taught Jokowi to swim and who generally kept an eye on him during riverside games, somewhat easing the worries of Sujiatmi, known to her neighbors as Bu Noto, about his safety.

In the years before he started school, Sujiatmi had help looking after little Jokowi from a nanny called Mukiyem.[42] Although in most Western countries only wealthy families are able to afford a nanny, in Indonesia even households with a very modest income may employ a part-time helper, often a woman from the immediate neighborhood without other employment. To be clear, Notomiharjo and Sujiatmi were not truly poor people. Though both came originally from impoverished villages, they were from families that were amongst the better off in those places, headed by a civil servant on one side and a local small businessman on the other. They belonged to a relatively mobile Javanese class during the early decades of Indonesia's independence, with at least some education and financial resources and a ready ability to move between rural and urban settings, not out of absolute desperation but in search of new and more exciting opportunities. Theirs were, in fact, the classic origins of the emerging, socially mobile modern Indonesian middle class, outside the small traditional elite of both town and country.

---

[40] Endah, *Jokowi Perjalanan Karya bagi Bangsa Menuju Cahaya*, 32.

[41] The origins of the friendship between Jokowi and Bandi is discussed in Deden Gunawan and Ibad Durohman, "Masa Kecil dan Cerita-cerita Tersembunyi tentang Jokowi," *detikNews*, https://news.detik.com/berita/d-3396869/masa-kecil-dan-cerita-ceritatersembunyi [accessed March 17, 2019].

[42] Gunawan and Durohman, "Kisah Mulyono Menjadi Joko Widodo."

Nonetheless, they did live in close proximity to precarity and severe poverty, and in the 1950s and 1960s there was often a fine line between people in such conditions, and the likes of Notomiharjo and Sujiatmi. Notomiharjo's decision to turn away from a career in village governance to try to establish himself as an entrepreneur made them particularly vulnerable, though the extended Javanese family network would always protect them from absolute destitution.

Growing up, Jokowi often saw neighbors who were sick but were unable to buy medicine or receive hospital care for lack of money, and he saw how they dealt with their situation, turning to the homemade remedies which could be obtained easily and cheaply. He also saw directly the way his mother struggled to care for his younger sisters when they fell sick. She did not use expensive medicines, and did not go to a doctor, but relied instead on herbal remedies that could be prepared at home.[43] He also saw some of his playmates drop out of school because their parents could not pay the fees.[44] This sharpened his awareness of his parents' commitment to his own education.

"Whatever the condition of our family, you all must go to school," his father had told them.[45]

As a quiet child, Jokowi did reportedly receive some hostile attention from bullies at school. However, there were no serious consequences and he had no significant difficulties in his early education. The only slight bump in the road came in his teenage years when he failed to gain a high enough mark for entry to his first choice of senior high school. But he went on to complete his schooling successfully in another institution.

Wood and Metal: Jokowi's Student Years

The timber business had colored Jokowi's childhood. He grew up with the smell of wood from the moment he woke up in the morning until he went to sleep at night, and he expected from an early age to become a timber entrepreneur himself. But he heeded his father's firm emphasis on the value of education, and on graduating high school he went on to a place at Gadjah Mada University (UGM) in Yogyakarta, sixty kilometers west

---

[43] Endah, *Jokowi Memimpin Kota Menyentuh Jakarta*, 30
[44] Ibid.
[45] Idrus Marham, *Keutamaan Jokowi: Studi Kepemimpinan Nasional dalam Perspektif Kesinambungan Pembangunan* (Bekasi: Penjuru Ilmu, 2017), 129.

of Surakarta. UGM was, and remains, one of Indonesia's most prestigious state universities. Jokowi's choice of academic specialism was entirely determined by his background, and by his intended future career: he studied in the Forestry Faculty.

Jokowi began his university studies in 1980, graduating five years later. One of his former lecturers, Kasmudjo, remembers him as a conscientious and disciplined student, though he also notes that this was the norm amongst UGM students at the time. Kasmudjo also recalls that Jokowi was still committed to helping out in his family business throughout his university days.

"I remember that he used to go back and forth by motorbike from Solo-Yogya, just to help out in his family's furniture business," Kasmudjo says.[46]

The forestry program had a practical emphasis and Jokowi and his classmates often left the campus on field trips to forest areas. According to one of his fellow students, Adriana (one of just eight women in the eighty-strong cohort, and now herself a UGM lecturer), this created a particularly strong bond amongst them. Jokowi would look back fondly on his student days and the friendships he made at the time, and according to Adriana, once he had graduated and begun his career, he would sometimes contact his former classmates to arrange nostalgic get-togethers.[47]

The early 1980s were a time of political stability and improving standards of living in Indonesia, and university campuses were not the hotbeds of protest politics they would become in the subsequent decades. For Jokowi, student life was mainly a matter of hard work on his studies, frequent returns to his family in Surakarta, as well as friendship with his fellow forestry students. He was an active member of a student mountaineering club and made at least one long-distance trip, to Sumatra, to climb a mountain. He also maintained the interest in heavy metal music which he had first encountered at fourteen at junior high school,[48] and which prompted various international media reports about the "heavy metal president" after his rise to political fame. Metallica, Megadeth, and

---

[46] "Teman Seangkatan Harap Jokowi Bisa Bawa Indonesia Makin Maju," Universitas Gadjah Mada, October 21, 2019, https://ugm.ac.id/id/berita/18612-teman-seangkatan-harap-jokowi-bisa-bawa-indonesia-makin-maju [accessed October 8, 2020].

[47] Ibid.

[48] Dom Lawson, "Joko 'Jokowi' Widodo's metal manifesto," The Guardian, July 11, 2014, https://www.theguardian.com/music/2014/jul/11/joko-jokowi-widodos-metal-manifesto [accessed October 8, 2020].

Napalm Death were among the enduring favorites he discovered during his student years.[49] Jokowi's genuine lifelong heavy metal fandom was demonstrated in later years when, as governor of Jakarta, he was always keen to attend the concerts of visiting international metal bands. In 2017, he even paid Rp11 million out of his own pocket to be allowed to keep for personal use a signed, limited vinyl edition of Metallica's *Master of Puppets* album, gifted by the Danish government and thus initially declared a state asset.[50]

Jokowi completed his university studies in 1985. The subject of his dissertation project shows that he was still firmly focused, as he had been since childhood, on a career in his hometown timber industry. The dissertation was titled "A Study on Plywood Consumption Patterns in End Use in the Municipality of Surakarta."[51]

Like many of his fellow forestry students, Jokowi had hoped to gain an initial graduate post in Indonesia's state-owned forestry company, Perhutani, but he did not succeed in the stringent entry test for prospective employees.[52] He was, however, able to find a post with another state operation, a post that would take him a long way from Central Java.

A Perfect Couple: Marriage and Early Career

One day in early 1987 a young couple, newly married, could be seen descending from a plane that had just arrived from Java at Blangbintang Airport in Banda Aceh at the northernmost tip of Sumatra, more than 2,000 kilometers from their home city of Surakarta. They were carrying large suitcases containing clothes and personal effects, and were about to begin a new life.[53] The man was employed as a surveyor at a wood processing

[49] Michael Bachelard, "Indonesia's likely new President Joko is a Megadeth fan but this is no cause for alarm," *Sydney Morning Herald*, July 9, 2014, https://www.smh.com.au/world/indonesias-likely-new-president-joko-is-a-megadeth-fan-but-this-is-no-cause-for-alarm-20140710-zt1r7.html [accessed October 8, 2020].

[50] Eli Meixler, "Indonesia's President Paid $800 to Keep a Limited-Edition Metallica Album," *Time*, February 22, 2018, https://time.com/5172101/indonesia-president-joko-widodo-metallica-master-of-puppets/ [accessed October 8, 2020].

[51] "Terungkap, Ternyata Ini Lho Judul Skripsi Jokowi saat Kuliah di UGM," *Surya Malang*, January 15, 2017, https://suryamalang.tribunnews.com/2017/01/15/terungkap-ternyata-ini-lho-judul-skripsi-jokowi-saat-kuliah-di-ugm [accessed October 8, 2020].

[52] Switzy Sabandar, "4 Kenangan Jokowi Saat Kuliah di Fakultas Kehutanan UGM," *Liputan6*, December 19, 2017, https://www.liputan6.com/news/read/3201101/4-kenangan-jokowi-saat-kuliah-di-fakultas-kehutanan-ugm [accessed October 8, 2020].

[53] Endah, *Jokowi Memimpin Kota Menyentuh Jakarta*, 48.

plant in this remote and troubled province. The woman was just settling into her new role as a housewife.

The then 25-year-old Joko Widodo had begun working at the plant the previous year. When he first took up the job he was still unmarried, though he had a sweetheart in his hometown. He had recently graduated as a Bachelor of Forestry and planned to work hard in that discipline. But he did not intend on a long-term career employed by others. What he really wanted was to take on the timber business that had been started by his parents. But he knew that to take that business to the next level he needed a wider range of experience. So, as soon as the first job offer came along, it was an opportunity that he seized. He was recruited and sent with five other recent forestry graduates[54] to a factory belonging to a state-owned company named PT Kertas Kraft Aceh, which produced heavy-duty paper for cement sacks and other industrial purposes.[55]

After several months working in Aceh, he decided to marry the woman he had been dating since the beginning of his time at university. He returned briefly home to Surakarta for the wedding, on December 24, 1986.[56] The girl was named Iriana and he had now brought her along to his new place of work.

"I'll just go along," Iriana had said. "If we are married then I must accompany you. It's no problem to live in the forest."[57] It was a typically calm and pragmatic response to a challenging career move by her husband. She had already left university to get married,[58] and was now going to live in rudimentary conditions in a remote location in a far-off province with a reputation for instability.

Jokowi had not initially imagined that his new workplace would be in the middle of the forest. The word "factory" had suggested an urban location, but in fact the plant was sited in an isolated area, close to its

---

[54] "Ternyata Jokowi Pernah Bekerja di Perusahaan Milik Prabowo di Aceh Tengah Pemasok Bahan Baku PT KKA," *Bangka Pos*, February 19, 2019, https://bangka.tribunnews.com/2019/02/19/ternyata-jokowi-pernah-bekerja-di-perusahaan-milik-prabowo-di-aceh-tengah-pemasok-bahan-baku-pt-kka?page=all [accessed October 8, 2020].

[55] Ferdian Ananda Majni, "Kisah Kehidupan Jokowi di Gayo," *Media Indonesia*, January 13, 2018, https://mediaindonesia.com/read/detail/140562-kisah-kehidupan-jokowi-di-gayo [accessed September 11, 2020].

[56] Ibid.

[57] Endah, *Jokowi Memimpin Kota Menyentuh Jakarta*, 47.

[58] Andhika Prasetia, "Jokowi: Iriana Dulu Kuliah di Muhamadiyah, Semester 6 Saya Ajak Kawin," *detikNews*, November 19, 2018, https://news.detik.com/berita/d-4307951/jokowi-iriana-dulu-kuliah-di-muhamadiyah-semester-6-saya-ajak-kawin [accessed September 11, 2020].

supply of raw timber. The company provided onsite accommodation for its employees. However, the housing turned out to be only a longhouse partitioned with wooden slats. "The barracks are good," Jokowi recalls his wife calmly saying at her first sight of their new lodgings, though he also recalls that she was unable to hide her shock at the rudimentary conditions.

The factory was in the middle of a large forest of the indigenous Sumatran Merkus pine in the Gayo Highlands of Central Aceh, close to the foot of Mount Burni Telong.[59] It was far from any villages. During the day, only the roar of a wood-cutting machine could be heard. At night, there was only the sound of the wind and the occasional cry of an animal. Sometimes herds of wild pigs would emerge from the forest and create a disturbance around the barracks.[60]

At that time, Aceh was not the peaceful area it is today. A long-running insurgency with roots in the colonial era was continuing at a low level. Armed insurgents were active and sometimes clashed with the military, and there were frequent rumors about these clashes. (A more extreme insurgency would erupt the following decade and continue sporadically, despite international peace efforts, until a final settlement in the aftermath of the 2004 tsunami, which devastated coastal Aceh.) However, the young couple were not daunted by such rumors. And they often spent time away from the factory and the longhouse, in the regional cities of Banda Aceh or Lhokseumawe in search of civilization and excitement.[61] Everything was far removed from the lively atmosphere in Surakarta where they had grown up, and their recent sophisticated student life. Sometimes, when he had a weekend off, Jokowi took Iriana to explore the villages in the hills near the factory. Colleagues from the time recall that Jokowi still kept up his childhood hobby of fishing and would encourage them to join him on trips to mountain lakes. They also recall night-time games of dominos and listening to rock music at the plant base camp.[62] As a surveyor, Jokowi often had to travel deep into the forest, and he reportedly suffered at least one bout of malaria during his time in Aceh.[63]

Jokowi's anxiety about taking Iriana to such an extreme location in the early days of their marriage, at a time when they were still adjusting to

---

[59] Thayrun, *Jokowi Pemimpin Rakyat Berjiwa Rocker*, 15.

[60] Endah, *Jokowi Perjalanan Karya bagi Bangsa Menuju Cahaya*, 41–43.

[61] Ibid., 48.

[62] "Ternyata Jokowi Pernah Bekerja di Perusahaan Milik Prabowo," *Bangka Pos*, February 19, 2019.

[63] Endah, *Jokowi Perjalanan Karya bagi Bangsa Menuju Cahaya*, 48.

wedded life and still getting to know one another properly, was dispelled by Iriana's calmness. His concern that the situation would make her fearful and panicked was met with a simple response, "But you'll be there."[64]

Iriana was born in Surakarta in 1963. According to Jokowi's mother, she knew from early on that Iriana would be the first and last girlfriend of her eldest child.

"She was a friend of my second child," Sujiatmi recalled.[65]

The couple have their own recollections of the start of their romantic relationship, though there is some good-natured disagreement about how exactly things developed.

"She was always coming to my house with the excuse of looking for my sister," Jokowi says.

But Iriana remembers things differently. "Oh no. He was the one chasing me. He was the one who liked me first."[66]

She proved to be a steadfast partner, and would later be as calm and pragmatic in accepting the challenges which would come with her husband's move into politics and rapid ascent to the national stage as she had been when he had asked her to accompany him to the Acehnese forest many years earlier. When asked in recent years about the pressures of public life, she has responded, "Everyone has a saturation point. But I am grateful for this public mandate. It makes me happy. With a happy heart, one seldom feels tired. If you are tired, take a rest."[67]

Raising a Family and Rising in the Business World

The next chapter of Joko Widodo's life began with Iriana's pregnancy. When they discovered that they were expecting a child, Joko asked Iriana to return to their hometown of Surakarta while he himself continued to work in Aceh. He followed her home for the arrival of their son, Gibran Rakabuming Raka, who was born on October 1, 1987. They would go on to have two more children, a daughter, Kahiyang Ayu, born in 1991, and a second son, Kaesang Pangarep, born in 1994. Initially, Jokowi continued working in Aceh, but he found it difficult to endure separation from his young family. He left PT Kertas Kraft Aceh in 1989 and returned permanently to Surakarta.

---

[64] Ibid.

[65] Ambarita, *Jokowi Spirit Bantaran Kali Anyar*, 80.

[66] Thayrun, *Jokowi Pemimpin Rakyat Berjiwa Rocker*, 13.

[67] Zaenuddin H. M., *Jokowi Dari Jualan Kursi Hingga Dua Kali Mendapatkan Kursi* (Jakarta: Ufuk Press, 2012), 88–89.

Jokowi (back row center) as a young child in the 1960s.

Jokowi (front right) and fellow students from the Mapala Silvagama club at Gadjah Mada University heading off on a hiking trip in the 1980s.

Jokowi (squatting right) on a trip with fellow student adventurers.

A group of Gadjah Mada University students about to board a bus to the mountains. Jokowi is squatting front right.

Jokowi (seated bottom left) with fellow student mountaineers posing on the slopes of one of Indonesia's volcanic mountains.

Jokowi (wearing cap) demonstrating his campsite cookery skills during a trip with other student mountaineers.

ABOVE Surakarta, Jokowi's hometown, is a sprawling low-rise city in the heart of Java centered on a kraton (royal palace).

LEFT The Kali Anyar river, which flows through the northern neighborhoods of Surakarta, was the site of Jokowi's childhood. His family lived in a series of rented houses on its banks.

Jokowi and other family members with his maternal grandparents, Wiroredjo (standing far left) and Sani (seated center), in the early 2000s. Sani died in 2015 at the age of 100.

Jokowi's parents, Sujiatmi and Wijiatno Notomiharjo, pose with wedding gifts for the bridal couple, Surakarta, 1986.

Miyono, Jokowi's eldest maternal uncle and furniture-manufacturing mentor, at Jokowi and Iriana's wedding.

Jokowi and Iriana on their wedding day in Surakarta, 1986.

The mountainous forested Gayo region of Aceh in northernmost Sumatra where Jokowi began his career after graduating with a degree in forestry from Gadjah Mada University.

Jokowi and Iriana on their wedding day, flanked by Jokowi's parents, Sujiatmi and Wijiatno Notomiharjo.

Jokowi and his mother offer prayers during a pilgrimage to the grave of his father during the 2014 presidential election campaign. Jokowi's father, Wijiatno Notomiharjo, died in 2000 and is buried in a family grave complex near his home village of Gondangrejo in the countryside north of Surakarta.

Jokowi with his beloved mother Sujiatmi at the start of his 2014 presidential campaign. Until her death in 2020, he always sought her blessings for any major life or career decision.

Jokowi and Iriana on their Haj, the Muslim pilgrimage to Mecca, in 2003, shortly before Jokowi's political career began. At the time, Jokowi was a successful businessman in early middle age, a period of life when many Indonesian Muslims make the pilgrimage.

ABOVE AND LEFT
Jokowi with
workers in his
furniture factory
in the 1990s.

Jokowi showcasing the products of his furniture company to international buyers.

Jokowi and fellow ASMINDO members. His leadership role in this business association sowed the seeds of his political career.

Jokowi with a colleague in front of the Palais Garnier in Paris during a business trip to France in the late 1990s.

Jokowi with a colleague on the road in Europe in the 1990s, exploring export markets for Indonesian furniture.

F. X. Hadi Rudyatmo, Jokowi's deputy during his time as mayor of Surakarta. A veteran local politician, Rudyatmo took over as mayor of Surakarta when Jokowi moved to Jakarta.

Basuki Tjahaja Purnama, better known as Ahok, Jokowi's deputy during his time as governor of Jakarta.

Jokowi watches Megawati Sukarnoputri, leader of the Partai Demokrasi Indonesia Perjuangan (PDI-P), during an event in 2004 at the start of their political relationship.

Jokowi with his first political partner, F. X. Hadi Rudyatmo. The pair governed Surakarta as mayor and deputy from 2004 to 2012.

Jokowi and F. X. Hadi Rudyatmo in traditional *wayang* costume, celebrating Surakarta's Javanese heritage.

During his term as Surakarta's mayor, Jokowi began to attract attention in international development circles. Here he speaks at a United Nations conference on housing and urban development in Kenya in 2009.

Jokowi showing off his early taste for heavy metal music when he was mayor of Surakarta.

BatikSolo Trans, a modern bus service running across Surakarta launched in 2010, was one of Jokowi's early infrastructure successes.

Jokowi as governor of Jakarta, a stepping-stone away from the presidency of Indonesia.

Jokowi on a *blusukan* site visit meeting Jakarta residents during his time as the city's governor.

The Jakarta MRT, a transformational infrastructure project, was stuck at the planning stage for around half a century before finally being kick-started during the Jokowi governorship.

Prabowo Subianto, Jokowi's former backer for the Jakarta governorship and two-time rival for the presidency, delivering a speech.

Jokowi with Megawati, long-standing chair of PDI-P and one of the most powerful backroom figures in Indonesian politics.

Jokowi speaking to a group of rural residents in Tegal, Central Java, in 2018 during a ceremony to issue official certification of land tenure. Land insecurity is a decades-old issue for many Indonesians, particularly in rural areas, where formal titles can be difficult to obtain.

Jokowi meeting with farmers and agricultural industry leaders on a *blusukan* visit to a rural farming community in Lampung, Sumatra, during the early days of his presidency.

Jokowi explains the KIS (Healthy Indonesia Card) program to the managing director of the International Monetary Fund, Christine Lagarde, during a visit to a Jakarta hospital in 2018.

Schoolchildren pose with their KIP (Smart Indonesia Cards), which provide educational support funds for underprivileged families with the aim of reducing the school drop-out rate.

A new *embung* (irrigation reservoir) in Giriroto, the home village of Jokowi's mother, Sujiatmi. During Jokowi's childhood, the lack of irrigation meant that farmers in the village were unable to cultivate their fields all year round.

Pujon Kidul, a mountain village in East Java, which has successfully used a Village Fund allocation to develop tourism facilities run by residents.

Sukarno (third from left) outside the courthouse during his 1930 trial by the Dutch colonial authorities.

Sukarno casting his ballot at Indonesia's first—and for a long time only—general election in 1955.

Sukarno, Indonesia's first president (1945–1967).

Suharto, Indonesia's second president (1967–1998).

Suharto, flanked on the right by his deputy, B. J. Habibie, announces his resignation on May 21, 1998, ending his three-decade New Order presidency and ushering in the Reformasi period.

LEFT Indonesia's third president, B. J. Habibie, served for just 71 days, but his short presidency provided a transition between the New Order and the Reformasi period.

BELOW B. J. Habibie on the campaign trail for Golkar during the last New Order election in 1997.

TOP A massive PDI-P rally fills the streets of central Jakarta in 1999 in the run-up to the first proper democratic election since 1955.

LEFT Indonesia's fourth president, Abdurrahman Wahid, popularly known as Gus Dur, at the World Economic Forum meeting in 2000. He served from 1999 to 2001.

Megawati Sukarnoputri, who served as Indonesia's fifth president from 2001 to 2004, remains an influential figure as chair of PDI-P. Her backing was vital in Jokowi's rise to the Jakarta governorship and onwards to the presidency.

Susilo Bambang Yudhoyono, popularly known by his initials SBY, was Indonesia's first directly elected president. Shown here at the United Nations in 2007, he served two terms, from 2004 to 2014, and bolstered Indonesia's image internationally.

Jusuf Kalla, vice president during Jokowi's first term. A highly experienced politician, he had served in the same role under Jokowi's predecessor, SBY, and was thus debarred from running with Jokowi for a second term because of the constitutional two-term limit.

Jokowi's choice for his second-term running mate surprised many: Ma'ruf Amin, a senior Muslim cleric.

ABOVE Jokowi, flanked by Iriana and outgoing president Susilo Bambang Yudhoyono, heading for the presidential palace on October 20, 2014, for Jokowi's inauguration.

LEFT Jokowi's first official portrait after becoming the seventh president of the Republic of Indonesia.

Having left the secure job in Aceh, Jokowi decided to continue an apprenticeship of sorts in the trade while working for CV Roda Jati, the company owned by his mother's older brother, his Pakdhe Miyono.[68] That company, which still exists today, specialized in the manufacturing of high-quality furniture. The timber trade in general and the furniture business in particular was a challenging environment in the 1980s, with fierce competition, demanding buyers, and difficulties obtaining permits and confirming the legality of the raw timber. Jokowi had to get to grips with all of this. The unwritten rules for dealing with corrupt officials were also something that he had to understand. These were experiences that gradually informed a commitment to the ideal of a clean and transparent social order, and a desire to clean up the mafia-infested business world, which often created challenges for a young would-be entrepreneur.

Like his father before him, Jokowi was determined to become fully independent and to develop his own business. His early attempts at this ended in repeated failure, probably due to a surfeit of youthful enthusiasm which was not tempered by sufficient caution.[69] In 1988, he ventured to open his own furniture business under the name CV Rakabu, a name taken from a part of the name of his first son. With just three employees at the outset, the company had a shaky start. At one point in the early days, Jokowi was tricked into providing a large order that ultimately was not paid for. However, he rose again from this setback in 1990, with a capital loan of Rp30 million from his mother,[70] and later expanded the business further with help from a state scheme to support SMEs.[71] The repeated early business failures ultimately provided him with excellent experience and knowledge of the potential pitfalls, and also enhanced his resilience in the face of setbacks.

CV Rakabu grew into a successful company through the 1990s. In 1991, Jokowi made his first overseas business trip to showcase the company's products at an expo in Singapore,[72] and he would soon be a regular on the furniture expo circuit. As the 1990s progressed, Jokowi managed

---

[68] Thayrun, *Jokowi Pemimpin Rakyat Berjiwa Rocker*, 18.

[69] Compare this with other examples of business innovation in Tom Kelley and Jonathan Littman, *The Art of Innovation* (Manhattan: Penguin Random House, Inc., 2001).

[70] Walter Isaacson, in *Steve Jobs* (New York: Simon & Schuster, 2011), 295, shows how Jobs founded Apple after a bankruptcy and the company went on to become one of the biggest in the world.

[71] Adam Tyson and Budi Purnomo, "President Jokowi and the 2014 *Obor Rakyat* controversy in Indonesia," *Critical Asian Studies* 49, no. 1 (2017): 120.

[72] Endah, *Jokowi Memimpin Kota Menyentuh Jakarta*, 58.

to establish his family in solid middle-class comfort. Iriana was eventually able to set up her own business, a wedding hall close to the neighborhood where Jokowi grew up, but far removed from the rustic environment of his childhood. And Jokowi himself became widely respected in the local business community and the wider Indonesian furniture industry.

It was during this period that the man called Mulyono at birth, and who had been known as Joko Widodo since early childhood, got the name he now continues to use: "Jokowi." It came about through his international connections in the furniture business. A French furniture importer named Bernard Chene had established a business relationship with Jokowi's uncle, Miyono.

"One day his uncle introduced him [Jokowi]. He was a graduate from forestry. I asked him if he was able to produce some teak furniture and he told me, 'Yes, why not?'" Chene recalls. "Immediately I did trust him, and we started like that in business."

For a French-speaker, the name "Joko Widodo" was something of a mouthful, and Chene already had various other Indonesian contacts named Joko. So he came up with an abbreviated alternative: "If you don't mind, perhaps I will call you only 'Jokowi'?" he said.[73] The name stuck, and though it was originally only used between Chene and Jokowi, its catchy and unique quality would prove useful during future election campaigns.

The heyday of the furniture industry in Indonesia was 2002,[74] even though the wider economy had not fully recovered from the 1998 financial and political crisis that had brought an end to Suharto's rule and kickstarted the Reformasi era.[75] The weak Indonesian currency, in fact, helped the export element of the furniture trade to develop rapidly. One by one, new entrepreneurs sprang up, aiming to export furniture to American and European markets. In Surakarta and its surroundings at the time, there were around 280 entrepreneurs in the furniture export business.

The mushrooming of the furniture export market created new problems for the industry in the form of an aggressive price war. It was in the midst of this price war that Jokowi initiated the formation of the Greater

---

[73] "Panggil Jokowi Saja," YouTube, https://www.youtube.com/watch?v=j2fHG6hjwh8 [accessed October 8, 2020].

[74] "Kata Rekannya di Solo, Jokowi Itu Sosok 'From Zero to Hero,'" *Kompas*, July 23, 2014, https://regional.kompas.com/read/2014/07/23/15352691/Kata.Rekannya.di.Solo.Jokowi.Itu.Sosok.From.Zero.to.Hero [accessed August 31, 2019].

[75] Sintong Arfiyansyah, "Utang dan Trauma Krisis Ekonomi 1998," *detikNews*, https://news.detik.com/kolom/d-4558270/utang-dan-trauma-krisis-ekonomi-1998 [accessed July 10, 2019].

Surakarta Commissariat of the Indonesian Furniture and Handicraft Industry Association (Asmindo). He was already a committee member of Asmindo at a national level, and on July 11, 2002 he was chosen as the first chairman of the new Regional Commissariat,[76] leading an organization of more than a hundred and forty local furniture and handicraft entrepreneurs.[77]

Through a program arranged by the Ministry of Trade, Asmindo Greater Surakarta under Jokowi's chairmanship held a series of exhibitions abroad to open new markets in Asia and Europe. As chairman, Jokowi worked to provide new opportunities for his members, and he gained an understanding of the difficulty of penetrating foreign markets. He also made a "mission trip" to Eastern Europe, which had been previously closed to Indonesian commercial access.

It was through this activity as a senior business figure and trade association chairman that Jokowi, who was already relatively well known among middle-class Surakarta people connected with the timber industry, first gained the attention of the wider community. And it was on the basis of his profile and success as a business leader that it was first suggested that he might consider entering the world of politics and running as a candidate for mayor of Surakarta.

His journey to business success had been long, with false starts and failures along the way. But it had been a journey that his upbringing, education and work experience had all directly informed. Now, however, he would need to redeploy those skills, and to call on all the life lessons he had gathered on the banks of the Kali Anyar, in visits to his ancestral villages, at university, in the forests of Aceh, in the timber workshops of Surakarta, and in his own personal life. His rapid journey to the very top of the Indonesian political scene was about to begin.

---

[76] Endah, *Jokowi Perjalanan Karya bagi Bangsa Menuju Cahaya*, 75.
[77] "Kisah Awal Jokowi Terjun ke Dunia Politik," *detikNews*, https://news.detik.com/ berita/d-2645557/kisah-awal-jokowi-terjun-ke-dunia-politik [accessed August 29, 2019].

"Radiant Without Corruption": a poster for Jokowi's 2005 mayoral campaign.

Chapter Three

Stepping onto the Political Stage: From Mayor of Surakarta to Governor of Jakarta

On a July day in 2006, a large procession could be seen moving through the streets of Surakarta. It was a colorful affair, with marching bands, horse-drawn carriages, and ceremonial guardsmen in the traditional uniforms of the royal Javanese courts. Local dignitaries were on hand, too, but the core of the procession belonged to a group of around a thousand men and women from the informal bottom rung of the city's workforce. They were street vendors who had finally been persuaded to leave their traffic-clogging, litter-spilling place of commerce around Banjarsari Park in the north of the city, to a purpose-built new market area at Pasar Klitikan Notoharjo, several kilometers to the south. The procession had been organized to mark the relocation. Also taking part was the man who had brought the whole thing about. Just one year into the job, Jokowi was already making his mark on Surakarta.

The peaceful relocation of a group of informal street vendors may seem a fairly trivial affair. But, in fact, Jokowi had managed to solve a persistent social problem that had prompted middle-class grumbling for years, and that previous city administrations had wrangled over at great length without ever achieving a solution. What is more, he had done it in double-quick time and without the sort of violent clashes that have often ensued when the authorities intrude on the livelihoods of working-class Indonesians. The slogan that echoed around the July 2006 march was "We have all won."

Street vendors, many selling food from mobile carts or tented pavement stalls, others hawking clothes, toys, simple souvenirs, or household items, are a part of life in every Indonesian city and an important aspect of the informal economy. Street vending is a traditional fallback for working class people in times of personal or national economic crisis. Those laid off from a salaried job can always turn to selling homemade snacks on the street with minimal start-up capital (during the Covid-19 crisis, some out-of-work Indonesians turned to a hi-tech variant of this tradition, selling food via digital marketplace platforms).[1]

The number of street vendors had mushroomed after the economic crisis which brought down Suharto. By 2002 there were around 6,000 of them in Surakarta alone.[2] One of the largest concentrations was gathered at Banjarsari, around a park and monument commemorating the Indonesian revolution. For local residents, the vendors were a nuisance, creating traffic jams, litter, and antisocial behavior, and having a negative impact on legitimate businesses in the area. Locals had complained to officials for years, going as far as to boycott Independence Day commemorations in 2004 in protest.[3] City authorities had been seeking a solution since 1998, but without success.

Jokowi came to power in Surakarta promising to clean up Banjarsari by August 17, Independence Day, the following year. But he soon discovered how entrenched and intransigent the vendors were, having been fighting relocation since the late 1990s. It would have been possible to demolish their makeshift stalls and clear the area by force, but Jokowi was mindful of his own childhood experiences when city officials moved in to demolish illegal housing on the Kali Anyar riverbank. He embarked instead on an exhaustive round of dozens of lunch meetings with the vendors and with the NGOs fighting their corner. It turned into a six-month process of dialogue.

"I came to know the condition and situation of the street vendors 100 percent," Jokowi says.[4]

Officials and local academics were tasked with collecting data on the vending community. A new location was identified with a promise of free equipment, training, and affordable loans for business development, all at a cost of around Rp9 billion.[5] Eventually, all 989 of the Banjarsari vendors agreed to relocate to a new purpose-built market area at Pasar Klitikan

[1] CNA, "COVID-19 Crisis In Indonesia: How Will The Poor Recover?" https://www.youtube.com/watch?v=HirsHt-PLCA&t=1s [accessed October 9, 2020].
[2] Rushda Majeed, "Defusing a Volatile City, Igniting Reforms: Joko Widodo and Surakarta, Indonesia, 2005–2011," Princeton University, 2012, 4.
[3] Ibid., 3.
[4] Ibid., 8.
[5] Ibid.

Notoharjo.[6] The move, marked by the celebratory traditional procession, was completed a month ahead of Jokowi's self-imposed deadline of Independence Day 2006. Most of the vendors subsequently reported significant improvements in their incomes in the more spacious and orderly new location, while the authorities were able to start collecting licensing fees and taxes from them for the first time.

If the street vendor relocation of Jokowi's first year in public office is still often cited today in discussions of his career, it is for good reason. It neatly encapsulates the modus operandi that gained him national and international attention as mayor of Surakarta, and that propelled him onwards and upwards to the presidency. He had managed the relocation through a formidable outlay of time and effort, generous public spending, and meaningful dialogue with the people affected, listening to their concerns and aspirations and attempting to create an equitable solution, which, in the end, boosted the local economy and raised tax revenues.

Why Politics?

Why did Jokowi, already in his forties, with a family, a successful business, and a comfortable middle-class lifestyle he had worked hard to achieve, decide to move abruptly into the rough-and-tumble of Indonesian politics?

Jokowi's father, Wijiatno Notomiharjo, had himself shunned a possible career in politics and public service with all its twists and turns. He had refused to consider taking on his father's position as *lurah* of Kragan, and had turned instead to the business world of his in-laws (though he did become interested in politics in the late 1990s, and was briefly involved with the PDI-P, later to be his son's own party of choice, at a local level).[7] Jokowi, himself steeped in the timber trade from earliest childhood, might have been expected to do the same and, indeed, that was the direction he maintained for the first four decades of his life. But then he began to find himself drawn inexorably towards politics. He had already become a leader in the furniture business, and various people in Surakarta began

---

[6]"Dialogue, Negotiation, and Mutual Respect: An Indonesian Mayor's Successful Approach to Relocating Street Vendors," *Tadamun*, November 4, 2014, http://www.tadamun.co/dialogue-negotiation-mutual-respect-indonesian-mayors-successful-approach-relocating-street-vendors/?lang=en#.X4Bj1mhKjIV [accessed October 9, 2020].

[7]Ika Ningtyas, "Benarkah Ayah dan Kakek Jokowi Pernah Menjadi Ketua PKI Boyolali?" *Tempo*, November 14, 2019, https://cekfakta.tempo.co/fakta/477/fakta-atau-hoaks-benarkah-ayah-dan-kakek-jokowi-pernah-menjadi-ketua-pki-boyolali [accessed May 20, 2021].

to suggest, in all seriousness, that he might consider running for public office. These suggestions came initially from those closest to him, friends and colleagues who were not themselves from a political background. In particular, a group of local business leaders decided that they should field a candidate in the upcoming mayoral elections in an attempt to tackle the bureaucracy and corruption that had long blighted their interactions with the Surakarta authorities. Having run a test to identify the most "fit and proper" person, they pinpointed one man as the perfect fit: Jokowi.[8]

Jokowi was initially reluctant. He tended to see politics as a world of meaningless noise and competing interests, a world full of chaotic conflict and jostling action.[9] In the furniture industry, the only noise was that of the wood-cutting machinery. In politics, meanwhile, the noise came from the many competing sides who *main kayu* in the Indonesian idiom, literally "play wood," to play rough and dirty. This perception of the political world is a common one in Indonesia. Politics is often viewed with particular disdain by those in the entrepreneurial private sector, the business-minded middle class within which Jokowi had firmly established himself.[10] Politics is viewed as unreliable, oppressive, and corrupt.[11]

Jokowi's personal interactions with the authorities had also colored his view. As a child he had been evicted by government officials from his home on the banks of the Kali Anyar. And when he became a businessman, he had experienced the difficulty of breaking through the bureaucratic barricade and negotiating official corruption. He had observed the brutality of Indonesian politics. He had grown up during Suharto's New Order, and had been trying to make his way as a young entrepreneur during its final, chaotic period as the economy collapsed and political violence erupted. Besides Jakarta, Surakarta had been one of the places worst affected by the rioting and looting of 1998. Jokowi had also seen the initial public optimism of the Reformasi period revert rapidly to cynicism.

He did, however, recognize the ultimate purpose of politics, beyond its often problematic exercise, and this, again, had some connection to the figure of his paternal grandfather, and the various village legends in Kragan about Mbah Wiryo's bravery and fine human qualities. Jokowi recognized

---

[8] Michael Bachelard, "Joko Widodo: man with a mission," *The Sydney Morning Herald*, June 14, 2014, https://www.smh.com.au/lifestyle/joko-widodo-man-with-a-mission-20140609-39rui.html [accessed October 9, 2020].

[9] A. Bakir Ihsan, *Etika dan Logika Berpolitik* (Bandung: Remaja Rosdakarya, 2009), 19–20.

[10] Andrew Gamble, *Politics: Why It Matters* (Cambridge: Polity Press, 2019), 1.

[11] Muchtar Buchori, *Indonesia Mencari Demokrasi* (Yogyakarta: Insist Press, 2005), 38–39.

that politics at base, in the mode of Indonesia's revolutionary heroes who went on to become its first generation of civilian leaders, was supposed to be about liberation, social justice, and a shared sense of purpose. As a village *lurah*, Mbah Wiryo had occupied one of the lowest tiers of Indonesian regional government (below the regency/municipality level, the cascade of administrative subdivisions continues, through *kecamatan* or districts, right down to individual neighborhoods). A *lurah* was tasked with nothing more than the decent governance of his own community. For Jokowi, this was not so very different from the prospect of becoming mayor of Surakarta. The city was his own community, after all, and a place he had remained committed to throughout his university education and work experience in Aceh, and which he had never shown any inclination to leave for good.

More practically, governance is about problem-solving, and in his own business and in his industry leadership role, Jokowi had a clear track record for that. He had developed the common conviction that, if he were ever given the chance, he would be able to make a better job of it than the people currently in power. Of course, many late entrants to politics arrive with similar self-belief. But Jokowi was actually able to make good on the promise of his own idealism.

The question of whether leaders are born or made is an old and ultimately unanswerable one. But there is little doubt that the qualities which carried Jokowi to the mayordom of his hometown arose from experience. The personal values he gained from his parents and the local community on the banks of the Kali Anyar clearly prepared him for the dialogic approach and natural connection with the *wong cilik* which became his political trademarks. Meanwhile, his background in a notably "end-to-end" business sector forged a particular mindset with regards infrastructure, economics, and logistics, as well as a particularly hands-on managerial approach.

But it was clear from the outset that Jokowi did not have an archetypal personality in terms of Indonesian political leadership. The two radically contrasting men who dominated Indonesia's first half-century of independence remain the touchstones of political style in the country: Sukarno, mercurial, charismatic, and capable of driving forward an agenda through force of personality; and Suharto, possessed of a distinctly monarchical air of cool authority. The enduring potency of these leadership models would be aptly demonstrated in the persona adopted by Jokowi's main rival during the presidential elections of 2014 and 2019. But from the start of his political career in Surakarta, Jokowi himself has never invited ready comparisons with either the first or second president of the Republic of

Indonesia. At a push, a reasonable comparison might be made with the warm and informal personability of the fourth president, Abdurrahman Wahid. But while Jokowi's formidable ability to connect with the public in face-to-face encounters is well attested, on the podium or the TV screen he remains a less forceful personality than Wahid. Indeed, he has routinely been described as "unassuming." This has often been turned against him by his opponents, who have described him as *plonga-plongo*, slack-jawed, and perhaps slow-witted, and various other insulting epithets. During each of his campaigns for election, this line of attack has tended to be associated with a dismissal of his seriousness as a contender; while following each of his victories it has been redeployed to question his competency.

Perhaps the most telling insight to his personality is, in fact, his response to all of this: *Aku rapopo.* This colloquial Javanese phrase literally means "I'm okay" or "I have no problem," but it also implies a sense of being unhurt but also accepting of an attack. Jokowi first began routinely to use it in response to personal and political attacks in the run-up to his first presidential campaign.

"If you want to attack me, you're welcome; if you want to make fun of me, you're welcome. After all, the public can filter out what's true and what's not true. If you want to support me, you're welcome; if you don't want to support me, you're welcome. *Aku rapopo, aku rapopo…*" he said at the time.[12] This casual unflappability and lack of vindictiveness or defensiveness turned out to be a valuable asset in terms of electoral appeal, an appeal first revealed in the Surakarta mayoral elections of 2005.

Connecting with the PDI-P

Jokowi's success in the role of chairman of the Greater Surakarta Commissariat of Asmindo (the Indonesian Furniture and Handicraft Industry Association) had caught the attention of established political parties in Surakarta, and several made approaches as it became known that he was thinking about running for election. As part of the widening of democracy in the Reformasi era, decentralization was underway at the time, and municipalities were due to directly elect their mayors and vice-mayors for the first time. Initially, Jokowi refused requests from the various parties who came courting. But, eventually, he aligned himself with PDI-P, becoming

---

[12] Alsadad Rudi, "Alasan Jokowi Gunakan Istilah 'Aku Rapopo,'" *Kompas*, March 25, 2014, https://megapolitan.kompas.com/read/2014/03/25/1704217/Alasan.Jokowi.Gunakan.Istilah. Aku.Rapopo [accessed September 14, 2020].

a member in 2004, the first time in his life that he had had a specific political affiliation.

Although he could potentially have found himself a comfortable place in any of the many nationalist parties, PDI-P was a particularly good fit for Jokowi's political outlook, with its strong established base amongst the *wong cilik*, the little people from amongst whom Jokowi himself had risen. As a fresh face, he had something to offer the party in Surakarta, too: the mayoral elections were fast approaching and PDI-P was still looking for a strong candidate.

At this point, the figure of Fransiskus Xaverius Hadi Rudyatmo, generally known as F. X. Hadi Rudyatmo, and informally as Rudy, appeared to make up for Jokowi's shortcomings in terms of experience. Rudy was a veteran local politician from a working-class background, whose own political apprenticeship had been at a grassroots level, serving first as chair of his local *rukun tetangga*, or neighborhood association, the lowest of all subdivisions in Indonesia's administrative structure (two levels below even that headed by a *lurah* like Jokowi's grandfather).[13] Rudy had risen through the ranks of the Surakarta branch of the PDI-P, becoming its chairman in 2000. In a fairly common Indonesian electoral arrangement, the party nominated the less politically experienced figure seen to have significant leadership potential, Jokowi in this case, and paired him with a solid political veteran as running mate. While Jokowi had an existing profile amongst the middle class business community, Rudy's grassroots party background would help to connect with working-class voters. He also had extensive experience in the practicalities of voter mobilization essential for any effective campaign. And there was one other factor involved in the arrangement: Rudy was from a Javanese Catholic family. This may not have been as significant a disadvantage as one might assume in a place like Surakarta, where almost a quarter of the population belongs to Christian denominations. But by nominating a Muslim with a Catholic running mate, both men solidly Javanese by background and deeply rooted in the local community, PDI-P had actually created a ticket that represented the city's demographics well.

Before he finally committed to run, Jokowi felt that he needed to gain the approval of his family. At first they did not all support his desire to enter the political arena.[14] The view of politics held by Jokowi's extended

---

[13] "Fransiskus Xaverius Hadi Rudyatmo," *Viva*, https://www.viva.co.id/siapa/read/160-fransiskus-xaverius-hadi-rudyatmo [accessed September 14, 2020].

[14] Yon Thayrun, *Jokowi Pemimpin Rakyat Berjiwa Rocker* (Jakarta: Noura Books, 2012), 31.

family at that time was the standard one: a harsh world of intrigue and jostling for position. Life as a businessman seemed much calmer. Gibran, Jokowi's eldest son, frankly expressed his opposition to his father's political ambitions at the time: "Why are you running for mayor? I do not agree with it. I prefer my father as he is now, the one who isn't an official and doesn't play at politics," Gibran, who would eventually develop his own political ambitions, reportedly said at the time.[15]

However, Jokowi presented his mayoral candidacy as an opportunity to pursue social justice and to improve the conditions of Surakarta residents such as those amongst whom he had grown up.

"I feel guilty if I'm just busy thinking about business. Imagine, there are many small traders, marginalized people and people who are treated unfairly. That haunts me. It's like a call going out to me," Jokowi told his son. In the end, his family, including Gibran, gave their blessing, and he was then officially put forward as candidate, the last to be nominated for the 2005 election. A complete political newcomer, he was now running for the highest public office in his hometown.

The Joko Widodo-F. X. Hadi Rudyatmo pair, which had the endorsement of the PKB as well as PDI-P, ran under the slogan *Berseri Tanpa Korupsi*, "Radiant Without Corruption." They took the largest share of the vote, 36 percent, just over the 30 percent threshold required to avoid triggering a run-off.[16] They had beaten Achmad Purnomo-Istar Yuliadi (PAN), Hardono-Dipokusumo (Golkar, Demokrat, PKS),[17] and incumbent Slamet Suryanto who, with running mate Hengky Nartosabdo, was backed by a coalition of fourteen small parties but who received the smallest share of the vote.

Jokowi had become the sixteenth mayor of Surakarta since Indonesia gained its independence and the first to be directly elected by the people. The personality forged on the banks of the Kali Anyar, in rented houses, in furniture workshops, in his uncle's timber warehouse, and on the international expo circuit, had already been tempered in his role as chairman of Asmindo's Surakarta branch and as a member of Asmindo at a national level. This had given him experience of leadership. But would it translate successfully into local government and into the world of politics more broadly?

---

[15] "Kisah Awal Jokowi Terjun ke Dunia Politik," *detikNews*, https://news.detik.com/berita/2645557/kisah-awal-jokowi-terjun-ke-dunia-politik [accessed July 23, 2014].

[16] Majeed, "Defusing a Volatile City, Igniting Reforms."

[17] Thayrun, *Jokowi Pemimpin Rakyat Berjiwa Rocker*, 28.

Transforming Surakarta

The arrival of Jokowi and Rudy in office provided a shock to the enervated Surakarta civil service. Unannounced checks, promotions based on performance rather than merely on time served, and abrupt sanctions for corruption and incompetence became the order of the day, to widespread public approval. Hotlines were set up to allow members of the public to report corruption, make general complaints, and put their concerns directly to officials, and a "One Stop Service" office was organized to streamline the notoriously convoluted processes of applying for permits, identity cards, and official documentation. Budget transparency was another key focus. Budgets for individual projects were published online and in the press, and the overall annual budget, with all its allocations, was circulated publicly.[18]

The mayor and his deputy had an excellent working relationship, and came up with a carefully coordinated approach and a careful division of labor within the Surakarta Secretariat. Broadly speaking, Jokowi handled the administration's vision and communication, while Rudy, with his superior political experience, handled implementation.[19] Rudy was generally able to corral the city legislators into supporting his and Jokowi's projects, and the pair benefited from a DPRD (regional legislature) dominated by their own PDI-P and coalition of supporting parties.

A central element of Jokowi's style of governance and policy making emerged during his first term in Surakarta: *blusukan*. This Javanese term might be translated as "going to a place to gather information." For Jokowi, it meant getting out of the office on frequent site visits, whether to view projects already underway or simply to meet the public. By the time he became president, security arrangements and the attendant media circus meant that Jokowi's *blusukan* were often highly coordinated affairs. But in Surakarta in the early days, they were often genuinely impromptu and unannounced trips to traditional markets, slum neighborhoods, and building sites with flustered civil servants in tow.

"I always went to the people," Jokowi has said of his time as mayor. "Show up, and you solve 90 percent of the problem. Then we follow through with the other 10 percent."[20]

Blusukan also informed Jokowi's ideal of *nguwongke wong cilik*,

---

[18] Majeed, "Defusing a Volatile City, Igniting Reforms," 14.
[19] Ibid., 5.
[20] Ibid., 18.

"humanizing the little people," as deployed in his long deliberations with the street vendors of Banjarsari. And many of his other policies in Surakarta were aimed at bettering the lot of the sort of people amongst whom he had grown up. There were programs to upgrade or replace the housing of the city's poorest residents, with proper title to the properties arranged as part of the package. And Jokowi also developed a card-based healthcare program which prefigured the larger programs he put in place in Jakarta and then nationally, ensuring that insurance coverage was available to all residents beyond the poorest demographic which had already received support via existing national programs.

These policies suggest a decidedly working class-focused approach. But, in fact, Jokowi's overwhelming popularity in Surakarta rested on his building a broad base via a balanced policy portfolio. He had initially been suggested as a mayoral candidate by local business leaders, after all, and his efforts to smooth out bureaucracy and foster investment meant that they were well satisfied with their man. He ended up with the enthusiastic support of both the *wong cilik*, the slum dwellers and street vendors, and of his own small-town entrepreneur class. To illustrate this fine policy balance, on the one hand he got rid of a long-standing bylaw which banned construction of any new buildings taller that the highest point of the Surakarta Kraton, the royal palace, finally opening up Surakarta to the malls, modern office blocks, and high-rise hotels seen in other Indonesian cities, to the approval of investors and the middle classes.[21] On the other hand, he banned new malls from being built in the vicinity of existing traditional markets to safeguard the livelihoods of small vendors.

The apparent contradiction here gives rise to the difficulty non-Indonesians sometimes have in making sense of Jokowi and Indonesian politics more generally: policies reliant on massive public spending for the benefit of the poorest, the sort of thing which might be expected of a solidly left-wing government in Europe, in the same portfolio as red tape-slashing, tax break-offering reforms designed to cheer the investor class, typically the preserve of right-leaning parties elsewhere. But, in fact, this is typical of the ideologically blended approach which Indonesian politicians from Sukarno onwards have pursued and the nationalist tradition to which Jokowi is affiliated, an ethos that has some parallels

---

[21] Christian von Lübke, "Maverick mayor to presidential hopeful," *Inside Indonesia*, February 23, 2014, https://www.insideindonesia.org/maverick-mayor-to-presidential-hopeful [accessed October 11, 2020].

with a Western social-democratic position but which is also determined by economic nationalism.

Although not every one of Jokowi's efforts in Surakarta was an unqualified success (overall poverty rates remained stubbornly high; some street vendor relocation projects proved less economically successful than that from Banjarsari; and the health insurance program was sometimes hampered by poor public awareness of its requirements, as would be the later Jakarta and national program), there were few who would have disputed the idea that the city had palpably changed for the better by the end of his first term. Public transport had been transformed and previously neglected areas of the city such as Jalan Slamet Riyadi and Jalan Ngarsopuro had been rejuvenated.[22] There was a marked and visible improvement to the general cleanliness of the streets and numerous successful infrastructure developments. Surakarta was also attracting external investment and seeking opportunities to host international events. Indeed, after just five years, the city had been identified both nationally and internationally as an example of "best practice" in city governance[23] and used as a case study in Indonesian and foreign universities. It had been a rare example in Indonesia of a genuinely transformational mayoral term and an apparent success story of decentralization and Reformasi. (Jokowi's example was subsequently followed by another PDI-P-affiliated mayor, Tri Rismaharini, who has overseen an arguably even more dramatic positive transformation of the larger Javanese city of Surabaya.)

It was no surprise when Jokowi was re-elected for a second term as mayor of Surakarta in 2010, again with F. X. Hadi Rudyatmo as running mate. But the scale of the victory was an astonishing indication of public approval: the pairing took 90.09 percent of the vote.[24] Running again under a PDI-P banner, this time they picked up extra endorsements from PAN and PKS. On polling day, they lost the popular vote at just one polling station out of 932 across Surakarta. Their only challengers, Eddy S. Wirabhumi and Supradi Kertamenawi, who were backed by the Partai Demokrat (Democratic Party) and endorsed by Golkar, only garnered 9.91 percent.[25]

---

[22] Ibid., 26.
[23] Tim Bunnell, Rita Padawangi, and Eric C. Thompson, "The politics of learning from a small city: Solo as translocal model and political launch pad," *Regional Studies* 52, no. 8 (2018).
[24] Ibid., 23.
[25] "Kemenangan Fenomenal Jokowi-Rudy," *Kompas*, May 25, 2010, https://regional.kompas.com/read/2010/05/21/03402631/%20Kemenangan.Fenomenal.Jokowi-Rudy [accessed October 11, 2020].

The unassuming former furniture entrepreneur was clearly a political force to be reckoned with. He had also shown a natural aptitude for the optics of politics. Early in his first term, he had announced that he would not be taking his mayoral salary and would be returning his pay checks to the city coffers. On the one hand, this was a relatively painless gesture for a man who was already well-established financially: Jokowi's personal wealth, including assets, was assessed at around US$1.5 million at the time.[26] His family business was continuing successfully, and the meager Rp6.2 million mayoral salary[27] was one he could do without. But it sent a clear message to the public about Jokowi's motivations. He was already approaching middle age. He had already achieved financial success and set his family up for the future. His entry into politics was motivated only by an idealistic commitment to public service. To underscore the message, he made a point of flying economy class when on official duty and eschewed the usual mayoral perk of a brand-new official car, continuing to use the old vehicle of his predecessor. When he finally replaced the mayoral car during his second term, it was with a with a prototype for a possible new national car brand, designed and built by students of a local vocational high school.[28]

Although Jokowi is sometimes portrayed as a naïve idealist, his sophisticated media savvy was detected by outside observers early in his career. In 2011, a study tour from the Thai city of Pak Kret visited Surakarta to learn from its various successes. The Thai visitors later reported their impression that Jokowi paid much "attention to the public relations" and appeared to have "influenced the media so much."[29] Crucially, however, this eye for effective public relations was backed by indisputable achievements on the ground.

By this time, Jokowi, the skinny, heavy metal-loving maverick who had transformed Surakarta, was on his way to becoming a household name across Indonesia. Admiring stories about his achievements were starting to appear in national print and broadcast media. In 2010, he was given the national Bung Hatta Anti-Corruption Award (named for Indonesia's first vice president), and the following year the Home Affairs Ministry

---

[26] von Lübke, "Maverick mayor to presidential hopeful."

[27] Majeed, "Defusing a Volatile City, Igniting Reforms," 6.

[28] Kusumasari Ayuningtyas, "Jokowi's Esemka to start mass production next year," *The Jakarta Post*, December 8, 2014. https://www.thejakartapost.com/news/2014/12/08/jokowi-s-esemka-start-mass-production-next-year.html [accessed October 11, 2020].

[29] Bunnell et al., "The politics of learning from a small city," 1069.

named him the country's best mayor. Many people, both media observers and political actors, were beginning to wonder if his success in Surakarta might be transferable onto bigger political stages.

Taking the Capital

The governorship of Jakarta is the highest profile local government role in Indonesia and one of the most challenging in the world. It involves administering a complex and densely populated capital city which is home to around 10 million people, double the entire population of New Zealand or Ireland, and twenty times bigger than Surakarta. Jakarta residents had voted for their first directly elected governor in 2007, with the job going to veteran local politician Fauzi Bowo. Although Foke, as Fauzi Bowo was popularly known, had heavyweight political backing and had achieved some individual successes in his first term, many Jakarta voters were frustrated by the lack of serious progress in addressing the notoriously congested city's myriad problems. As the end of Fauzi Bowo's first term approached, various potential challengers began to emerge.

Late in 2011, scholars from the University of Indonesia, working with a political consultancy, ran a "Looking for the Best Jakarta Governor Candidate" survey. Instead of simply measuring public popularity, the survey took account of perceived capabilities and qualities for running the city. The potential candidate with the highest score was Jokowi.[30] By this time, thanks to his Surakarta successes, Jokowi himself was increasingly convinced that he might have what it took to govern Jakarta, and so were some very senior Indonesian political figures.

On March 18, Jokowi was officially nominated for the gubernatorial race by PDI-P, on the decision of the party chair and former president, Megawati. In putting Jokowi forward for the Jakarta job, Megawati was partnered by Prabowo Subianto, leader of Gerindra or Partai Gerakan Indonesia Raya (Great Indonesian Movement Party), who had agreed to fund the campaign costs. One of Jokowi's first major political backers on the national stage was thus the same man who would go on to become his opponent in two of the bitterest elections in Indonesian history before eventually joining his government as a minister in 2019, a particularly dramatic manifestation of the many twists and turns of Indonesian politics.

---

[30] Abdul Hamid, "Jokowi's Populism in the 2012 Jakarta Gubernatorial Election," *Journal of Current Southeast Asian Affairs* 33, no. 1 (2014): 89–90.

It has sometimes been suggested that by running for governor of Jakarta with the direct backing of these two political giants, Megawati and Prabowo, Jokowi had somehow been "bought," and would no longer be his own man. But this somewhat patronizing view relies in part on the idea of Jokowi as a political ingénue, admittedly an image he had himself helped to cultivate. Indonesian politics is certainly transactional, but in 2012 Megawati and Prabowo needed Jokowi as much as he needed them. The pair had been running mates in the 2009 presidential election (with Megawati as the presidential candidate and Prabowo running for vice president), but they had been decisively beaten by Susilo Bambang Yudhoyono. Despite her solid party base, Megawati had struggled to find personal success at the polls, while Prabowo was seen by some as the epitome of elite New Order continuity in the Reformasi era, having been a senior military office in the regime's turbulent later years and having been married for a time to one of Suharto's daughters. If Jokowi would benefit from their organizational support and financial backing, then they would gain significant political capital from associating with a fresh, non-elite, and wildly popular figure. It was a quid pro quo scenario.[31]

Prabowo had identified a perfect running mate for Jokowi, another political outsider who had emerged through local elections. Basuki Tjahaja Purnama, better known as Ahok, had been elected regent of East Belitung (his home regency, part of an island province off the east coast of Sumatra) the same year that Jokowi had become mayor of Surakarta. Though Ahok failed in a subsequent run for the provincial governorship, he had gone on to take a parliamentary seat for Golkar in 2009. Now he switched allegiance to Gerindra and teamed up with Jokowi.

Ahok was a distinctive, somewhat abrasive character, very different from the mild-mannered Jokowi. He was also very unusual in that not only was he a Protestant Christian but he was also ethnically Chinese, making him a "double minority." In the Bangka-Belitung province, with its large ethnic Chinese population, this had not been hugely noteworthy, but on the national stage it was significant. Historically, very few Chinese Indonesians have had high-profile national-level political careers.

Despite their different backgrounds and characters, Ahok and Jokowi gelled well and presented a refreshingly informal image on the campaign trail. Jokowi proved to have something approaching pop star appeal at street level, attracting excited crowds wherever he went. The pair branded

---

[31] von Lübke, "Maverick mayor to presidential hopeful."

their campaign with the initials "JB," which stood for both "Jokowi-Basuki" and Jakarta Baru, "A New Jakarta." In a brilliant piece of visual branding, indicative of Jokowi's hands-on business background, the pair also adopted a campaign uniform of matching plaid shirts. The shirts' black, red, and white check echoed both the red-black PDI-P party colors and the red and white of the Indonesian flag. But they also sent an important message: these were not the ceremonial batik shirts more commonly favored by Indonesian politicians; Jokowi and Ahok looked like they were dressed for hard work. The shirts quickly became a sort of unofficial team uniform for Jokowi's supporters, and a tailor from Jokowi's old neighborhood in Surakarta was tasked with producing hundreds of them for the campaign.[32]

Despite neither man being a Jakarta native, they ousted the incumbent, taking 53 percent of the final vote. Back in Surakarta, F. X. Hadi Rudyatmo took over as mayor until the end of Jokowi's original term, before being re-elected in his own right in 2016.

A Truncated Governorship

Jakarta is twenty times bigger than Surakarta, but as governor Jokowi was essentially able to scale up the same approach he had taken in his hometown. He and Ahok made their salaries public and publicized their administrative budgets. City government budgetary meetings were publicly broadcast on YouTube, and there were clampdowns on corruption within the administration. For residents, an online tax system was launched to simplify the process and reduce tax fraud. Jokowi was even able to organize a repetition of the iconic early success of his first year in office in Surakarta. Using the same patient "humanizing the little people" dialogue-based approach that had worked at Banjarsari, in 2013 he was able to arrange the willing relocation of around 1,000 street vendors from Tanah Abang to a purpose-built center at Block G.[33] There were also similar successes based on similar methods when it came to relocating slum dwellers from the banks of revitalized reservoirs.

Urban rejuvenation progressed. Jokowi raised the wages of provincial workers by 30 percent; and hundreds of new TransJakarta and Kopaja buses

---

[32] Ikrob Didik Irawan, "Suparto Senang Bisa Buat Baju Kotak Jokowi," *Tribun Jogja*, April 14, 2012, https://jogja.tribunnews.com/2012/04/14/suparto-libatkan-penjahit-smk-buat-20-ribu-kemeja-kotak-jokowi [accessed October 15, 2020].

[33] Bunnell et al., "The politics of learning from a small city," 1070.

were added to the city's rickety public transport network.[34] Even more significantly, a long-delayed and desperately needed metro project was finally hustled from the drawing board to the construction stage (when Jokowi became governor, Jakarta was one of the only major Asian capitals without an MRT system). And a health insurance card scheme, similar to that pioneered in Surakarta, was launched to provide cover for those residents not insured under existing social welfare programs. As with the later national roll-out, the initial emphasis was simply on achieving universal coverage, and at times Jakarta's hospital system struggled to cope with the extra demand. But Jokowi did begin to improve provision. Various hospital wards were reclassified for public patients, and extra doctors were recruited. The Healthy Jakarta Card (KJS; Kartu Jakarta Sehat) was then followed by the Clever Jakarta Card (KJP; Kartu Jakarta Pintar) for poor students, with education funds directly accessible through the ATM system.

Jokowi also continued his regular *blusukan*, touring working-class districts and construction projects. Ahok seldom accompanied him on these trips,[35] and the two men established a division of labor not unlike that with Rudy in Surakarta. While Jokowi went onto the ground, Ahok was back in the office knocking civil service heads.

All the while, Jokowi's national popularity was increasing. He was now a familiar figure to Indonesians all over the country, and with the next presidential election due in mid-2014, speculation rapidly mounted that he might run for the top job. By the start of the year he was topping all credible polls of potential candidates, and though there had been no official announcement, it was widely rumored that he would be nominated by PDI-P.[36] The announcement was a long time coming. The decision over whether Jokowi would be the party's candidate was down to the PDI-P chair, and Megawati spent a long time mulling her options. As late as November 2013, she was reportedly still considering another presidential run herself.[37] But, finally, on the afternoon of Friday, March 14, 2014 word

34 "Kinerja Jokowi Sebagai Gubernur DKI Jakarta," https://www.kaskus.co.id/thread/52da4732f-8ca175a7b8b47ef/kinerja-jokowi-sebagai-gubernur-dki-jakarta/ [accessed January 19, 2014].

35 Sita W. Dewi, "Jokowi takes Ahok on 'blusukan,'" *The Jakarta Post*, February 28, 2014, https://www.thejakartapost.com/news/2014/02/28/jokowi-takes-ahok-blusukan.html [accessed October 13, 2020].

36 Ibid.

37 "For 4th time, Megawati considers her presidential luck," *The Jakarta Post*, November 20, 2013, https://www.thejakartapost.com/news/2013/11/20/for-4th-time-megawati-considers-her-presidential-luck.html [accessed October 13, 2020].

came through: PDI-P would be backing the former furniture salesman from the banks of the Kali Anyar for the presidency.[38]

Eleven days later, Jokowi faced one of the few public protests in his brief stint running Jakarta. A crowd of several hundred people, calling themselves the Koalisi Masyarakat Jakarta Baru, the "New Jakarta People's Coalition," gathered in front of Jakarta's Balai Kota, the City Hall on the southern side of Medan Merdeka. They were protesting not because they disapproved of the way Jokowi had been running the city. Far from it, they were so enthusiastic in their support that they wanted him to stay on to finish the job.

"It's not time for him to leave us yet!" one of the protesters, a woman named Lena, told reporters. "If Jakarta has already become outstanding in five or ten years' time, then Jokowi can become president!"[39]

But the governor himself had already set his sights on the building on the opposite side of Jakarta's great central square. Jokowi was heading for the Istana Merdeka, the Presidential Palace.

---

[38] Peter McCawley, "Indonesia: Jokowi declares for presidency, but what does he stand for?" The Lowy Institute, March 17, 2014, https://www.lowyinstitute.org/the-interpreter/indonesia-jokowi-declares-presidency-what-does-he-stand-for [accessed October 13, 2020].

[39] "Geruduk Balai Kota, Warga Tolak Jokowi Jadi Calon Presiden," *Viva*, March 25, 2014, https://www.viva.co.id/arsip/491428-geruduk-balai-kota-warga-tolak-jokowi-jadi-calon-presiden [accessed October 13, 2020].

The highest office: the presidential inauguration, 2014.

Chapter Four

Becoming President: The 2014 Campaign and a New Political Approach

Monday, October 20, 2014, 10.26 a.m. Western Indonesia Time. The sky was clear. The clocks on the walls seemed to be ticking slower than usual. The television stations were carrying live reports, covering an event of great significance for Indonesia. For the first time, someone popularly perceived as an outsider was about to enter the presidential palace. A tall, thin man with a certain passing resemblance to Barack Obama (another world leader who had broken the electoral mold), he had disproved the theory that Indonesia's highest office would only ever be accessible to members of a narrow political elite.

Jokowi stood calmly on the stage in the Sidang Paripurna I Room, inside the iconic Nusantara Building with its distinctive double roof, shaped like the spread wings of the mythical Garuda, at the heart of the parliamentary complex in Jakarta. The ceremony was led by Chief Justice Hatta Ali. Everyone present in the room waited. Jokowi began to read his presidential oath.

"*Bismillahirrahmanirohim*. By God, I will fulfill my obligations as President of the Republic of Indonesia as well as possible and as justly as possible, upholding the 1945 Constitution, carrying out all its laws and regulations in the most straightforward manner and serving the nation and state."

Seventeen heads of state attended the inauguration, including the prime ministers of Indonesia's neighbors, Australia, Malaysia, and Singapore, and the leaders of most other countries in the region. Also present were senior representatives of major world powers, including deputy speaker of the Chinese Parliament Yan Junqi, US Secretary of State John

Kerry and Russian minister of industry Denis Valentinovich.[1]

Outside the building, it is estimated that over a million people had come out onto the streets of Jakarta, creating a boisterous, celebratory atmosphere. At the Hotel Indonesia roundabout, a long-standing focal point of mass public gatherings in the Indonesian capital, a huge crowd was gathering to follow along the route of Jokowi's journey from parliament to the presidential palace. Millions more watched the inauguration on television all across the country, not least in Jokowi's hometown Surakarta, and beside the Kali Anyar river.

What was in Jokowi's mind when he stood up and took the oath and received the mandate from the citizens of the Republic of Indonesia? Did he have time to think back on his life's journey since childhood on the banks of that river, to this point, standing at the center of the attention of all the people of Indonesia?[2] He was now the supreme leader of a country with a population of almost 270 million.

For many Indonesians, Jokowi's election was a victory of the people. This was a new chapter in the country's political history. This time, the president did not have "blue blood." He did not come from the military or the established political or social elite. He was an ordinary citizen, like most other Indonesians. This, finally, looked like proper democracy, a forum that provides the opportunity for anyone to become president.[3] Jokowi had already proven himself a highly effective political leader in his previous roles as mayor of Surakarta and governor of Jakarta, and many of his simple but effective actions there had cut through, and been comprehended by voters at all levels of society. But it remained to be seen whether the same energetic development approach could be scaled up again, this time to the vast field of a huge archipelagic nation.

A Hard-won Election

At the start of the year, many people had assumed that Jokowi would have an easy ride all the way to the presidential palace. At the time, polls gauging public enthusiasm for potential presidential candidates were routinely

---

[1] "Siapa Saja Tamu Negara yang Hadir di Pelantikan Jokowi?" *Tempo*, October 19, 2014, https://nasional.tempo.co/read/615490/siapa-saja-tamu-negara-yang-hadir-di-pelantikan-jokowi [accessed October 14, 2020].

[2] Ipho Adhita Wahanani, *Program Perilaku Hidup Bersih dan Sehat (PHBS) Menuju Solo Sehat 2010* (Surakarta: Universitas Sebelas Maret (UNS), 2010), 66.

[3] Haryatmoko, *Etika Politik dan Kekuasaan* (Jakarta: Penerbit Buku Kompas, 2003), 91.

showing him with support in the region of 35 percent, while the eight other figures widely believed to be in contention were mainly on single digits.[4] But that was before the formal nominations came through and the field thinned. It was also before the legislative elections of April 2014, in which PDI-P performed disappointingly. While the party still took the single biggest share of the vote, they failed to get the hoped for 25 percent, which would have allowed them to nominate their own presidential candidate without requiring the backing of other parties. Instead, they had to put together a coalition to endorse their ticket. Jokowi had stated early on that he would not promise cabinet posts in advance to backers, which made coalition building tricky. As the campaign proper got underway, it quickly became apparent that it would be a close and hard-fought battle between Jokowi on the one hand, and on the other the political heavyweight who had provided the crucial financial backing for his gubernatorial campaign just two years earlier: Prabowo Subianto.

Jokowi was paired with political veteran Jusuf Kalla, who had previously been affiliated with both Golkar and the Partai Demokrat, and who had served as vice president during Susilo Bambang Yudhoyono's first term. They were backed by a coalition of PDI-P, PKB, Nasdem, Hanura, and the small Indonesian Justice and Unity Party (PKPI; Partai Keadilan dan Persatuan Indonesia). Prabowo, meanwhile, was partnered with Hatta Rajasa of PAN, and was backed by Golkar, his own Gerindra Party, and most of the main Muslim parties.

The stylistic contrast between the two main candidates could not have been starker. Prabowo had had an international upbringing, spending parts of his childhood and youth in Singapore, Hong Kong, Malaysia, Switzerland, and the United Kingdom. He had had a high-profile military career, serving as head of the Army Strategic Reserve Command at the end of the New Order years, and he was a very wealthy businessman in his own right. He was also an exceptionally confident and fluent speaker.

Prabowo's deep New Order roots, and in particular his association with its military excesses, alarmed some liberal Indonesians and many foreign

---

[4] "For 4th time, Megawati considers her presidential luck," *The Jakarta Post*, November 20, 2013, https://www.thejakartapost.com/news/2013/11/20/for-4th-time-megawati-considers -her-presidential-luck.html [accessed October 13, 2020]. The other figures initially considered as likely contenders were cabinet minister Dahlan Iskan, businessman and Golkar stalwart Aburizal Bakrie, Hanura leader and former general Wiranto, and outgoing chief justice Mahfud M. D., as well as Prabowo, Megawati, and the two eventual vice presidential candidates, Hatta Rajasa and Jusuf Kalla. Yusril Ihza Mahendra and Suryadharma Ali also expressed intentions to run before the final nominations were confirmed.

observers, and international commentaries began portraying the election as a sort of battle for the country's soul, pitting a would-be dictator against the last great hope of Indonesian democracy. This decidedly hyperbolic discourse made no allowances for the overblown rhetoric of the campaign trail, nor for the tempering coalitions backing both men and the inevitable horse-trading that would ensue, whoever won, and it has ultimately proved unhelpful for Jokowi. Like Barack Obama just a few years earlier, the initial wave of overinflated expectation could only ever lead to disappointment, and even to rapid claims of "betrayal," though in Jokowi's case much of this was initially confined to overseas newspaper columns and was hardly reflective of actual Indonesian public opinion.

But whichever way the 2014 election went, it would ultimately be a reaction to the disillusionment that had set in during Susilo Bambang Yudhoyono's term. Corruption remained endemic; the same old people seemed to be in charge; and the progress of Reformasi had been disappointing. By Yudhoyono's final term it was not unusual to hear people claiming that things had been better under Suharto (who had died in 2008). With a "strong leader," the argument went, Indonesia had been better run. A meme began to appear, not only on Indonesia's burgeoning social media but also on T-shirts, bumper stickers, even plastered across the tailgates of trucks,[5] featuring the New Order president, apparently waving smugly from beyond the grave, and the Javanese words *Piye Kabare?! Enak Jamanku To?!*" (How's it going? It was nice back in my day, wasn't it?).

This nostalgic discourse did not serve Jokowi well. His relaxed and humble personality was key to his popularity, but it did nothing to suggest the "firm hand" that some claimed Indonesia badly needed. Prabowo, meanwhile, was able to capitalize on this: his otherwise problematic background certainly suggested "strength." He was also a more impressive orator than Jokowi, with a knack for channeling potent political ghosts. On the campaign trail he dressed in a retro white safari suit and black *peci* (cap), and did a passable impression of Sukarno at the microphone, while at the same time deploying dog-whistle references to "strong leadership."

Jokowi, meanwhile, stuck firmly to the belief that the approach which had won him Surakarta and Jakarta would work at a national level. He spent much time campaigning at street level, where the response was always enthusiastic. He had campaign staffers with a good grasp of social

---

[5] Alex Palit, "Piye Kabare, Enak Jamanku To?!" *Tribun*, October 23, 2013, https://www.tribunnews.com/tribunnews/2013/10/23/piye-kabare-enak-jamanku-to [accessed October 23, 2013].

media and a focus on young urban first-time voters.[6] His supporters even sought to capitalize on the comparisons with Obama, as blue-and-red images of Jokowi appeared, mimicking Obama's iconic two-tone "Hope" poster. Although undoubtedly a genuine reflection of his personality, the Jokowi "brand," the down-to-earth leader with a humble background and a rare capacity for getting things done, had been carefully curated since his first term in Surakarta. This is hardly surprising given that Jokowi was a successful businessman, who knew how to brand high-quality furniture products effectively and how to promote them to domestic and international markets. The trouble in 2014 was that his opponent was offering a different product altogether, one pitched on very different terms which had an alarming capacity to cut through. As polling day approached, Jokowi's once enormous lead dwindled until only a hair's breadth separated the two men in the polls.

By this stage the campaign had developed a very dirty underbelly. Malicious rumors about Jokowi were circulating widely. Particularly notorious was a tabloid newspaper named *Obor Rakyat* which, at the height of the campaign, published spurious accusations about the integrity of Jokowi's Muslim faith and a ludicrous but widely repeated claim that he was ethnically Chinese and had communist sympathies (the latter a particularly potent libel in Indonesia), as well as the allegation that he was a puppet of more powerful political and business figures. Around half a million copies of the paper were distributed throughout Java.[7] "Fake news," as it would later come to be known, would be an even more prominent feature of the subsequent 2019 campaign.

Ultimately, both Jokowi and Prabowo were offering solutions to Indonesia's perceived problems firmly rooted in the nationalist tradition. But one emphasized positivity and continuing progression while the other arguably offered a kind of retreat. This was underscored by the names of the rival coalitions backing the candidates. The Jokowi-supporting parties were dubbed the Koalisi Indonesia Hebat, the "Awesome Indonesia Coalition" (*hebat* could also be translated as "cool" or "great" in the sense of a colloquial exclamation of approval). Prabowo's grouping, meanwhile, would come to be known as the Koalisi Merah Putih, the "Red and White Coalition" (KMP), referring to the national flag.

---

[6] Adam Tyson and Budi Purnomo, "President Jokowi and the 2014 *Obor Rakyat* controversy in Indonesia," *Critical Asian Studies* 49, no. 1 (2017): 123.
[7] Ibid., 125.

While some of the critical commentary around Prabowo's electoral pitch was overblown, it could certainly be argued that his rhetoric and style prefigured the populism that would sweep other countries, not least the USA, just a few years later. The difference, of course, is that when Indonesia went to the polls on July 9, 2014, Prabowo did not win.

The immediate aftermath of the election was somewhat messy, with both men announcing victory based on the quick counts, and Prabowo then rejecting and appealing the result. But in the end it was a clear victory for Jokowi and Kalla, though by no means a landslide. They took 53.15 percent of the vote.

Sailing towards a Greater Indonesia

In his inaugural speech on October 20, Jokowi laid out the agenda for his presidency: "This is the moment for us to unite with our hearts and our hands. This is the moment for us to continue in the next very difficult test of history, to achieve and realize an Indonesia which is sovereign in the political field, independent in the economic field, and with a sense of character in its own culture."

This three-part aspiration was taken directly from a Sukarno concept, *Trisakti*, meaning "Three Powers" or "Three Sacred Forces." Jokowi had mentioned Trisakti as a guiding principle of his own politics as early as 2012, during his Jakarta gubernatorial campaign.[8] By citing it again at the outset of his presidency he set a firmly nationalist tone, in keeping with Indonesia's major political traditions, in keeping with the ethos of PDI-P, and in keeping with the one direct trace of a political heritage in his own background: the figure of his grandfather, the Kragan *lurah*, Lamidi Wiryo Mihardjo, whose own political affiliation had been with Sukarno's PNI.

Jokowi had further elaborated Trisakti with his own Sukarnoesque Sanskrit coinage: *Nawacita*, meaning "Nine Ideals." This had been unveiled during the campaign as the core of Jokowi's 42-page "Vision and Mission" statement. Now in his first presidential speech, he reiterated its importance as the foundation of his development ideology. In summary, Nawacita's nine elements were as follows:

---

[8]Laurel Benny Saron Silalahi, "Jokowi selalu teringat trisakti Bung Karno," *Merdeka*, June 23, 2012, https://www.merdeka.com/peristiwa/jokowi-selalu-teringat-trisakti-bung-karno.html [accessed October 15, 2020].

1. Protection of Indonesian citizens;
2. Good governance;
3. Development of Indonesia from the peripheries;
4. The eradication of corruption;
5. Improvements to the quality of life of all citizens;
6. An increase in productivity and global competitiveness;
7. Economic independence;
8. The initiation of a "mental revolution" through education reforms with an emphasis on strengthening "national character";
9. A strengthening of Indonesia's ethos of "unity in diversity".[9]

While these principles may seem somewhat vague and even anodyne, concise philosophies of this sort are a traditional element of Indonesian political thinking, with Pancasila being the most famous example. Throughout his first term Jokowi would seek to align his policy decisions with the "Spirit of Nawacita."

Nawacita placed particular emphasis on the oft-discussed Indonesian concept of *gotong-royong*. Originally a vital feature of cohesion at the level of the Javanese village, involving a carefully maintained balance of debts and credits in time, labor and material within a discrete social unit, it has been scaled up to a national level to imply a more straightforward ideal of "mutual cooperation" or "shared burdens."

Jokowi's speech continued: "I am sure that this enormous historical task will be carried out together with unity, with gotong-royong, and with hard work. Unity and gotong-royong are the conditions for us to become a great nation. We will never be great if we are trapped in division and disunity. And we are never truly independent without hard work.

"The government that I lead will work to ensure that all people in all corners of the country feel the benefit of government services. I also invite all state institutions to work in the same spirit in carrying out their respective duties and functions." [10]

The speech was notable for its emphasis on the idea of a task requiring completion, and there was a particular stress on the word "work."

---

[9] Anita Rachman and Ben Otto, "How Well Is Jokowi Keeping His Campaign Promises?" *The Wall Street Journal*, February 9, 2015, https://www.wsj.com/articles/BL-SEAB-5712 [accessed October 14, 2020].

[10] "Pidato Presiden Joko Widodo pada Pelantikan Presiden dan Wakil Presiden Republik Indonesia," Sekretariat Kabinet Republik Indonesia, October 20, 2014, https://setkab.go.id/pidato-presiden-joko-widodo-pada-pelantikan-presiden-dan-wakil-presiden-republik-indonesia-di-gedung-mpr-senayan-jakarta-20-oktober-2014/.

"I am sure this country will be stronger and more authoritative if all state institutions work to carry out the mandate given by our constitution. To the fishermen, laborers, farmers, *bakso* sellers, hawkers, drivers, academics, teachers, soldiers, police, businessmen, and professionals, I call on you to work hand in hand, work together, because this is a historical moment for all of us to move together, to work, to work and work."[11]

The speech also drew particular attention to Indonesia's defining geographical characteristic, a characteristic which has often been neglected in terms of the national conversation: this is a maritime country; most of Indonesia's total territorial area is covered with seawater. Jokowi argued that Indonesia had turned his back on the sea for too long.[12]

"We must work as hard as possible to restore Indonesia as a maritime country. Oceans, seas, straits, and bays are the future of our civilization. We have turned our backs on the sea, turned our backs on the ocean, and turned our backs on the straits and bays," he said. In stressing this point he used an ancient Sanskrit phrase, dating from the time of Majapahit, the greatest of Indonesia's precolonial states: *jalesveva jayamahe*. The phrase remains the motto of the Indonesian Navy, and translates roughly as "on the waters we are victorious."

"This is the moment for us to restore everything so that *jalesveva jayamahe*, in the sea we actually become victorious, so that the watchwords of our ancestors ring out once more," Jokowi said.[13]

This aspect of the speech echoed the themes of the victory address Jokowi had given three months earlier, when the election result was first announced. Late at night, Jokowi and Jusuf Kalla had spoken from the floodlit deck of a *pinisi*, the traditional sailing ship of the Bugis, the great maritime culture of southern Sulawesi, docked in the Sunda Kelapa Harbor in the north of Jakarta, a port synonymous with Indonesia's maritime history.[14] Then and in the inaugural speech, Jokowi explicitly portrayed himself as the "captain" and Indonesia as a "ship."

"As the captain trusted by the people, I invite all citizens of the nation to board the ship of the Republic of Indonesia and sail together towards a Greater Indonesia. We will develop strong sails, we will face all storms

---

[11] Ibid

[12] Nurulloh, *Presiden Jokowi Harapan Baru Indonesia* (Jakarta: Elex Media Komputindo, 2004), 106.

[13] "Pidato Presiden Joko Widodo."

[14] "Rock Star or Politician as Jokowi Takes Presidency," OPEMAM, October 21, 2014, http://www.opemam.org/node/6057 [accessed October 14, 2020].

and ocean waves with our own strength. And I will stand under the will of the people and the constitution," he said.[15]

But "work" was undoubtedly the overarching theme of the speech: "Therefore, work, work, and work is the most important thing. I am sure that through hard work and gotong-royong we will be able to protect the entire Indonesian nation and every drop of Indonesia's blood, improve public welfare, educate the nation, and participate in carrying out a world order based on independence, eternal peace and social justice."[16]

No one, however, faced a bigger job of work than the new president himself. Much had to be decided swiftly. The fate of stalled projects had to be determined.[17] Programs had to be budgeted for. The future of children in all corners of Indonesia depended on new assistance.[18]

Jokowi in the Nationalist Tradition

Sukarno first used the term Trisakti during his iconic *Tahun Vivere Pericoloso* (The Year of Living Dangerously) speech of August 17, 1964. He described Trisakti as a key tool in an ongoing national revolution. The Sanskrit-derived name indicated a political ideal consisting of the same three parts that Jokowi would cite half a century later: political sovereignty, economic independence, and a sense of cultural identity.

The key to Trisakti was Sukarno's notion of *kemandirian* (autonomy) in the specific sense of "standing on one's own feet." This had, in fact, been first expressed way back in the anticolonial struggle, during his trial for "disturbing public order" at Den Landraad Te Bandoeng, the Dutch district court in Bandung, on December 2, 1930.[19] In his rousing defense speech, which later became known as "Indonesia Accuses," Sukarno declared:

Honorable Judges, let us repeat it again: political power, independence, can only be brought about by the efforts of the Indonesian

---

[15] "Pidato Presiden Joko Widodo."

[16] Humas, "Dana Desa, Pemerintahan Jokowi Wujudkan Kedaulatan Desa," Sekretariat Kabinet Republik Indonesia, https://setkab.go.id/dana-desa-pemerintahan-jokowi-wujudkan-kedaulatan-desa/ [accessed May 3, 2019].

[17] "Ini Resep Jokowi Supaya Proyek Infrastruktur Tidak Mangkrak," *Suara*, February 26, 2017, https://www.suara.com/bisnis/2017/02/26/211337/ini-resep-jokowi-supaya-proyek-infrastruktur-tidak-mangkrak [accessed March 13, 2019].

[18] Keen Achroni, *Jokowi Memimpin dengan Hati* (Yogyakarta: Ar-Ruzz Media, 2018), 132.

[19] "Jejak Pledoi Fenomenal Bung Karno," *Hukum Online*, January 8, 2013, https://www.hukum-online.com/berita/baca/lt50ebec952d9a6/jejak-pledoi-fenomenal-bung-karno.

people themselves! Imperialism has had to hold us back; from the imperialist system, which lives on colonialism, we must expect no support in bringing an end to colonization.

Our fate is in our own hands; our salvation is within our own desire, in our own determination, in our own habits, in our own efforts. Our watchword is not pleading, not begging, not mendicancy ... our watchword must be noncooperation, or more truly: self-help—*Zelferwerkelijking, selfrehance!*—which we represent with the symbol of the buffalo's head![20]

Jokowi's own party is, of course, the PDI-P, which has a claim to the mantle of Sukarnoist nationalism. By directly affiliating himself to Sukarno's rhetoric and ideology (without, in any way, attempting to emulate Sukarno's style) Jokowi, the "political outsider," was signaling his own embeddedness in the nationalist political tradition. There is a widespread popular perception in Indonesia that Sukarno represents a sort of "pure" political ideology which existed before the corruption and cynicism of later decades. By drawing directly on Sukarno's Trisakti concept in laying out his own agenda, Jokowi was arguably taking a sort of "back-to-basics" approach, aligning himself with the political ideals of the wider public rather than any contemporary political elite.

"Playing Javanese": Culture and Politics

Indonesia's political scene has long been dominated by people of a Javanese background. This is largely because of simple demographics, and also because of Java's relatively advanced economic development and proximity to the national capital. (It is important to note, however, that culturally Jakarta is not in "Java"; the westernmost part of the island that bears that name is occupied by ethnically distinct Sundanese people, while the capital itself is a general melting pot which also has its own indigenous Betawi culture.)

The Javanese are by far Indonesia's largest ethnic group, numbering at least 100 million. Inevitably, various originally Javanese cultural manifestations have come to be seen as generically "Indonesian." The Sanskrit-based phrases used to determine ideological and political concepts—Pancasila,

---

[20] Sukarno, *Indonesia Menggugat* (Jakarta: Departemen Penerangan Republik Indonesia), 82, accessed from https://rowlandpasaribu.files.wordpress.com/2013/09/soekarno-indonesia-menggugat.pdf.

Trisakti, Nawacita, and so on—are particularly closely associated with classical Javanese culture. And phrases from colloquial Javanese frequently enter general Indonesian discourse (*wong cilik* and *gotong-royong*, for example). All of Indonesia's previous presidents have had a strongly Javanese heritage and upbringing, with the exception of B. J. Habibie, and even he, though born and raised in Sulawesi, was of aristocratic Javanese descent on his mother's side.

Inevitably, then, an impression of Javanese hegemony on the national political stage has sometimes fostered resentment in non-Javanese regions. This was especially the case during the rule of Suharto, whose own explicitly Javanese identity was particularly pronounced. He was seen by some critics as having used, or rather misused and distorted, Javanese ideals and ethics to perpetuate his own grip on power.

For example, amongst Suharto's most favored Javanese proverbs was *Jer basuki mawa beya*,[21] which might be translated as "Everything must be paid for," "Any achievement requires sacrifice," or, more bluntly, "There's no such thing as a free lunch." The proverb was deployed to convince people that Suharto's "developmentism" required sacrifice. The problem was that during his rule, those who had to bear the *beya* (sacrifice) and those who enjoyed the *basuki* (results) were generally not the same people. It is not surprising, then, that concerns have sometimes been raised about Jokowi's own deeply Javanese identity, and his frequent recourse to the proverbs and aphorisms typical of a Javanese worldview.

Seno Gumira Ajidarma, a writer and rector of the Jakarta Arts Institute (Institut Kesenian Jakarta), is one of those concerned about this aspect of Jokowi's public persona. In the newspaper *Koran Tempo* on August 2, 2019,[22] he highlighted a Javanese-language proverb, or *piwulang*, that Jokowi had used during an interview: *Lamun sira sekti, aja mateni; lamun sira pinter, aja minteri; lamun sira banter, aja mbanteri*. This proverb translates roughly as "Even if you are powerful, do not kill; even if you are smart, don't trick others; even if you are fast, don't overtake others." In an opinion piece titled "Javanese (Political) Arrogance?" Ajidarma read into Jokowi's use of this proverb, not an honorable pacifist sentiment, but a decidedly Suhartoesque veiled threat. The implication, he argued, typically Javanese in its indirectness, was not "I will not kill, trick or overtake you,"

---

[21] Mohammad A. Syuropati, *1800++ Peribahasa Jawa Lengkap dengan Arti dan Tafsirannya* (Yogyakarta: Kauna Pustaka, 2015), 88.

[22] Seno Gumira Ajidarma, "Arogansi (Politik) Jawa?" *Koran Tempo*, August 2, 2019, https://koran.tempo.co/read/444556/arogansi-politik-jawa [accessed August 13, 2019].

but "Never forget: I *am* powerful, smart and fast." Ajidarma also raised concerns more generally at the potential cultural arrogance of "playing Javanese" on the national stage.

But Eko Sulistyo, deputy IV of the presidential chief of staff and a personal friend of Jokowi since his entry to Surakarta politics, has countered Seno's criticism. In the same newspaper, he argued that these concerns lacked an analysis of the contemporary political structure, which has changed considerably since the fall of Suharto. Eko argued that there was an essential difference between Suharto's approach to power, often equated to that of a traditional Javanese king, and Jokowi's efforts to connect with the electorate. While Suharto did deliberately aim to instill a degree of fear through veiled threats, Jokowi intends to gain public support through a sense of shared origins.

Looking at this further, it should be reiterated that Jokowi is the only president since Suharto who has emerged from outside of hereditary elitism. (Suharto himself came originally from a very modest rural Javanese background; but he stepped into politics only after rising to the highest levels of the military.) Jokowi's popularity emerged in large part because he was widely believed to understand the concerns of the Indonesian people, and the *wong cilik* in particular. His leadership was accepted not because of repression or fear, but because of genuine popularity. Eko argued that whatever it might have implied coming from the mouth of Suharto, an expression such as *Lamun sira sekti* from Jokowi should genuinely be read as an ethos for the limiting of power through a model of non-violence.

Growing up on the banks of Kali Anyar, Jokowi had been steeped in the Javanese values of *welas asih* (compassion), *tepa selira* (empathy), and *andhap asor* (humility). He was also urged to be *pinter*, to pursue the highest possible education. Having reached that point, the phrase *Lamun sira pinter* was actually advice for himself: "Do not use your intelligence to *minteri* (fool) others."

Eko further argued that Javanese culture requires introspection as a means of managing power in a moral and harmonious manner. In Javanese philosophical understandings, the term *mateni* should not simply be read in the most superficial translation as "to kill." It can be interpreted as cutting off another person's means of sustenance, or closing opportunities for others. By using such moralistic Javanese proverbs, Eko argues, Jokowi, as president, is creating a reminder for himself, to place limits on his own potential power and to open the widest possible space for others.

Appointing a Cabinet and Identifying Development Priorities

Jokowi understood how difficult it would be to captain the ship of the republic which was now in his charge.[23] His first practical step was the appointment of a cabinet. The line-up was announced on October 26, a week after the inauguration. He had originally planned to make the announcement earlier, but the delay was caused in part by Jokowi's insistence that all potential ministers be vetted in advance by the Corruption Eradication Commission (KPK; Komisi Pemberantasan Korupsi) and the Financial Transaction Reports and Analysis Center (PPATK; Pusat Pelaporan dan Analisis Transaksi Keuangan). Eight of the original names were rejected during this process.[24] When finally unveiled, the 34-person cabinet featured 18 technocratic appointments and 16 figures from a political background. There were eight women ministers, a record number, including the first female foreign minister, Retno Marsudi.

Some commentators expressed disappointment at the fairly conventional cabinet configuration, with its mix of technocrats and politicians. But this was an inevitable result of the position Jokowi found himself in as president. The coalition building required after PDI-P failed to gain enough votes in the April parliamentary election to be his sole backer meant that there would always have to be a number of political appointees. And the fact that Jokowi himself had no leadership position within PDI-P meant that he was always likely to have to include some party nominations to the cabinet. Indonesian cabinets also typically feature some appointments influenced by the vice president. All this was indicative of the new and more complex challenges Jokowi would face as president. Running Surakarta and Jakarta he had, in a way, had more autonomy. Now he would have to negotiate the various powerful interests involved in a country where no single political party or interest group ever achieves outright dominance.

Nonetheless, the fact that Jokowi had been able to stick to his stated intention to vet ministers in advance, and that several had been knocked back, was significant. He also created a new structure for the coordinating ministries, reflecting the developmental emphases of Nawacita. He gave the ministerial team a name which reflected the ethos he had stressed in his inaugural speech, and which had characterized his own approach to both

---

[23] Achroni, *Jokowi Memimpin dengan Hati*, 228.

[24] Yeni Kwok, "Indonesia's New President Appoints a Cabinet of Compromise," *Time*, October 27, 2014, https://time.com/3540622/jokowi-cabinet-compromise-joko-widodo/ [accessed October 15, 2020].

his previous elected roles. This was to be the Kabinet Kerja, the "Working Cabinet." The name was an affirmation of Jokowi's own distinctive motto, "work, work, and work." It also came with a certain historical resonance: Sukarno had called his own 1959 ministerial team the Kabinet Kerja.[25]

Despite the high aspirations and the swift start, Jokowi and his new ministers faced a plethora of challenges. Indonesia had weathered the global economic crisis of the previous decade remarkably well, maintaining strong growth throughout. But the global economic climate remained uncertain. A good captain must understand the weather and be able to predict potential dangers on the voyage ahead. One of these, still beyond the horizon as Jokowi took office, was the threat of a major trade war between the United States and China. In that eventuality it would require deft decision making if the country were to avoid the fate of the mousedeer crushed between two fighting elephants, as the Indonesian proverb has it.

Jokowi has argued that global rivalry of this kind should not be viewed as healthy market-driven competition but as an attempt to inflict defeat. Constructive competition ought to involve working together to improve mutual quality, one country complementing the needs of another without attempting to achieve dominance or control. Yet, on the international scene dominance and control are often the obvious goals, with debt commonly used for leverage, especially against developing countries. As an experienced businessman, Jokowi felt that a strong economic foundation was essential to protect Indonesia from this scenario and that interactions with other nations ought to be carried out on an equal basis.[26]

He also felt that an "Indonesia-centric" future for the nation depended heavily on social justice, properly extended to all corners of the archipelago. The past mistake of concentrating development on Java has left many of Indonesia's peripheral areas underdeveloped. In remote regions infrastructure was still minimal and schools still lacked reliable teachers. And employment opportunities beyond Java and the major urban centers were often severely limited.

As well as promising to revive Indonesia's time-honored status as a maritime nation, Jokowi also emphasized its role as an agricultural country. He wanted to streamline the planning and implementation of state revenue and expenditure, just as he had done in Surakarta and Jakarta. And he

---

[25] M. C. Ricklefs, *A History of Modern Indonesia since c.1200*, 3rd edn (London: Palgrave, 2001), 322.

[26] Inu Kencana Syafi'ie, *Sistem Administrasi Negara Republik Indonesia* (Jakarta: Bumi Aksara, 2011), 82.

placed a strong emphasis on the enforcement of laws and regulations based on the four long-established pillars of Indonesian nationalism, namely, the Pancasila national ideology, the national slogan of *Bhinneka Tunggal Ika* (typically translated as "Unity in Diversity"), the Unitary State of the Republic of Indonesia, and the 1945 Constitution.[27] This, from a nationalist perspective, was seen as a powerful bulwark against religious radicalism, intolerance, and international terrorism.

As president, Jokowi intended to be optimistic and positive,[28] and to take a businessman's approach to problem solving, seeking opportunities within each challenge and emphasizing work rather than discourse. Although his terms in Surakarta and Jakarta are often portrayed as periods of radical and total change for those cities, in fact his approach often simply involved streamlining existing systems and completing the unfinished tasks of previous administrations. The famous Banjarsari street vendor relocation had, after all, been on the agenda for years before Jokowi became mayor. He came into the presidency with a similar approach. Despite his perceived "newness," he did not take a destructive or even a dismissive attitude towards the work that had been done by his predecessors.

One of the biggest infrastructure projects that had been initiated under Susilo Bambang Yudhoyono's administration was the Trans-Sumatra Toll Road, part of the Master Plan Percepatan dan Perluasan Pembangunan Ekonomi Indonesia (MP3EI), the "Master Plan for the Acceleration and Expansion of Indonesian Economic Development." Jokowi intended to finish the job. Another major unfinished infrastructure plan that Jokowi picked up for completion was the Jakarta-Cikampek elevated toll road. This is an important point: although his first term was defined by dramatic and fast-moving infrastructure developments across the country, many were based on incomplete or stalled existing projects.[29] Jokowi did not necessarily need to create big plans from scratch; many, in fact, already existed.

A notable example of this was the Mass Rapid Transport (MRT) system for Jakarta, which Jokowi started during his truncated term as governor.[30] The supporting work around this project included the completion of the Jatigede Reservoir construction, which was actually initiated as far back as the Sukarno administration (indeed, the idea for an MRT system itself

---

[27] Tjahjo Kumolo, *Nawa Cita untuk Kesejahteraan Rakyat Indonesia* (Jakarta: Penerbit Buku Kompas, 2017), 47–48.

[28] Alberthiene Endah, *Jokowi Memimpin Kota Menyentuh Jakarta* (Solo: Metagraf, 2012),198.

[29] Achroni, *Jokowi Memimpin dengan Hati*, 230–36.

[30] Bambang Susantono, *Revolusi Transportasi* (Jakarta: Gramedia Pustaka Utama, 2016), 111.

dated back to the 1960s). Also targeted for completion during his first term was the Trans-Papua Highway, the construction of which was started under the Suharto government.

At the outset, Jokowi's administration set a target of creating at least ten million new jobs during its five-year term, two million each year. But it was recognized from the outset that extensive new infrastructure would be essential to approaching that ambitious goal. Jokowi was eager to develop tourism, both domestic and international, in places well beyond the traditional centers of Bali and Java. However, regional airports were too small, or inadequate; their runways were not long enough; and many places with major tourism potential did not have an airport at all. He wanted to increase agricultural productivity, but existing reservoir, dam, and irrigation capacity amounted to only around 11 percent of the total requirement to maximize yields. He wanted to advance the fishing industry and improve the welfare of fishermen, and to exploit Indonesia's wider maritime potential as one of the largest archipelagic countries in the world as a route to prosperity.[31] But most ports were severely lacking in capacity and facilities. Meanwhile, the region-wide issue of territorial violations by foreign fishing vessels was a notable sore point.

There were also questions to be addressed about the future of Indonesia's rural communities, and also about its natural resources. The long-standing drift from villages to cities, the journey undertaken by Jokowi's own father in the late 1950s, continued, with all its attendant social problems, and with the consequent failure to exploit rural potential. There were also some ninety million hectares of forest nationwide, much of it left unproductive.[32] In the field of human resources, meanwhile, many Indonesian children were still failing to complete their schooling, typically because of financial pressure:[33] a lack of money for uniforms or equipment, or a need to drop out to help their parents to earn a living. Jokowi's own journey had been determined by his father's insistence on the importance of education regardless of financial constraints, and he was committed to following that lead as head of state. All these challenges were exacerbated by the persistent problem of inequality: inequality between cities and villages, rich and poor, west and east. In many remote, underdeveloped

---

[31] Nurulloh, *Presiden Jokowi Harapan Baru Indonesia*, 113–34.

[32] "Jokowi: Pengelolaan Hutan Harus Produktif, Kalo Tidak Percuma Saja," *Tempo*, October 25, 2017, https://nasional.tempo.co/read/1027893/jokowi-pengelolaan-hutan-harus-produktif-kalo-tidak-percuma-saja [accessed June 27, 2019].

[33] Achroni, *Jokowi Memimpin dengan Hati*, 132.

and outermost areas of Indonesia there was a strong sense of grievance, and of having been left behind.

The next five chapters of this book look closely at Jokowi's efforts to address each of these key policy areas in turn, from tourism to the development of infrastructure and social justice mechanisms in Papua, while also charting the narrative of his first five years in power.

Jokowi in 2016 on a visit to Raja Ampat, an emerging tourism hotspot in Eastern Indonesia.

Chapter Five

Building "New Balis": Tourism in Jokowi's Indonesia

Early Challenges: Jokowi's First Year in Office

Jokowi had come to office in an atmosphere of celebration, optimism, and heightened expectation. But in truth, the situation was an awkward one for a president hoping to move swiftly and decisively. The realpolitik had demanded pragmatic cabinet appointments. The economy was looking somewhat sluggish. He had inherited a number of thorny problems from the outgoing administration. And he also faced the classic difficulty for the president of any country with separate executive and legislative branches: a parliament firmly controlled by the opposition.

Jokowi's KIH, the "Awesome Indonesia Coalition," had just 207 seats in the DPR, while Prabowo's KMP, the "Red and White Coalition," accounted for 353 seats. Although Prabowo himself had no elected position and was not a member of the house, his own Gerindra Party was the third biggest in the DPR with 73 seats, and fully 63.04 percent of DPR members belonged to parties which had backed Prabowo for the presidency.

A clear signal of the power of the KMP-dominated parliament came early on. Traditionally, the speaker of the House had been appointed by the single largest party (which in 2014 was still PDI-P, with 109 seats). But the DPR now passed a new law which meant that the speaker would be appointed by parliamentary vote, and a few weeks before Jokowi's inauguration, Golkar's Setya Novanto was elected to the role.[1] It looked as

---

[1] "Indonesia's New Parliament Inaugurated; Clash on Speaker Voting," *Indonesia Investments*, October 2, 2014, https://www.indonesia-investments.com/news/todays-headlines/

though Jokowi would have to deal with a potentially hostile parliament as he attempted to realize his ambitious program.

Jokowi, however, was typically relaxed and casual about the parliamentary situation. "It's not a problem to have a minority," he told reporters shortly before his inauguration, noting that as governor of Jakarta he had not controlled a majority in the city's regional assembly, the DPRD. "I had a similar experience in Jakarta and it was not a problem to get things done. It's the same at the national level."[2]

But as it happened, the opposition coalition proved more fractious than the Jokowi-backing KIH. Competing factions emerged in Golkar, the biggest of the KMP parties, with one half pulling towards a new position supportive of the president. A similar situation emerged in PPP. And by September 2015, PAN, the party of defeated vice presidential candidate Hatta Rajasa, had switched sides altogether and joined Jokowi's KIH.

What had started out looking like a solidly anti-Jokowi parliament had tacked rapidly in the president's favor. This in itself presented a potential challenge. Jokowi's predecessor, Susilo Bambang Yudhoyono, had worked hard to establish a solid supporting coalition. But as a result, he had often been hampered by the competing agendas of the multiple parties which, in theory, gave him their backing. He also had shaky control over the coalition within the DPR. All this had contributed to the somewhat ineffectual reputation of his presidency.[3] The balance between the advantages of a notionally acquiescent DPR, on the one hand, and the advantages of fewer coalition partners clamoring for cabinet seats and pushing their own priorities, on the other, was one that Jokowi still had to work through during his first year in office. But in the short term, the fragmentation of the opposition coalition strengthened his position.

But there were still plenty of other problems to deal with, not least the sensitive issue of fuel subsidies. Indonesian motorists had enjoyed access to subsidized fuel ever since the country gained its independence in 1949.[4] At the outset, the rationale for this policy was solid: the country

---

indonesias-new-parliament-inaugurated-clash-on-speaker-voting/item2473 [accessed October 19, 2020].

[2] Kanupriya Kapoor, "Indonesian president-elect's principles could derail his reform," *Reuters*, October 7, 2014, https://www.reuters.com/article/us-indonesia-politics/indonesian-president-elects-principles-could-derail-his-reforms-idUSKCN0HW23H20141007 [accessed October 19, 2020].

[3] Ahmad Ibrahim Almuttaqi, *Jokowi's Indonesia and the* World (Singapore: World Scientific Publishing, 2020), xxii.

[4] Krithika Varagur, "Indonesia to Effectively Continue Fuel Subsidy," *VOA News*, March 19,

had its own oilfields with much unexploited potential and relatively low domestic demand. But as the decades passed, demand rapidly outstripped domestic supply and the subsidies became a huge financial burden on the state, accounting for up to 20 percent of fiscal expenditure by the 1960s.[5] Previous governments had attempted to remove the subsidies, but the country was developing rapidly and the more time passed, the more Indonesians became direct consumers of petrol and the more politically sensitive the issue became. Susilo Bambang Yudhoyono had attempted to reduce the subsidies in 2013, prompting nationwide street protests.[6] During the transition period between Jokowi's election and his inauguration, he had actually asked Yudhoyono to make further subsidy reductions before the end of his term, but the outgoing president demurred.[7] At the time, around 3 percent of Indonesia's entire GDP was still being spent on fuel subsidies.[8] Jokowi had plans for massive infrastructure investment and extensive expansion of healthcare coverage and education support, and he badly needed to free up that cash.

Just a month after his inauguration, the new president made his first move to increase the fixed price of consumer petrol and diesel. Then, in early January 2015, he moved to cut the subsidies further. There was some public opposition, but the fact that global oil prices were falling rapidly at the time cushioned the blow. For a while, prices at the pumps actually fell and Jokowi was able to free up around US$20 billion of government funding.[9] Later, when global oil prices began to rise once more, Jokowi intervened to fix prices at the pumps. But the main cost of this intervention would now have to be borne by Pertamina, the state-owned oil company.

At the same time, the Indonesian economy was looking decidedly sluggish, and the currency, the rupiah, was weakening. Partly in response to this and partly because he felt increasingly secure as parliamentary

---

2018, https://www.voanews.com/east-asia/indonesia-effectively-continue-fuel-subsidy#:~:-text=The%20Ministry%20said%20it%20would,while%20keeping%20pump%20prices%20unchanged [accessed October 19, 2020].

[5] Ibid.

[6] "Indonesia fuel prices rocket by 44% sparking protests," BBC, June 22, 2013, https://www.bbc.com/news/world-asia-23015511 [accessed October 19, 2020].

[7] Hans Nicholas Jong and Ni Komang Erviani, "Jokowi fails to persuade SBY on fuel subsidy," *The Jakarta Post*, August 28, 2014, https://www.thejakartapost.com/news/2014/08/28/jokowi-fails-persuade-sby-fuel-subsidy.html [accessed October 19, 2020].

[8] Varagur, "Indonesia to Effectively Continue Fuel Subsidy."

[9] Andy Nguyen, "President Jokowi's Economic and Energy Reforms: A Year in Review," The National Bureau of Asian Research, October 23, 2015, https://www.nbr.org/publication/president-jokowis-economic-and-energy-reforms-a-year-in-review/ [accessed October 19, 2020].

opposition crumbled, in August Jokowi reshuffled his "Working Cabinet." Six ministers, including three of the coordinating ministers, were replaced on the grounds of poor performance, mainly in relation to the economy. The replacements were mostly solid technocrats.[10] Former investment banker Thomas Lembong took over the trade portfolio and Darmin Nasution, former governor of Bank Indonesia, the country's central bank, became coordinating economic minister. Jokowi also announced a series of reforms intended to streamline procedures for businesses and to encourage investment.

In late October 2015, Jokowi headed for the USA for bilateral talks with Barack Obama, a man to whom he had often been compared. This was by no means his first overseas trip as president. There had been an early visit to Beijing in November 2014 for an APEC summit, and a G20 meeting in Australia soon afterwards, as well as various regional trips on ASEAN business and a foray to the Middle East. But the US trip was a particularly high-profile journey. It marked the end of his first full year in the job. The preceding twelve months had not been entirely straightforward, and Jokowi's public approval ratings had proven erratic, going from 72 percent before his inauguration to figures below 50 percent at various points, then climbing once again. Just as had been the case for his American counterpart, at the outset many of Jokowi's most enthusiastic supporters seem to have made no allowance for essential pragmatism, to have assumed that he would be able to govern entirely unbeholden to the legislature, entirely uninfluenced by the push and pull of practical politics, entirely untrammeled, in fact, by the very factors that restrain a democratically elected president from assuming absolute power. Despite the grumbling, in some areas Jokowi's presidency was already proving transformational. In Surakarta and Jakarta, he had been lauded for rolling up the sleeves of his trademark plaid shirt and getting things done. And there was no doubt that when it came to development, he was doing the same thing at a national level. One of the particular areas that was getting Jokowi's attention was tourism, and the unrealized potential of little-known destinations all across the sprawling Indonesian archipelago.

---

[10] "Jokowi inaugurates six new ministers," *The Jakarta Post*, August 12, 2014, https://www. thejakartapost.com/news/2015/08/12/jokowi-inaugurates-six-new-ministers.html [accessed October 19, 2020].

Pecinta Alam: At Home in the Great Outdoors

As a student at Gadjah Mada University (UGM) in the 1980s, Jokowi had a reputation as what is known in Indonesia as *pecinta alam*, a "lover of nature," one who revels in the outdoors. He was a member of Mapala Silvagama, a long-standing semiautonomous club for students within the Faculty of Forestry at UGM, which organizes hiking and camping trips and other outdoor activities with the aim of fostering enthusiasm for conservation and the natural world.[11] The appreciation for Indonesia's natural wonders that Jokowi developed as a student clearly carried over into his later tourism policies.[12]

According to one of his university friends, Hardanto Hartomosuharjo, Jokowi had a reputation among his fellow Mapala Silvagama members as an enthusiastic and energetic mountaineer. Indonesia has a strong tradition of student mountaineering. Many of the country's huge volcanic peaks are easily accessible from large urban centers, and on any given weekend their trails are busy with groups of young hikers aiming for the summit. Yogyakarta, where UGM is located, is a particularly appealing base for mountain lovers, surrounded as it is by some of Java's most dramatic summits, Merapi, Lawu, Sumbing, Sindoro, Merbabu, and others. Jokowi tackled many of these peaks as a student, and in 1984 he made a longer trip to Sumatra with a group of other Mapala Silvagama members to climb the 3,805-meter Gunung Kerinci, Indonesia's tallest volcano and the country's highest summit outside of the Sudirman Range in Papua. Hardanto says that "Of the several who took part, he was the first to reach the summit."[13]

Later, as a businessman, Jokowi made various trips abroad and saw the well-developed tourist industries of other countries, both within Southeast Asia and further afield, places where tourist infrastructure and public and government engagement with the industry appeared to be at a much higher level than in Indonesia. These experiences of international travel stuck with him.

As mayor of Surakarta, Jokowi had sought to develop the city's obvious tourism potential through improvements to infrastructure, widening

---

[11] Mapala Silvagama, http://www.mapalasilvagama.or.id/ [accessed September 17, 2020].

[12] Rimsky K. Judisseno, *Aktivitas dan Kompleksitas Kepariwisataan* (Jakarta: Gramedia Pustaka Utama, 2017), 46.

[13] Imanuel Nicolas Manafe, "Reunian Kembali, Teman Mapala Jokowi Cerita Petualangannya di Gunung Kerinci," *Tribun*, February 10, 2017, https://www.tribunnews.com/nasional/2017/02/10/reunian-kembali-teman-mapala-jokowi-cerita-petualangannya-di-gunung-kerinci [accessed August 28, 2020].

pavements, creating public gardens, and revitalizing decayed architecture. He also created events to attract domestic and international visitors, such as the Solo Batik Carnival, launched in 2008 and has since become an annual celebration. Later, as governor of Jakarta, Jokowi also sought to develop tourism potential. Although it is Indonesia's major gateway for international travel, the capital has long had a reputation as a chaotic and uninviting place, generally avoided by international leisure travelers. Changing such a perception internationally would be a lengthy process. But the vast potential for domestic tourism, and in particular the potential for short-term tourist activities for local residents, gained attention during Jokowi's gubernatorial term. On several occasions, local tourism potential was developed as a "by-product" of infrastructure projects. For example, during the redevelopment of reservoirs to act as flood buffers, Jokowi ensured that facilities were put in place to attract sightseers. Former slum neighborhoods alongside the Pluit and Ria Rio reservoirs were turned into parks, which today are visited by large numbers of Jakarta residents at weekends. But now, as president, Jokowi was faced with the challenge of boosting tourism on a much larger scale.

Unrealized Potential: A Stagnant Sector

Compared to many other much smaller countries in the region, Indonesia has long struggled to attract large numbers of international tourists despite the obvious potential of its rich cultural heritage and diverse and beautiful landscapes. The industry has received various blows over the decades, in particular the political turmoil of the late 1990s and the high-profile terrorist attacks of the early 2000s. Even disregarding these individual setbacks, Indonesian tourism has proved peculiarly stagnant compared to its endlessly booming counterparts in Thailand, Malaysia, and various other ASEAN member states.

According to the UN World Tourism Organization, in 2017 foreign tourist arrivals in Thailand totaled 35.4 million people, while neighboring Malaysia received 26 million visitors. Indonesia, meanwhile, was visited by just 12.9 million people that year. In this it lagged behind even Singapore, which, despite covering an area smaller than the Yogyakarta Special Region of Java, was visited by 13.9 million people in 2017.[14] Arrival numbers to

---

[14] Eric Rosen, "New Rankings Of The World's Fastest-Growing Tourism Destinations,"*Forbes*, September 6, 2018, https://www.forbes.com/sites/ericrosen/2018/09/06/new-rankings-of-the-worlds-fastest-growing-tourism-destinations/ [accessed July 5, 2019].

Indonesia have shown significant annual increases in the decades following the economic crisis of the late 1990s. But under close examination, those statistics are overwhelmingly dominated by arrivals to a single destination within Indonesia: Bali. Among the reasons for limited realization of tourism potential in other parts of the country are those of obvious practicality: poor facilities, difficult access, and limited information.

At the start of his presidency, Jokowi had made tourism a key development priority as both a way to boost economic opportunities for communities far from the country's conventional economic centers in line with the "development from the peripheries" element of his Nawacita framework,[15] and as an important source of foreign currency earnings in an era of global economic uncertainty. Accessibility and development of appropriate facilities were identified as key factors in opening up new areas.

When it came to attracting both foreign and domestic tourists, Jokowi noted that many traditional tourist spots, such as lakes, mountains, beaches, waterfalls, and more, were carelessly managed, with garbage and shabby informal food stalls spoiling the beauty. But the most significant problem was invariably a lack of infrastructure and a lack of connectivity between various potential tourist destinations.

One obvious example of Indonesia's neglected tourism potential could be seen in Lake Toba, North Sumatra. It is a stunning place, one of the largest volcanic calderas in the world surrounded by green mountains and home to the distinctive Toba Batak culture. Though it has attracted a trickle of international backpackers since the 1980s, and more recently a smattering of Indonesian student travelers, until recently it was never properly organized and managed as a tourist destination. The journey to the lake from Medan, the nearest large city, took around five hours on a narrow and poorly maintained road. The hotel facilities at the lake were basic and the level of service rudimentary. Lake Toba was one of very many such places, scattered all across Indonesia's vast archipelago. Jokowi wanted to unlock their unrealized potential.

Strategies and Approaches: Marketing, SEZs, and the "Ten New Balis" Program

To answer this challenge, Jokowi created the "Main Tourism Breakthrough" and "Four Pillars of Tourism" frameworks. The four tourism pillars were

---

[15] Alberthiene Endah, *Jokowi Memimpin Kota Menyentuh Jakarta* (Solo: Metagraf, 2012), 198.

tourism destinations, tourism industry, tourism marketing, and tourism institutions.[16] One of the simplest and most instantly effective measures to be put in place was the granting of free visit visas to travelers from a total of 169 different countries, a reform which instantly made Indonesia more competitive as a destination given that neighboring ASEAN member-states already had similar tourist visa arrangements.

Jokowi encouraged an energetic and hard-working approach to tourism amongst his staff, emphasizing it as a priority. In 2016, he issued Presidential Decree No. 3 concerning the Acceleration of the Implementation of National Strategic Projects.[17] Through this decree, the government began speeding up improvements to transportation, electricity, and clean water infrastructure to support the development of important tourism areas.[18]

But all the effort to improve infrastructure would be of little value in terms of increasing international tourism if people outside the country still had no idea of what Indonesia had to offer. It has often been noted that when it comes to international tourism, one small province, Bali, is generally better known than the vast country of which it is a part. Indeed, anecdotes are common about foreign tourists who arrive believing that Bali is a country in its own right, or even a part of Thailand or China! But while Bali has instant name recognition as a holiday paradise, popular perceptions persist of Indonesia as an obscure Third World nation despite its ranking as one of the twenty largest global economies.

As a former entrepreneur, Jokowi was fully aware of the importance of planned promotion and measurable targets when presenting a product, in this case Indonesia itself.[19] Marketing of high-quality products had been part of the work he had done at the very start of his entrepreneurial career, during his three-year apprenticeship at his *pakdhe*'s furniture company. It had also been central in both his own business and in promoting the wider Surakarta furniture sector in his role at Asmindo.

International marketing for tourism during Jokowi's first presidential term was carried out under the "Wonderful Indonesia" brand. A centerpiece of the campaign was the appearance of a Wonderful Indonesia

---

[16] Nursodik Gunarjo, *Nawacita Meretas Indonesia Maju* (Jakarta: Kominfo, 2016), 126.

[17] "Sektor Pariwisata Jadi Unggulan Pemerintahan Presiden Jokowi," *Suara*, December 11, 2018, https://www.suara.com/news/2018/12/11/133536/sektor-pariwisata-jadi-unggulan-pemerintahan-presiden-jokowi [accessed June 26, 2019].

[18] James J. Spillane, ed., *Pariwisata Indonesia: Siasat Ekonomi dan Rekayasa Kebudayaan* (Yogyakarta: Kanisius, 1994), 52.

[19] Tony Burhanudin, "Pariwisata Indonesia Kurang Promosi," *Marketing.co.id*, https://marketing.co.id/pariwisata-indonesia-kurang-promosi/ [accessed June 28, 2019].

advertisement across three digital billboards in Times Square, New York, in 2017, featuring images of Bali, komodo dragons, and the Raja Ampat archipelago in Papua. Further traditional advertising campaigns were subsequently carried out in other international locations. At the same time, marketing approaches that eschewed the traditional advertising model were also put in place. GenPI (short for Generasi Pesona Indonesia, "The Indonesian Charm Generation") and GenWI ("Generasi Wonderful Indonesia") were teams of millennial influencers tasked with promoting Indonesian tourism in cyberspace, to considerable effect.

Historically, successful tourist destinations have tended to develop over many decades through a combination of organic growth and sustained official interventions. Bali's world renown, outstripping even that of the wider country of which it is a part, is no accident. Tourism there was initiated by the Dutch colonial government as far back as the 1920s.[20] Sukarno later made efforts to promote the island internationally, and this continued throughout Suharto's rule. The huge tourist industry that exits in Bali today is the product of a full century of development.

To have any chance of emulating Bali's success in the new regions earmarked for tourism, Jokowi's administration recognized the need for sustained and well-integrated approaches. In line with this, a number of Special Economic Zones were developed, each involving a mix of hard infrastructure, such as improved airport and other transport facilities, and soft infrastructure, such as looser regulations, easier flow of goods in and out, and a reduction of bureaucracy. The legal umbrella for these SEZs had actually been put in place in 2009 by the previous administration, another example of Jokowi's approach of completing or expanding work initiated by his predecessors. The SEZ initiative was seen as well aligned with the ethos of Nawacita: to develop Indonesia from the periphery, to improve quality of life, to increase productivity and international competitiveness, and to move towards economic self-reliance.

A total of twelve locations were identified for the establishment of SEZs, all in peripheral areas away from established economic hubs. The most recent three sites were inaugurated by Jokowi in April 2019: Bitung in North Sulawesi, the Maloy Batuta Trans-Kalimantan (MBTK) SEZ in East Kalimantan, and Morotai in North Maluku, which has been specifically identified for a tourism focus. In total, these three SEZs are expected to

---

[20] Flores Tanjung et al., *Sejarah Pariwisata* (Jakarta: Yayasan Pustaka Obor Indonesia, 2017), 55–63.

attract investment of more than Rp100 trillion. All three, and all the other designated SEZs, require major infrastructure investment, with ongoing work slated for Jokowi's second term.

From the outset, the Jokowi administration's determined focus on infrastructure development led to criticism and even abuse from opposition figures and sections of the media, with the standard line of attack being that "people can't eat infrastructure." This has certain uncomfortable echoes of the similar criticisms leveled against Suharto's New Order regime, with its famed emphasis on developmentalism. But Jokowi has consistently made the point that his own administration's developmental focus is informed by his own personal experiences. In particular, he recalls the severe economic limitations placed on his own ancestral villages due to lack of access and infrastructure. Tourism, as a sector particularly suited to small and micro enterprises, has particular potential to improve the lives of large numbers of people in otherwise economically stagnant areas. But first, the tourists need to be able to get to those areas, hence the need for infrastructure.

During a visit to Hong Kong in May 2017, Jokowi spoke to local businesspeople about the next step in his ambitious plans for Indonesian tourism.

"You all know Bali, our famous island paradise?" he said. "With improved infrastructure, we will launch a program called 'Ten New Balis'."[21]

This plan received a certain amount of dismissive commentary, with detractors arguing the impossibility of instantly replicating from scratch a destination created by a century-long process of combined organic and orchestrated tourism development. In fact, the places identified for the program were not entirely "new" as tourist destinations. Lake Toba in North Sumatra; Tanjung Lesung in Banten; Kepulauan Seribu (the "Thousand Islands" off the coast of Jakarta); Tanjung Kelayang in Bangka-Belitung; the Borobudur temple area in Central Java; Mount Bromo in East Java; the Mandalika area of southern Lombok; Labuan Bajo in East Nusa Tenggara; Wakatobi in South Sulawesi; and Morotai, North Maluku: these were all places already on the tourist radar.[22] Some, such as Borobudur, were already visited by hundreds of thousands of people each year. Some, such as southern Lombok, had a long-established tourist profile that had somehow never properly flourished. And others, such as Bangka-Belitung,

---

[21] Francis Chan, "Jokowi plans to replicate Bali's success in 10 other Indonesian spots," *The Straits Times*, October 10, 2017, https://www.straitstimes.com/asia/jokowi-plans-to-replicate-balis-success-in-10-other-indonesian-spots [accessed September 18, 2020].

[22] Kementerian Pariwisata, *Kebijakan Pengembangan Destinasi Pariwisata Indonesia 2016–2019* (Jakarta: Kementerian Pariwisata, 2016), 126–27.

were places that had emerged relatively recently as new destinations for the Indonesian middle classes. Jokowi was not aiming to conjure up Ten New Balis from nowhere. Instead, he planned to take places with proven tourism potential and to give them a massive developmental boost.

An investment fund of around Rp280 trillion was required for the development of the program. This was drawn from the wider reprioritizing of funding. Less urgent budgets were cut to provide more cash for infrastructure development. Again, this received considerable criticism, the financial return of infrastructure such as reservoirs and bridges not being immediately obvious or measurable. But when it comes to tourism, the direct returns tend to be easier to see, and more rapid. A new airport, for example, quickly brings more visitors to a particular region.

Overall, Jokowi's Ministry of Tourism set a financing and investment target of Rp500 trillion for nationwide tourism development by 2024, with the largest allocation going to the Ten New Balis program,[23] and the remainder for development in a further 88 Strategic National Tourism Areas. This funding requirement was to be met through government investment worth Rp170 trillion and private investments of Rp35 trillion, in addition to private financing from banks worth Rp230 trillion, Rp10 trillion from non-bank financier, and Rp45 trillion from the capital market.

The combined funding approach was intended to boost private sector confidence and to provide assurance that, unlike some major development projects under previous administrations, there would be no abandonment in years to come. Furthermore, from the outset Jokowi deployed his usual *blusukan* approach to the supervision of these developments, with site visits and surveillance of funding allocations in each destination. And more generally, budget allocations to the Ministry of Tourism were increased for solving problems related to the "New Balis" development program. In 2019, it was noted that a further Rp6.4 trillion had been disbursed.

Transformations on the Ground

One of the first places to receive attention under the Ten New Balis program was the beautiful but long-neglected Lake Toba. Silangit Airport, the closest to the lake, was dramatically upgraded. It had been inaugurated as a passenger airport by Susilo Bambang Yudhoyono in 2005 but had a short runway and very limited services, mainly from other airports within

---

[23] Gunarjo, *Nawacita Meretas Indonesia Maju*, 126–27.

the North Sumatra region. Of the few domestic and international tourists who did visit Toba, almost all arrived through the much larger international airport in Medan, before tackling the long and uncomfortable road trip to the lake. But under Jokowi's program the Silangit runway was extended and the terminal enlarged. In 2017, the national airline Garuda operated the inaugural international flight from Singapore.[24] Direct flights from Jakarta and other Indonesian hubs were also launched, and Air Asia began flying direct from Kuala Lumpur. Work also began to develop a toll road from Medan to Parapat, the main town on the lake.

Drawing on experiences running right back to his time as chair of Asmindo's Surakarta branch, Jokowi recognized that a lack of coordination had been a major factor undermining past tourism development initiatives in Indonesia. It was essential, therefore, to ensure oversight and communication amongst stakeholders in each of the destinations earmarked for development. Lake Toba spans seven different regencies, each with its own tourism officials, so an overarching Lake Toba Authority Implementing Body was formed, involving key representatives from each regency.

From one "New Bali" in the west to another in the east, Labuan Bajo is a clear example of how tourism has been neglected in the past. This port town at the western tip of Flores in East Nusa Tenggara is the gateway to the Komodo National Park, home to the famous giant lizards, designated a UNESCO World Heritage Site in 1991.[25] Despite the iconic status of the local wildlife, and despite the area's obvious beauty, with scattered islets, white-sand beaches, and well-preserved coral reefs, for decades Labuan Bajo attracted little more than a trickle of low-budget backpackers.

The problem was obvious: Labuan Bajo was simply too difficult to reach. In the past, many tourists arrived by boat straight from Bali. They would typically sleep aboard the boats and then return directly to Bali, often without ever disembarking in Labuan Bajo town and without putting any money, other than park entry fees, into the local economy. Labuan Bajo residents were, for the most part, mere spectators of tourism. There was a long-established airport but it had a short runway and could only

---

[24] Pramdia Arhando Julianto, "Garuda Indonesia Layani Penerbangan Internasional Singapura-Silangit," *Kompas*, September 25, 2017, https://ekonomi.kompas.com/read/2017/09/25/095700126/oktober-garuda-indonesia-layani-penerbangan-internasional-singapura-silangit [accessed September 17, 2020].

[25] "Manggarai Barat dan Kemenpar Dorong Taman Nasional Komodo dan Labuan Bajo Jadi Destinasi Wisata Alam Dunia Indonesia," *Travel News*, http://www.indonesiatravel.news/pariwisata/manggarai-barat-dan-kemenpar-dorong-tn-komodo-dan-labuan-bajo-jadi-destinasi-wisata-alam-dunia/ [accessed July 1, 2019].

accommodate small propeller planes. For domestic tourists from the big cities of western Indonesia, traveling to Labuan Bajo for a holiday would typically take longer and cost more than going overseas to a well-developed destination in another ASEAN country.

All that changed under Jokowi's tourism development program. He began by ordering the expansion of the Labuan Bajo airport. The terminal building was expanded and beautified and the runway was extended, allowing larger planes to land. This itself was another previously planned but long-stalled project which Jokowi had hustled to the finish line.[26] Direct flights were launched from Jakarta, Surabaya, Denpasar, Lombok, and Kupang. Local road infrastructure was also improved, and the port facilities were upgraded. Training was provided to local people in tourism. And perhaps most importantly, Labuan Bajo was promoted on a large scale to foreign countries. The wider plan for Labuan Bajo also stipulated the formation of the Labuan Bajo Tourism Authority Agency through Presidential Regulation No. 32 of 2018, dated April 5 2018. As a result, tourism has developed significantly, bringing economic benefits to the surrounding community. Indeed, so dramatic was the uptick that local authorities had to consider the possibility of a temporary closure of the national park to allow for rejuvenation.[27]

One of the most important points to note about Labuan Bajo's rapid emergence as a tourism hotspot is the shift in the tourist demographic. Previously, the area was visited almost exclusively by international travelers, mainly from Australia, Europe, and North America. But since the infrastructure improvements and the launch of direct flights from Jakarta and Surabaya, locals working in the industry have reported a dramatic increase in numbers of domestic tourists,[28] a change which, perhaps, bodes well for the sustainability of the industry there in light of the impacts of 2020's global pandemic on international travel.

While developments at Lake Toba and Labuan Bajo were likely to facilitate a broad tourist demographic, elsewhere there was a focus on specific emerging markets. One such place was the Mandalika region of southern Lombok. Despite its close proximity to Bali, despite its very obvious assets

[26] https://www.jejakpiknik.com/rentalmobil-labuan-bajo/ [accessed June 22, 2019].

[27] Karla Cripps, "Indonesia's famed Komodo Island may close for one year," CNN, April 1, 2019 [accessed September 21, 2020].

[28] "Sektor Pariwisata Jadi Unggulan Pemerintahan Presiden Jokowi," Suara, November 12, 2018, https://www.suara.com/news/2018/12/11/133536/sektor-pariwisata-jadi-unggulan-pemerintahan-presiden-jokowi [accessed July 6, 2019].

in the form of unspoilt beaches and spectacular coastal landscapes, and despite the fact that a certain amount of tourism infrastructure had been present for decades, this was a region that had never truly flourished. To rectify that, there has been a new focus on a specific emerging tourism market which Indonesia is very well placed to exploit, namely, "halal tourism."

In 2016, Indonesia took a swathe of prizes at the Abu Dhabi-based World Halal Tourism Awards, with individual destinations in West Sumatra, Aceh, and Lombok all gaining accolades. In general, halal tourism can be defined as tourism products aimed at facilitating the traveling needs of devout Muslims, typically in the form of travel packages that conform to the rules of life for observant Muslims. It is a rapidly expanding market, the global value of which was projected to reach US$220 billion in 2020 before the Covid-19 pandemic rocked the industry. Even countries with majority non-Muslim populations, such as Thailand and South Korea, have begun pursuing the potential of the halal market in recent years. Clearly Indonesia, as the world's largest Muslim-majority nation, is particularly well placed to take advantage of this. The sharp increases in tourist arrivals in Indonesia between 2015 and 2019 have been boosted by the country's profile as a halal destination.[29]

In the Mandalika region of Lombok, one of the Ten New Balis and a tourism-focused SEZ, Qatari investors agreed to disburse funds of up to US$500 million for the development of halal tourism. The idea has begun to emerge that Nusa Tenggara Barat, the province comprising Lombok and neighboring Sumbawa, in general, and the Mandalika SEZ, in particular, might become synonymous with halal tourism in years to come.

However, Jokowi recognized that segmentation of the tourist industry ought not be taken to an extreme point with Lombok effectively partitioned from the rest of the archipelago for tourism purposes. For example, the issue of separating male and female tourists on an open beach would not only put off non-Muslim visitors, it might also be out of line with local cultural norms. In recognition of this, limits have been placed on the extent of exclusive provisions for halal tourism. And the development of more general appeal in Mandalika has not been neglected, for example, in the establishment of the "Mandalika Circuit" for MotoGP motorcycle racing. In 2019, Dorna Sports, the commercial rights holder for MotoGP, signed a contract with the Indonesia Tourism Development Corporation

---

[29] Kementerian Pariwisata, *Kebijakan Pengembangan Destinasi Pariwisata Indonesia 2016–2019* (Jakarta: Kementerian Pariwisata, 2016), 5.

to create an international racing circuit in southern Lombok, intended to host its first race in 2021.[30]

Once again, plans for development in this isolated and economically stagnant region of Indonesia were not a new invention of the Jokowi administration; they had actually been in place since 1989. But the project had stalled, particularly because of difficulties around land acquisition. Jokowi moved to expedite matters and end the decades-long delay. During the inauguration of the area on October 21, 2017, he asked Mandalika managers to make clear rules and contracts with investors, and warned against attempts to stall the development with bad practice and under-the-table deals. A strict limit was also issued to avoid further time wasting: "If investors go six months without any activities on the land they own, their [development] permits must be revoked, because there are many [others] who are interested in investing in this Mandalika SEZ," Jokowi said at the time.

During Jokowi's first term, developments in the Mandalika SEZ progressed rapidly, with new hotels, the Batu Jai Praya water treatment plant, improvements to the long-delayed new Lombok International Airport, the 150 kV Kuta Main Substation, the upgrading of Lembar Port, and improved roads.[31] All were supervised through the classic Jokowi approach of *blusukan* site visits, underscoring the idea that the SEZ and New Balis programs were equitable and not governed by political favoritism or a practice of rewarding supportive voters: Lombok was a region that had overwhelmingly voted for Jokowi's opponent during the presidential election.

Opening up Hidden Tourism Destinations

Jokowi's tourism strategies have been by no means focused entirely on the Ten New Balis. The ethos of integration as an ideal in wider development policies always allows for the deliberate exploitation of tourism as a "by-product" of other developments, as in the case of the city parks built alongside upgraded reservoirs in Jakarta. The Dana Desa village funding scheme (see Chapter 8) can also be used for small-scale community tourism projects. And Jokowi's penchant for getting out of Jakarta and making his trademark *blusukan* visits to far-flung corners of the archipelago has

---

[30] "Lombok Jadi Tuan Rumah MotoGP 2021," *Koran NTB*, February 21, 2019, https://koranntb.com/2019/02/21/lombok-jadi-tuan-rumah-motogp-2021/ [accessed June 27, 2019].

[31] Endah, *Jokowi Memimpin Kota Menyentuh Jakarta*, 97.

at times proved to be a catalyst for tourism development. One example of this is Mandeh Beach in Pesisir Selatan Regency, West Sumatra.

West Sumatra is a beautiful region, with the rugged Bukit Barisan mountain range sweeping down to the wild Indian Ocean shoreline. It has long had a low-key tourist industry around the main city, Padang, and in the upland town of Bukittinggi. But distance from major cities and poor overland connections have long limited visitor numbers, both domestic and international.

Towards the end of his first year in office, Jokowi visited the South Pesisir Regency, which lies fifty-six kilometers to the south of Padang. During the trip he asked to see the Mandeh Beach area, known as a local beauty spot. He was struck by the spectacular view from the high ground above the coast, with its panorama of beaches and offshore islets.[32]

Speaking to reporters during the visit, he said, "I was surprised when I entered this area. I saw from above how great God's grace is to us. We should be grateful for that beauty."[33] He immediately ordered the acceleration of the development of the Mandeh Integrated Marine Tourism Area (Kawasan Wisata Bahari Terpadu Mandeh), with the aim of encouraging more visitors and boosting the local economy.[34] Mandeh was then used as a pilot project for the development of tourist areas in West Sumatra. It went on to win first place in the "Most Popular Hidden Paradise" category at the Anugerah Pesona Indonesia national tourism awards in 2017.

Of course, the 2015 trip to Mandeh was not Jokowi's first visit to West Sumatra. This was the province he had traveled to as a student in 1984 along with other members of the Mapala Silvagama club, to climb Gunung Kerinci. The lush green mountain landscapes made an impression on the young traveler, as did the distinctive local architecture in the South Solok Regency, seen en route to the mountain. "I remember very well when going to Kerinci via South Solok. I admired the traditional houses, which were very pretty and very beautiful," he recalled thirty-five years later.[35]

[32] "Presiden Jokowi Takjub Keindahan Kawasan Mandeh," *Tempo*, October 10, 2015, https://nasional.tempo.co/read/708358/presiden-jokowi-takjub-keindahan-kawasan-mandeh/full&view=ok [accessed July 8, 2019].

[33] Joko Susilo, "Presiden berharap pariwisata Mandeh angkat perekonomian lokal," *Antara*, October 11, 2015, https://www.antaranews.com/berita/522901/presiden-berharap-pariwisata-mandeh-angkat-perekonomian-lokal [accessed July 8, 2019].

[34] "Ini Yang Selalu Diingat Jokowi akan Solok Selatan," *Radio Teman Sejati*, October 2, 2018, https://radiotemansejati.com/2018/02/10/ini-yang-selalu-diingat-jokowi-akan-solok-selatan/ [accessed July 8, 2019].

[35] Andhika Prasetia, "Jokowi Serukan Indonesia Hijrah: Ada Proses, Tak Bisa 1-2 Tahun," *detikNews*, November 7, 2018, https://news.detik.com/berita/d-4292040/jokowi-serukan-indonesia-hijrah-ada-proses-tak-bisa-1-2-tahun [accessed July 9, 2019].

Jokowi ordered the minister of public works and public housing to provide assistance to revitalize South Solok's *rumah gadang*, the striking traditional houses of the Minangkabau people, with their sweeping roof-lines and sharp finials. These wooden buildings are often decades or even centuries old, and though some local families use them as guesthouses, the cost of their upkeep is high and many have fallen into disrepair through lack of funds. The program was warmly welcomed by residents, who take a great deal of cultural pride in the houses. Indeed, South Solok is often known as "the land of a thousand rumah gadang." The revitalization project was intended to let residents maximize the value of these buildings as a tourism asset.

These tourism developments, smaller in scale than the major infra-structure investments around the designated Ten New Balis, were concrete examples of what Jokowi has described as a new understanding of the word *hijrah* (taken from Islamic history, but also used in a secular sense in Indonesian to mean "migration"): a *hijrah* from poverty to prosperity, from inequality to economic justice. Speaking to a group of young entrepreneurs in Jakarta in November 2018, Jokowi stressed that this process was not one that could be completed overnight, but it was nonetheless something that could be expedited by relatively simple material interventions, such as those designed to boost tourism in West Sumatra.[36]

Tourism, beginning at the level of the local day-trip sector, has the potential to revitalize local economies across Indonesia. In an emerging tourist destination, people who might previously have had no option other than the usual sort of migration, from rural areas to cities, to escape a working life limited to farming or fishing (as had been the case in Jokowi's own ancestral villages of Kragan and Giriroto) can explore different possibilities without ever leaving their home community. Those who are good at cooking provide food to visitors and may, in time, become successful restaurateurs. Those who are good at foreign languages become tour guides. Those who are inclined to drive become tourist drivers. The residents of previously marginalized areas can work according to their talents and interests.

---

[36] Erinaldi, "Kawasan Wisata Mandeh, Surga Tersembunyi Terpopuler," *Liputan6*, November 28, 2017, https://www.liputan6.com/regional/read/3177288/kawasan-wisata-mandeh-surga-tersembunyi-terpopuler [accessed July 6, 2019].

Aiming to Overtake Thailand and Malaysia

The "people don't eat infrastructure" line of criticism has been a standard one throughout Jokowi's time in office. It was something he addressed directly during a 2019 television interview.

"Yes, it is true. The infrastructure we build is not to be eaten. How can you tell people to eat cement, eat asphalt? [But] it's not like that. Infrastructure is not for eating, but this infrastructure can bring food closer to the community. This infrastructure can create jobs. Infrastructure can accelerate the mobility of goods, the mobility of people, so everything becomes easier and cheaper," Jokowi said.[37]

Tourism, with its potential for an unusually rapid return on infrastructure investment, has been an area where this approach has been clearly vindicated. Indeed, prior to the shock delivered to the global tourism sector by the Covid-19 pandemic of 2020, Jokowi's tourism development policies could be seen as one of the major successes of his first term, with tangible transformations delivered in individual destinations around the country. In the years before Jokowi's presidency began, the Central Statistics Agency (BPS) had recorded relatively modest year-on-year increases in tourist arrivals: 8.8 million arrivals in 2013, rising to 9.4 million in 2014. But from 2015 the pace began to pick up dramatically: 10.41 million foreign tourists visited that year. The sector's growth as a component of GDP was also well above the average for other industries, and the growth of foreign exchange earnings provided by tourism, namely 13 percent, was the highest of any sector.

The following year numbers were up again to 11.5 million, with the rate of increase still accelerating. According to the Ministry of Tourism's records, tourism growth from January to December 2017 reached 22 percent, far above the global average of 6.4 percent. In 2018, a total of 15.8 million foreign tourists visited Indonesia, well over double the number of a decade earlier. This very significant increase was able to generate foreign exchange earnings amounting to US$17 billion that year. Indonesia's tourism growth in 2018 ranked top in ASEAN, third highest in Asia, and ninth in the world.

By this stage, tourism's contribution of foreign exchange revenue had surpassed the contribution of oil, gas, and coal, and was second only to

---

[37] Mukti Ali Qusyairi, *Jalinan Keislaman, Keumatan, & Kebangsaan: Ulama Bertutur tentang Jokowi* (Jakarta: Republika, 2018), 166.

palm oil (which earned US$22.9 billion in 2017). Tourism looked set to become Indonesia's largest foreign exchange earner within a few years, and Jokowi's stated aspiration to see the country overtake Thailand and Malaysia as an international destination did not seem unrealistic.[38] In those countries, the industry was already mature and arguably at saturation point in many places. In Indonesia, meanwhile, the barely realized potential seemed unlimited.

"The comparison is Thailand. Visits of foreign tourists there are up to 35 million. Malaysia, meanwhile, gets 27 million. We have many legendary places, better places. So why can't we [be like that too]? We must be optimistic that we can [achieve the same]," Jokowi said during a broadcast interview in August 2019.[39] Here, on display, was the optimism which had been a key part of his character since his early attempts in business,[40] an optimism which, throughout his first term, he clearly brought to bear on his development policy initiatives.

For Jokowi, a particular vindication of the focus on tourism was in the fact that by this stage the industry was providing direct employment for well over 10 million Indonesians. As the second decade of the twenty-first century moved to its close, there was great optimism about the future of this sector though, of course, no one could have predicted the shock coming to the tourism industry in 2020.

---

[38] "Presiden Yakin Pariwisata Motor Penggerak Ekonomi," *Inilah*, https://m.inilah.com/news/detail/2473618/presiden-yakin-pariwisata-motor-penggerak-ekonomi [accessed July 6, 2019].

[39] Qusyairi, *Jalinan Keislaman, Keumatan, & Kebangsaan*, 132.

[40] Dwitri Waluyo and Endra S. Atmawidjaja, *Infrastruktur Meningkatkan Daya Saing* (Jakarta: Kementerian PUPR RI, 2017), xii.

A huge new intersection on the eastern outskirts of Jakarta.

Chapter Six
Energizing the Archipelago: Infrastructure and Energy Policies

Taking Charge: The Second Year of the Jokowi Presidency

Coming to power in late 2014, Jokowi's position had been far from ideal. He had faced an opposition-controlled and potentially obstructionist DPR, and a perception amongst some observers that he was still beholden to the powerful leadership of his own party. But by the time twelve months had passed, things had changed dramatically. And they continued to shift as the second year of his presidency got underway.

As the Prabowo-backing KMP, the "Red and White Coalition," fragmented, Jokowi found the parliamentary arithmetic moving in his favor. Soon he could count 386 backers in the DPR, a majority. Of course, a majority could have brought its own problems, as it had done for Jokowi's predecessor. The transactional norm of Indonesian politics has traditionally involved buying parliamentary support with promises of cabinet positions, which can leave a president surrounded by ministers with competing agendas. But Jokowi played a different game to Yudhoyono. Instead of attempting to coax opposition parties to cross the house with promises, he was able to benefit from their own internal divisions. Under Indonesian law, changes in the leadership of any party have to be registered and recognized by the Ministry of Law and Human Rights, so tacit government approval can tip the balance in favor of one or other faction during a party civil war. The factions inclined to shift to the Jokowi-backing coalition eventually came out tops in both Golkar and PPP.

But shifts of allegiance did not result in instant rewards, as they typically might have done under previous presidents. PAN, which had gone over to

Jokowi's coalition in September 2015, had to wait almost a year before it got a cabinet position. And when cabinet posts did go to members of the newly supportive parties, they were typically not the most significant ones.[1] It was a canny approach, borne of both principle and firmness, which belied the idea that the genial, easy-going Jokowi was a naïve leader and a pushover for more ruthless figures. But where had this steeliness come from? The answer, of course, was that by the time he reached the presidential palace, Jokowi was hardly an amateur. He was a decade into his political career, and had served in two powerful positions at the top of their respective tiers of regional government. He had also been paired at the start of his career with a hard-nosed political operator in the form of F. X. Hadi Rudyatmo, a man adept at wrangling with legislative bodies. Jokowi had taken note, and as president he turned out to be tougher than some people had expected.

The most significant shift in the party political weather came with Golkar's move into the government coalition. In July 2016, the party went as far as to endorse Jokowi for the next presidential race, still three years off. This endorsement, from the party with probably the most sophisticated nationwide infrastructure,[2] meant that Jokowi was no longer as dependent on his own party, PDI-P. During his first year in office, there had been a perception, at least partly justified, that Jokowi had at times had to act on the basis of the wishes of his party leadership. Although he was Indonesia's head of state, within PDI-P Jokowi was a mere cadre and Megawati was his boss. This situation had not helped his first-year approval ratings. But by the middle of 2016, he was looking a lot more like his own man.

In July, Jokowi overhauled his cabinet, bringing in some significant figures, not least Sri Mulyani Indrawati as finance minister. She had already done the same job for Susilo Bambang Yudhoyono during his first term, and had then left Jakarta for New York, where she became managing director of the World Bank. A hugely respected figure internationally, *Forbes Magazine* had once acknowledged her as amongst the world's most powerful women.[3]

The newly emboldened president made it clear to his refreshed cabinet who was in charge: "The first thing I want to say, especially to new ministers, there's no such thing as a vision or mission of a minister,

---

[1] Ahmad Ibrahim Almuttaqi, *Jokowi's Indonesia and the World* (Singapore: World Scientific Publishing, 2020), 29.

[2] Ibid., 30.

[3] Ina Parlina and Haeril Halim, "Jokowi's new Cabinet: Who's the boss now?" *The Jakarta Post*, July 28, 2016, https://www.thejakartapost.com/longform/2016/07/28/whos-the-boss-now.html [accessed October 20, 2020].

we only have the vision and mission of the president and vice president. All ministers must follow the vision and mission that we outline and all policies decided during either plenary or limited cabinet meetings," he said as he opened the first meeting with the new cabinet.[4]

One of the motivations behind the reshuffle, and in particular the appointment of the new superstar finance minister, was that the Indonesian economy was still proving stubbornly sluggish. This was largely due to external factors, well beyond the president's control. The fragile global economy meant that demand for Indonesia's natural resources, a key pillar of its economy for decades, had been weak for several years. The slowdown in China had had a noticeable impact.[5] But there were things that could be done domestically to boost growth. In particular, the roll-out of the massive infrastructure projects that Jokowi had promised needed to be speeded up.

The month after the cabinet reshuffle, during his speech to mark Indonesia's Independence Day commemorations on August 17, Jokowi declared 2016 "the year of development acceleration." It was a rather more prosaic title than those that Sukarno had chosen during his own Independence Day speeches during Jokowi's earliest childhood: "The Year of Victory," "The Year of Living Dangerously," and so on. But its aspirations were far more concrete, and indeed achievable. The government, Jokowi said, would be focusing on "breakthrough measures to eradicate poverty, unemployment and social inequality." And the first of these measures would be expediting infrastructure development.

"We will develop areas such as Entikong, Natuna and Atambua," he said, citing remote locations on Indonesia's frontiers, "so that the world sees Indonesia as a great nation that pays attention on every inch of its land."[6]

By the end of his second full year in office, Jokowi's approval ratings were solid once more, at around 65 percent,[7] and progress on infrastructure was key to the public enthusiasm. In the third year of his presidency, he would face some serious challenges, including threats to Indonesia's culture of pluralism and the commitment to "unity in diversity" underscored in the Nawacita vision. But support for his development policies

---

[4]Ibid.

[5]Jonathan Emont, "Visionary or Cautious Reformer? Indonesian President Joko Widodo's Two Years in Office," *Time*, October 10, 2016, https://time.com/4416354/indonesia-joko-jokowi-widodo-terrorism-lgbt-economy/ [accessed October 20, 2020].

[6]Chris Blake and Karlis Salna, "Jokowi Vows to Develop 'Every Inch' of Indonesia's Islands," *BloombergQuint*, August 16, 2016, https://www.bloombergquint.com/onweb/jokowi-vows-to-develop-every-inch-of-indonesian-archipelago [accessed October 20, 2020].

[7]Almuttaqi, *Jokowi's Indonesia and the World*, 31.

would not waver, with his highest approval ratings specifically linked to infrastructure development.[8] This was hardly surprising, for by the middle of his first term some dramatic transformations were underway.

Left Behind: Memories of Childhood Villages

As a child, Jokowi often made visits to his mother's home hamlet, Gumuk Rejo in Giriroto village, in the Ngemplak District of Boyolali Regency, Central Java. For a child from the crowded urban environment of the Kali Anyar riverbank, the village seemed a place of peace and fertility. He would explore the ricefield embankments and wander through expanses of sugarcane or along the edge of a seldom-used railroad. Little Jokowi saw an expanse of greenness stretching in all directions. But in truth, Gumuk Rejo was not a particularly fertile area.

The name of the hamlet means "prosperous hill," but its residents lived in straightened circumstances. There were only dirt roads. In the dry season, the air was dusty and scented with cow dung. When it rained, the roads became muddy, with puddles and potholes here and there. Most of the population worked as farmers or laborers on the rain-fed fields, while a smaller proportion worked in the wood handicraft sector.[9] In the prolonged dry season, the ricefields were parched due to the scorching sun. There was little technical irrigation and few reservoirs and dams, and throughout the middle part of the year the farmers could not cultivate the fields because of the lack of water.[10] Amongst the villagers there was an inevitable sense of alienation from urban society. They felt left behind, not only physically but psychologically. They had little access to good roads, bridges, piped water, or electricity.[11]

For Jokowi today, the recollection of the villages of his childhood informs an approach to infrastructure development with an emphasis on connectivity, beginning at the village level. Transport facilities, reservoirs, bridges, national border posts, and toll roads are intended to build connectivity, create access between villages and cities, and between regions,

---

[8] "Jokowi approval rating survives protests and inequality," *Nikkei Asia*, August 1, 2017, https://asia.nikkei.com/Features/FT-Confidential-Research/Jokowi-approval-rating-survives-protests-and-inequality?page=2 [accessed October 20, 2020].

[9] Wawan Mas'udi and Akhmad Ramdhon, *Jokowi: dari Bantaran Kalianyar ke Istana* (Jakarta: Gramedia Pustaka Utama, 2018), 6.

[10] Alberthiene Endah, *Jokowi Perjalanan Karya bagi Bangsa Menuju Cahaya* (Solo: Tiga Serangkai, 2018), 41–43.

[11] Mas'udi and Ramdhon, *Jokowi: dari Bantaran Kalianyar ke Istana*, 89.

opening up new potential for economic activity and improving people's welfare.[12]

The developmental emphasis of Nawacita was formulated in the National Medium-Term Development Plan, which outlined goals for his first term. Jokowi intended to build 2,650 kilometers of new roads across Indonesia and to repair an existing 46,770 kilometers. He also intended to build new airports and seaports and to extend the existing rail network.[13] In "the year of development acceleration," road building, in particular, moved forward apace.

Rolling out the Toll Roads

Each year, as the week-long Lebaran holiday that marks the end of Ramadan approaches, millions of Indonesians take to the roads, heading for hometowns and ancestral villages to spend the festive period with their families. And each year for decades, the Indonesian press has documented the almost unimaginable traffic congestion caused by the exodus around Jakarta. For particularly dramatic footage, photographers and cameramen have long headed for the Jomin Intersection, towards the eastern edge of Greater Jakarta, where various routes out of the city join the main coast road towards Semarang and Surabaya, known as the Pantura Line ("Pantura" being short for *pantai utara*, "northern beach"). Until recently, at the peak of the Lebaran exodus, even a motorcycle could take three hours to negotiate the junction; for a car it could be more like ten hours.[14] The problem was that the Jomin Intersection was the point of connection for the Jakarta-Cikampek Toll Road, a modern multilane carriageway, with the Pantura Line, a colonial-era highway built more than 200 years ago by the Dutch governor general, Herman Willem Daendels.

Daendels' road was originally known as De Grote Postweg, "the Great Post Road." It was built, beginning in 1808, at an enormous cost in cash and lives of local laborers. But stretching a thousand kilometers along the northern littoral of Java, it arguably remained the greatest single infrastructure

---

[12] Dedi Mahardi, *Indonesia Butuh Jokowi* (Jakarta: Buana Ilmu Populer, 2018), 117.

[13] Eijas Ariffin, "Financing Jokowi's infrastructure ambitions," *The ASEAN Post*, October 9, 2018, https://theaseanpost.com/article/financing-jokowis-infrastructure-ambitions [accessed October 21, 2020].

[14] "Simpang Jomin Menuju Jalur Pantura Macet Parah," *Okezone*, December 25, 2014, https://news.okezone.com/read/2014/12/25/340/1083935/simpang-jomin-menuju-jalur-pantura-macet-parah [accessed October 20, 2020].

project the island had seen until the twenty-first century. It greatly changed the dynamic of the place: the overland journey from Batavia (the colonial name for Jakarta) to Surabaya was reduced from around a month to just nine days. It allowed the Dutch to knit a politically fragmented landmass into a single colonial possession, and also allowed the beginnings of an integrated, island-wide cash economy. And Daendels' Post Road, renamed as the Pantura Line, remained Java's main trunk road long after Indonesia gained its independence. However, as the annual traffic chaos at the Jomin Intersection clearly demonstrated, it was no longer up to the job. Coming into office, Jokowi was determined to complete work on an upgraded cross-island route, the Trans-Java Toll Road. Yet again, this was not a new vision. It had been planned since 1995, but had never been completed.

Indonesia was, in fact, one of Southeast Asia's pioneers when it came to the development of modern toll roads. The country's first was the 59-kilometer Jagorawi Toll Road, which connects Jakarta, Bogor, and Ciawi. It was constructed by PT Jasa Marga and opened in 1978.[15] At the time, the project came in for considerable criticism. Private vehicle ownership was uncommon at the time, even in Jakarta, and there appeared to be little need for such a large and expensive road development. But the Jagorawi Toll went on to become a catalyst for local economic development, with factories, residential areas, schools, universities, and more springing up along its route.[16] However, Indonesia was slow to replicate this pioneering project, while other countries in the region forged ahead with road building. Since the 1970s, Malaysia has built 3,000 kilometers of toll roads; China has created 280,000 kilometers.[17] Indonesia had been left behind, but Jokowi aimed to change this.

The initial target was the completion of 1,150 kilometers of toll road to connect Merak on the western tip of Java with Banyuwangi in the east. Sections of toll road already existed around the major cities. But the bulk of the traffic along the route still used the 200-year-old Pantura Line, which in many places passes right through the middle of towns and markets, creating serious traffic bottlenecks.

Work progressed rapidly during Jokowi's first term. Between 2015 and

---

[15] "Jakarta-Bogor-Ciawi (Jagorawi)," Jasamarga-Indonesia Highway Corp, www.jasamarga.com/public/id/infolayanan/toll/ruas.aspx?title=Jakarta%20-%20Bogor%20-%20Ciawi%20(%20Jagorawi%20) [accessed April 30, 2019].

[16] Hologram Jokowi speech at Gedung Tri Brata, Jakarta, March 28, 2019.

[17] "Laporan 4 Tahun Kinerja Jokowi," maritim.go.id, https://maritim.go.id/konten/laporan-4-tahun-kinerja-jokowi-jk/ [accessed February 12, 2019].

2018, 616 kilometers of toll road were built on the Trans-Java route, double the entire toll road building across Indonesia in the previous thirty-five years. By 2019, an unbroken toll road extended as far as Probolinggo, east of Surabaya, with the final stretch slated for completion in 2021.

The spectacular shift in the pace of road construction was achieved through the expediting of land acquisition, always a major cause of delays in Indonesian building projects, and a reapportioning of toll concessions away from private companies that had failed to achieve progress to state-owned enterprises.

"I hope the completion of this toll road will have an effect on the economy, especially for industrial areas and special economic zones," said Jokowi when inaugurating central sections of the route in 2018.[18]

The completed Trans-Java Toll Road, like its colonial-era predecessor, will allow for a dramatic improvement in economic integration across the island, linking to improved national, provincial, and district roads, and greatly reducing journey times. The road journey from Jakarta to Semarang previously took at least ten hours, but is now routinely completed in six hours; the trip between Jakarta and Surabaya, Indonesia's two biggest cities, used to take a full twenty-four hours at times, but is now routinely completed in around twelve hours. This allows for greater economic integration between these major urban centers, but also for smaller communities all along the route, with readier access to urban markets for farmers and manufacturers in rural areas, and better connections between once-isolated villages and the cities.[19]

A large part of this economic boost is an automatic, organic result of the road construction, like the developments that emerged along the route of the original Jagorawi Toll through the 1980s. But opportunities for micro, small, and medium enterprises have also been deliberately built into the road expansion program, with rest areas developed every 10–20 kilometers along every stretch of toll road to allow local businesses access to the market provided by the thousands of passing motorists.[20] These rest areas are intended as a storefront for regional economic potential, where locally

---

[18] "Tol Trans Jawa dan Denyut Nadi Pantura," VOA, https://www.voaindonesia.com/a/tol-trans-jawa-dan-denyut-nadi-pantura/4712032.html [accessed April 27, 2019].

[19] "Jalan Tol Meningkatkan Produktivitas," bpjt.pu.go.id, http://bpjt.pu.go.id/berita/presiden-resmikan-pengoperasian-tol-pejagan-pemalang-dan-integrasi-sistem-transaksitol [accessed February 15, 2019].

[20] Interview with Central Java governor, Ganjar Pranowo, at the inauguration of the Trans-Java Toll Road in Pejagan, Pemalang, November 9, 2018.

produced crafts, food and drinks, furniture and clothing can be marketed.

New economic centers around toll roads continue to appear.[21] The Trans-Java Toll Road has also boosted domestic tourism within Java, with attractions across the island, from the pilgrimage destinations around Demak and Kudus to the mountains east of Surabaya now in much easier reach of visitors from Jakarta.

Jokowi's road building has not, of course, been restricted to Java. Similar toll road developments were launched during his first term in Sumatra, Sulawesi, Kalimantan, and Papua. Sumatra, in particular, has long been hampered by poor connectivity, something which Jokowi understood well from his time working in Aceh in the 1980s.[22] The developing Trans-Sumatra Toll Road, which will ultimately be far longer than its equivalent on neighboring Java, is intended to become the main artery connecting the whole island.

Weaving the Nation from the Air

Clearly, in a vast archipelagic nation like Indonesia roads are not the only required form of transport infrastructure for developing connectivity. A number of airports were redeveloped or upgraded under Jokowi's tourism development framework. But during his first term there was also a wider program of improvements to Indonesia's air transport infrastructure.[23]

Since the deregulation of the domestic airline sector in 2000, Indonesia's airline industry has developed rapidly. What was originally a limited and expensive travel option, dominated by state operators with only a few private and military-owned rivals, rapidly became wildly competitive with numerous privately owned airlines and aggressive ticket discounting. For even those on modest incomes, air travel quickly began to replace ferries for interisland journeys. Even between major cities within Java, flights were sometimes comparable in cost to travel by bus or train on the same route. After a series of fatal accidents and bankruptcies in the late 2000s, regulations were tightened and ticket prices rose somewhat.[24] But air

---

[21] Rinto Heksantoro, "Menpar Nilai Tol Trans Jawa Bantu Konektivitas Wisata di Jateng," *detikTravel*, February 19, 2019, https://travel.detik.com/travel-news/d-4429051/menpar-nilai-tol-trans-jawa-bantu-konektivitas-wisata-di-jateng [accessed October 20, 2020].

[22] Endah, *Jokowi Perjalanan Karya bagi Bangsa Menuju Cahaya*, 40–42.

[23] Nawacita Institute, *Wujud Kerja Nyata* (Jakarta: Republika, 2017), 240.

[24] "Deregulasi Penerbangan Indonesia Dan Akibatnya," *Runway Aviation News*, January 31, 2015, https://web.archive.org/web/20151222111416/http://www.runway-aviation.com/deregulasi-penerbangan-indonesia-dan-akibatnya/ [accessed September 22, 2020].

travel was by then firmly established as the principal means of stitching the vast Indonesian nation together. However, air connectivity beyond the main cities remained limited by a lack of investment in regional airports, many of which had rudimentary terminal facilities and runways too short to accommodate the medium-sized jets which are the workhorses of Indonesia's major domestic airlines.

For Jokowi, transport infrastructure development was in line with the priorities he outlined at the start of his presidency, drawing on Sukarno's Trisakti conception of the ethos of Indonesian nationalism, and elaborated in the Nawacita framework. It was particularly relevant to the goal of economic independence. Better transport infrastructure leads to cheaper transportation, more efficient exchange of goods and services between different regions, and domestic products that are better able to compete with their imported equivalents.[25] This aligned with the sixth point of Nawacita: "to increase people's productivity and competitiveness in the international market so that the Indonesian people can advance and rise together with other Asian nations."

Speaking in 2018, Jokowi said: "In the past four years, we have pursued efforts to encourage the emergence of new economic pockets. Therefore, the development of connectivity infrastructure, be it airports, ports, or railways, is important. This is not just for show."[26] Connectivity, he argued, was key to well-balanced development, dispersed from the old economic centers of Java.

During his first term, a total of ten new airports were established, namely, Letung (Riau Islands), Namniwel (Maluku), Miangas (North Sulawesi), Morowali (Central Sulawesi), Werur (West Papua), Maratua (East Kalimantan), Koroway Batu (Papua), Kertajati International Airport (West Java), Aji Pangeran Tumenggung Pranoto Airport (East Kalimantan), and Tebelian (West Kalimantan). Elsewhere, existing airports were upgraded and delayed projects expedited. In Yogyakarta, where Jokowi had been based during his student days at Gadjah Mada University, a stalled replacement for the old and overcrowded Adisutjipto Airport was finally completed, ahead of the revised schedule. Other existing airports were

---

[25] "Infrastruktur Menjalin Konektivitas Memangkas Kesenjangan," PresidenRI.go.id, www.presidenri.go.id/berita-aktual/infrastruktur-menjalin-konektivitas-memangkas-kesenjangan.html [accessed April 29, 2019].

[26] Ihsanuddin, "Presiden Jokowi: Infrastruktur Bukan untuk Gagah-gagahan," *Kompas*, October 25, 2018, https://nasional.kompas.com/read/2018/10/25/14285161/presiden-jokowi-infrastruktur-bukan-untuk-gagah-gagahan [accessed October 21, 2020].

upgraded to international status, as was the case with the Radin Inten II Airport serving the Lampung region of southern Sumatra, allowing for new potential in tourism and investment in an area that had previously served mainly as an agricultural hinterland for the populous provinces of Java to the east.

"There are so many tourist attractions in Lampung. Then there are a lot of business and investments in Lampung. This will support the speed of growth of this Radin Inten II Airport," Jokowi said during the inauguration of the new terminal.[27] Djalaluddin Airport at Gorontalo, an isolated city in Sulawesi, also received a major upgrade to its terminal under Jokowi's direction in 2016.[28] Where previously it had space for only 250 passengers, it could now accommodate 2,500 people, a tenfold increase.

The Nusantara Pendulum: Seaports and East–West Connectivity

In his inaugural speech in 2014, Jokowi had spoken of his desire to strengthen Indonesia's identity as a maritime nation. Despite the obvious fact that the world's largest archipelagic state has a huge amount of seawater within its frontiers, observers have long noted an Indonesian tendency to turn its back to the ocean. This tendency has arguably exacerbated the historical concentration of economic development in Java. Jokowi's goal was to move beyond the idea of the sea as a barrier and to return to the attitudes of the more distant past when it was, in fact, the main means of communication. Prior to the construction of the Great Post Road, the colonial foundation of the Pantura Line, by far the quickest way to travel between Batavia (Jakarta) and Surabaya was by sea even though both cities were in Java. Jokowi's maritime vision was to use the sea to unite Indonesia through the concept of a grand connecting "Sea Highway."[29] He also sought ways to exploit Indonesia's highly strategic location at the junction between the Indian and Pacific Oceans and the South China Sea, the very location that had allowed both its great precolonial trading states and the European colonizers who usurped them to flourish.

From his past as a furniture exporter, Jokowi was well aware of Indonesia's deficiencies in the entrepot trade. A major project to develop

---

[27] Accessed at http://presidenri.go.id/berita-aktual/resmikanterminal-barubandara-radin-inten-ii-di-lampung.html.

[28] Endah, *Jokowi Perjalanan Karya bagi Bangsa Menuju Cahaya*, 38.

[29] "Pelabuhan Bitung," Aroengbinang, https://www.aroengbinang.com/2017/11/pelabuhan-bitung.html [accessed February 15, 2019].

the Bitung International Port in North Sulawesi, the northernmost tip of Indonesia, was intended to address that problem. This development took place within the framework of the Special Economic Zone network, as both an international maritime trade gateway and a hub for connectivity throughout the northern and eastern regions of Indonesia.[30] This was linked to another key Jokowi development concept: the "Nusantara Pendulum" (Nusantara is a term dating from the historical Majapahit period, generally translated today as "the Archipelago" and sometimes used as a synonym for Indonesia itself). This rested on the idea of a sea highway running from Sabang and Belawan in the far west to Sorong in the far east, with Bitung as a strategic staging post on the route. The establishment of such an east–west maritime highway would, it was hoped, go a long way towards addressing key imbalances between the regions of Indonesia. Poor connectivity has long meant that consumer prices in remote eastern regions are far higher than in the more developed west of the country, despite the fact that communities in the east are typically markedly poorer than those in the west. The disparity in the prices of basic commodities and building materials is a persistent source of complaint amongst voters in areas such as Maluku and Papua, places which also tend to complain of general government neglect in terms of services and infrastructure.[31]

The establishment of a 5,000-kilometer sea highway, complete with effective modern ports and a continuous traffic of shipping, would, in theory, overcome much of the disparity by greatly simplifying the logistics of inter-regional goods transport. And, as with new toll roads and upgraded airports, the improved connectivity should, in theory, boost the wider economy in all places linked to the sea highway. For Jokowi this was a prime example of Indonesia-centric development: massive and evenly distributed infrastructure investment throughout the country, aimed at economic growth and regional development, and serving as a foundation for social justice.

Lighting up: Energy Issues

During Jokowi's childhood, electricity was something of a luxury. Although his own family had access in their own home on the banks of the

---

[30] Eko Sulistyo, *Konservatisme Politik Anti Jokowi* (Jakarta: Moka Media, 2019), 251.

[31] "Manfaat Laut Sangat Besar," Coordinating Ministry for Maritime & Investment Affairs, May 31, 2016, https://maritim.go.id/manfaat-tol-laut-sangat-besar/ [accessed October 21, 2020].

Kali Anyar, many of their neighbors did not. In the villages of Jokowi's grandparents, meanwhile, dark nights, broken only by a few flickering oil lamps, were the norm.[32] Very few villages at that time, even in relatively well-developed Java, had mains electricity. It was only in the 1980s that the Suharto government extended a village electricity program (known in Indonesian as Listrik Masuk Desa, "Electricity Comes to the Village," or LMD), financed through a mix of direct state expenditure, loans from foreign donor agencies, and international development grants.[33] Even this program was still mainly restricted to Java.

As recently as 2012, Indonesia's rate of electrification only reached 76.56 percent of the population. While in urban areas 92 percent of people had direct access to electricity, in the countryside only 59 percent had electricity at home, a worse ratio even than in countries like Laos.[34] By the time Jokowi came to power, the nationwide electrification rate had reached 84.35 percent. But that still meant that over 15 percent of all Indonesians had no direct access to mains electricity. Inevitably, this brought to mind the village communities of Jokowi's childhood and informed a determination to complete the program of electrification,[35] bringing Indonesia in line with other more developed ASEAN nations, such as Singapore, Brunei, and Malaysia (100 percent electrification) and Thailand (99 percent). Jokowi understood, from first-hand experience, the significance of a home electricity supply: the difficulties of schoolchildren and students attempting to study at night without proper lighting; the challenges for tailors and other craftspeople attempting to complete orders by oil lamp; and the impossibility for fishermen in remote areas of preserving a catch for distant markets. As a former businessman, he also understood the challenges for entrepreneurs presented by an unreliable mains supply, recalling the frequent instances when the power would drop out and the machinery in his furniture workshop would fall silent. He set a target of 99 percent electrification for the end of his first term.[36]

---

[32] Alberthiene Endah, *Jokowi Memimpin Kota Menyentuh Jakarta* (Solo: Metagraf, 2012), 21.

[33] Aryono, "Politik Listrik Orde Baru," *Historia*, https://historia.id/politik/articles/politik-listrik-orde-baru-v27zd [accessed August 29, 2019].

[34] Maxensius Tri Sambodo, *Akses Listrik & Kesejahteraan Masyarakat* (Jakarta: LIPI Press, 2016), 2.

[35] Ibid.

[36] "Menuju Rasio Elektrifikasi 99 Persen pada 2019," Ministry of Energy and Mineral Resources, http://ebtke.esdm.go.id/post/2018/04/27/1945/menuju.rasio.elektrifikasi.99.persen.pada.2019 [accessed July 4, 2019].

Indonesia's difficulties with electricity were down to a combination of infrastructure and supply. The vast scale and uniquely challenging geography of the country presented infinitely greater challenges in delivering mains supplies to all communities than was the case in most neighboring countries. This was exacerbated by the fact that the base supply had failed to keep pace with population growth and industrialization.

By 2014, Indonesia's electricity production had only reached 55,000MW, and eleven out of the country's twenty-three regional electricity networks experienced a chronic supply deficit, resulting in frequent "load shedding," or rolling blackouts. The cost of production, meanwhile, was rising, with many power plants still using imported fuel oil.

Making Electricity Affordable

The first element of Jokowi's policy on electricity was firmly in line with his wider "pro-rakyat" credentials: a free electricity installation program for underprivileged families.[37] This program began in West Java where 235,756 people were living without their own mains supply from the state energy provider, PLN (Perusahaan Listrik Negara). Many of these people obtained a limited supply by renting a connection via an extension cable from neighbors, a common practice in poorer communities across the country and one that had been very familiar to Jokowi during his Kali Anyar childhood. The new program, which was funded through a consortium of thirty-five state-owned enterprises and one subsidiary,[38] got underway in 2018.

"In West Java Province, there are approximately 200,000 houses without electricity. Some have no electricity; some do have it already but are connected to neighbors or parents. So, now we will connect them independently," Jokowi said during the launch of the program in Bogor in December 2018.

During the first wave, the program provided free installation of a 450VA mains connection to 130,248 families, with a target of completion across the province by December 2019. The cost to a private household of installing a mains connection outside of the program was typically around Rp1

---

[37] "Renstra," Direktorat Jenderal Ketenagalistrikan, djk.esdm.go.id/pdf [accessed April 30, 2019].

[38] "PLN: Ada 235.756 rumah tangga Jabar yang tak punya biaya menyambung listrik," *Kontan*, January 25, 2019, https://industri.kontan.co.id/news/pln-ada-235756-rumah-tangga-jabar-yang-tak-punya-biaya-menyambung-listrik [accessed April 30, 2019].

million, well beyond the means of many of the poorest families. But after the free connection is provided under the program, poor families are faced with a monthly bill of around Rp25,000–Rp30,000, typically less than the charge for an informal hook-up from a neighbor.

One beneficiary of the program was 52-year-old Eni Nurbaini from Bekasi. Eni makes a living from a small shop run from the front of her house.

"Previously, trading was only possible until late afternoon, just after sunset when it got dark. Now, thank God, I can continue until 9 pm. So [the electricity supply] has increased my income," she says.[39]

In other parts of Indonesia, networks were expanded to take in isolated areas previously cut off from the mains supply altogether. One such place was Nangka Island in Bangka-Belitung Province, an island group off the southeast coast of Sumatra. Nangka is home to around seventy families and previously had no government electricity supply. However, under the network expansion program, a 2x100KW Diesel Power Plant was installed by PLN on the island.

"Finally, Nangka Island gets light!" said Alie, head of the Nangka hamlet. According to Alie, the cost of kerosene for lighting was previously a major burden for community members. "The people here are mostly fishermen. After sunset, at 7 o'clock at night, the children would be asleep. They couldn't go over their lessons from school because of the limited lighting."[40]

In extremely remote areas, classified as having "3T" characteristics (*terdepan*, *terluar*, and *tertinggal*, that is, at the frontier, outermost, and underdeveloped), where installation of generating plants or connection to larger networks has not proved immediately possible, Jokowi's government has distributed energy-efficient solar lighting equipment. Although this has come in for some criticism, with some industry commentators arguing that it should not be used as a long-term solution,[41] and that it should not be included in the figures for the government's electrification targets,[42] it clearly makes a significant material difference to the lives of people in such long-neglected places.

---

[39] "Tinjau Langsung Program Sambungan Listrik Gratis di Bekasi," PresidenRI.go.id, PresidenRI.go.id/beritaaktual/tinjau-langsung-program-sambungan-listrik-gratis-di-bekasi.html [accessed July 4, 2019].

[40] "Menuju Rasio Elektrifikasi 99 Persen pada 2019," Ministry of Energy and Mineral Resources.

[41] Vincent Fabian Thomas, "LTHSE Dinilai Bukan Solusi Jangka Panjang Elektrifikasi di Desa," *Tirto*, February 27, 2019, https://tirto.id/dhTZ [accessed September 23, 2020].

[42] Vincent Fabian Thomas, "IMEF Ragukan Klaim Pemerintah Soal Rasio Elektrifikasi 98 Persen," *Tirto*, January 17, 2019, https://tirto.id/deBB [accessed September 23, 2020].

To tackle the bigger problem of the inadequate network supply nationwide, in 2015 Jokowi launched the "35,000 Megawatts of Electricity for Indonesia" program, with a five-year timeframe and an investment of Rp110 trillion. The aim of the program was to achieve a dramatic 35,000MW increase in the country's existing production capacity of 55,000MW, which in itself had taken seventy years to develop. The key problem under previous administrations had arguably been a failure either to anticipate future development or to keep pace with current changes. Supply networks, production capacity, and fuel availability never properly matched population growth or the pace of industrialization.

During Jokowi's first term, extra capacity was built into existing networks, such as the Java-Bali system to reduce the problem of load shedding, essential to encourage investment growth in the manufacturing sector which demands reliable supplies.[43] Efforts were also made to reduce fuel dependence on foreign suppliers. Indonesia has long relied heavily on a supply of fuel oil from Singapore because of the deficiency of its own refineries. But under Jokowi's administration, steps were taken to reduce this deficiency, with the signing of a contract for the implementation of the expansion of the capacity of the Balikpapan oil refinery in East Kalimantan.[44] This would involve the first newly constructed oil refinery since the Reformasi era (the last time Indonesia built an oil refinery was in Balongan, Indramayu, West Java, in 1994).[45] The Balikpapan redevelopment is intended to increase production by 100,000 barrels per day, reducing the burden of diesel imports by 17 percent. On completion, the upgraded Balikpapan refinery will also produce annually up to 230,000 tons of propylene, the raw ingredient of plastic. Balikpapan is one of four projects in the "Refinery Development Master Plan," which also includes two new "Grass Roots Refineries," all to be built by Pertamina, the state fuel company, with the aim of doubling production capacity by 2025.

---

[43] "Sistem Kelistrikan Indonesia Semakin Handal dan Ekonomis," PLN, https://www.pln.co.id/media/siaran-pers/2019/04/sistem-kelistrikan-indonesia-semakin-handal-dan-ekonomis [accessed May 1, 2019].

[44] Achmad Dwi Afriyadi, "Pertamina Mulai Kembangkan Kilang Balikpapan Awal 2019," *detikNews*, November 28, 2018, https://finance.detik.com/energi/d-4321183/pertamina-mulai-kembangkan-kilang-balikpapan-awal-2019 [accessed February 7, 2019].

[45] Raditya Hanung Prakoswa, "Kilang Minyak, Riwayatmu Kini," CNBC Indonesia, February 2, 2018, https://www.cnbcindonesia.com/news/20180202143456-4-3363/kilang-minyak-riwayatmu-kini [accessed February 8, 2019].

Boosting Renewable Energy

The oil-based refinery developments are intended to mitigate Indonesia's immediate energy demands, but steps have also been taken to address the longer-term future and the need to make a shift towards renewables. Clearly a tropical, volcanic, and maritime country like Indonesia has enormous potential for renewable energy, including geothermal, solar, and wind. But until recently, exploitation of this potential has been very limited due to a general lack of investment, limited technological knowhow, and an enduring skew towards fossil fuels sustained by subsidies.

However, the Indonesian authorities have become increasingly aware in recent years of renewable energy as an important solution for sustainable development.[46] The estimated renewable energy capacity of Indonesia is 441.7GW, with solar energy dominant. Currently, only around 2 percent of this potential is utilized, but development in the renewable sector has been highlighted as an important part of Jokowi's determination to achieve energy independence for Indonesia.[47]

Indonesia also has a national energy development road map as part of the National Energy Policy, outlined in Government Regulation No. 79 of 2014, which aims for a renewable energy mix (EBT) of 23 percent by 2025, increasing to 31 percent in 2050,[48] a target which Jokowi has committed to pursuing. In 2015, he formed a team to study the potential for renewable energy in Indonesia.[49] That same year, the Ministry of Energy and Mineral Resources indicated major upcoming budgetary increases for renewable energy, with a fivefold spending boost projected in the coming twelve months. The ministry also announced a project to install rooftop solar panels on government buildings, including the State Palace in Bogor.[50]

---

[46] Indrasari Wardhani, "Energi Terbarukan," WWF Indonesia, https://www.wwf.or.id/tentang_wwf/upaya_kami/iklim_dan_energi/solusikami/mitigasi/energi_terbarukan.cfm [accessed May 1, 2019].

[47] Cekmas Cekdin and Taufik Barlian, *Transmisi Daya Listrik* (Yogyakarta: Andi Publisher, 2013), 74.

[48] Aprillia Ika, "Bauran Energi Sudah Mencapai 11 Persen, Biomassa Paling Tertinggal," *Kompas*, January 26, 2018, https://ekonomi.kompas.com/read/2018/01/26/074000626/bauran-energi-sudah-mencapai-11-persen-biomassa-paling-tertinggal [accessed February 7, 2019].

[49] Wahyudin Sunarya and Giri Ahmad Taufik, *Pengantar Hukum Minyak dan Gas Indonesia* (Jakarta: Indorecht Publishing, 2018), 57.

[50] Khoirul Amin, "Govt to increase budget for new energy sources," *The Jakarta Post*, June 13, 2015, https://www.thejakartapost.com/news/2015/06/13/govt-increase-budget-new-energy-sources.html [accessed October 21, 2020].

By November 2017 the renewable energy mix in national power generation was recorded at 12.52 percent. The mix consists of hydroelectric at 7.27 percent, geothermal at 5 percent, and other renewables at around 0.25 percent. But steps to further increase production were underway by the end of Jokowi's first term. Private power companies have built hydroelectric power plants with a capacity of nearly 1,200 MW in 2017,[51] while Indonesia's geothermal potential—the largest in the world after the USA—is being developed, for example at the Sarulla Geothermal Power Plant in North Sumatra, which was projected to generate 3,300MW in 2019.

During Jokowi's first term, his administration also built two wind power installations, at Sidrap and Jeneponto in Sulawesi.[52] Indonesia's first wind farm is located at Mattirotasi village, Sidrap Regency, South Sulawesi. It has thirty wind turbines, occupying 100 hectares of hilly land which, fairly unusually in Indonesia, is exposed to consistent wind.[53] The Sidrap wind farm can generate up to 75MW, enough to supply more than 70,000 PLN customers with 900VA power. The second wind farm at Jeneponto has a 72MW capacity. Other wind farms are under development at Tanah Laut South Kalimantan, and Sukabumi, West Java.

The Sidrap plant lies in a beautiful region, around three hours from Makassar in the Watang Pulu hills. Jokowi himself was struck by the landscape with its dramatic ranks of turbines when he visited to inaugurate the site in July 2019.

"I see all the turbines spinning. This means that the wind here is more than enough. It feels just like the many windmills in—where? Yes! In Holland! It feels like the Netherlands, like Europe; but we are in Sidrap!" he said.[54]

[51] Aditya Budiman, "Jokowi: Potensi Panas Bumi di Indonesia Berlimpah," *Tempo*, December 27, 2016, https://bisnis.tempo.co/read/830736/jokowi-potensi-panas-bumi-di-indonesia-berlimpah [accessed February 7, 2019].

[52] "Peresmian PLTB Terbesar di Indonesia di Sulsel," PresidenRI.go.id, http://presidenri.go.id/beritaaktual/peresmian-pltb-terbesar-di-indonesia-di-sulsel.html [accessed February 8, 2019].

[53] Hendi, *Mengenal LISTRIK Lebih Baik dari Segala Sisi* (Jakarta: Elex Media Komputindo, 2016), 35.

[54] Ekky Imanjaya, *Amsterdam Surprises: Eksplorasi Kaya Rasa di Negeri Kincir Angin* (Jakarta: Lingkar Pena, 2010), 49.

Launching the KIS healthcare card.

Chapter Seven

Card Carrying: Education and Health under Jokowi

Hitting Turbulence: Jokowi's Third Year as President

As he marked the second anniversary of his inauguration, Jokowi appeared to be in a solid position: backed by a parliamentary majority without having ended up entirely beholden to the competing interests of a "big tent" coalition, and secure enough to have a degree of autonomy from his own party hierarchy. But there was serious trouble ahead. Just a couple of weeks later and many thousands of miles away, Donald Trump would win the US presidential election. The new American president would shortly pull out of the Trans-Pacific Trade Partnership, which Jokowi had signaled Indonesia was looking to join during his visit to Washington the previous year,[1] kick-starting a tense and wildly unpredictable period on the international front. But more immediately pressing for Jokowi was a brewing domestic storm. It pertained to the upcoming 2017 Jakarta gubernatorial election and it would put Indonesia's pluralism and democracy under considerable pressure.

When Jokowi stepped down as governor of Jakarta to take up the presidency, his deputy took over, just as had been the case in Surakarta two years earlier. Ahok continued as he had begun, outspoken, decidedly unconcerned with niceties, but indisputably effective. He went on with the work that Jokowi had begun, cleaning up the city, improving its infrastructure

---

[1] "Indonesia will join Trans-Pacific Partnership, Jokowi tells Obama," *The Guardian*, October 27, 2015, https://www.theguardian.com/world/2015/oct/27/indonesia-will-join-trans-pacific-partnership-jokowi-tells-obama [accessed October 22, 2020].

and public transport, and expanding social welfare programs. His approval ratings were sky-high, and most people assumed he would easily win a second term in his own right. This was noteworthy given Ahok's "double minority" status, both a Protestant Christian and of Chinese heritage. Prejudice against the long-established ethnic Chinese minority is deep-rooted in Indonesia, dating back at least to the Dutch colonial era.[2] It has generally kept Chinese Indonesians out of high-profile politics. That Ahok's track record seemed to allow him to cut through this was heartening for those committed to the ideal of pluralism in Indonesia. But then, in late 2016, everything fell rapidly to pieces.

In September, during a visit to the scattered island communities off the coast of Jakarta, Ahok made some offhand comments about sectarian-minded attacks on the legitimacy of his position as a non-Muslim governor of a Muslim-majority city. There was no immediate reaction, but the comments had been recorded and the recording began to circulate online, edited so that Ahok appeared not simply to be questioning the legitimacy of those who attacked him but of Muslim scripture itself. Uproar ensued, initially confined to social media but soon manifest in street protests. These protests were spearheaded by the FPI, the Front Pembela Islam or "Islamic Defenders Front," a notorious Islamist pressure group. But more reputable Muslim organizations soon weighed in to condemn Ahok. Official complaints were lodged with the police and there was growing pressure for him to be charged with blasphemy. A major protest outside the presidential palace in Jakarta on November 4 turned violent in its late stages. It was clear that the affair would not simply fizzle out, and though police launched an official investigation and actually charged Ahok on November 17, the pressure continued. Plans were revealed for an even bigger protest on December 2.

The background to the anti-Ahok movement is complex, many-faceted, and up for debate. Established hostility from the vocal sectarian Islamist minority met with a genuine sense of affront amongst a much wider body of Muslims, and also fed from an undercurrent of ethnic prejudice which

---

[2] The origins of anti-Chinese sentiment in Indonesia are manifold and linked to various historical resentments. In the colonial era, for example, the Dutch often leased exploitative revenue-collection mechanisms to ethnic Chinese entrepreneurs, while the notorious cronyism of Suharto's regime was associated with a small group of astronomically wealthy Chinese Indonesian tycoons, known colloquially as *cukong*. For insight into Suharto's "*cukong* extraordinaire," Liem Sioe Liong, see Nancy Chng and Richard Borsuk, *Liem Sioe Liong's Salim Group: The Business Pillar of Suharto's Indonesia* (Singapore: ISEAS Publishing, 2014).

had itself been stirred up anew by populist antipathy to extensive investment from China in Indonesia in recent years.[3] But there is little doubt that Ahok's political rivals were very ready to profit from the situation, and, to a greater or lesser degree, to exacerbate it. Attendance at the December 2 protest was boosted by cash distributed to demonstrators by "political groups" to cover travel costs and food on the day.[4] And of course, Ahok's political rivals were also Jokowi's political rivals.

The upcoming gubernatorial vote was something of a dress rehearsal for the 2019 presidential campaign. Ahok was backed by PDI-P, Golkar, Hanura, and Nasdem, an endorsing coalition much the same as that expected to support Jokowi for re-election two years later. The main rival, meanwhile, was Anies Baswedan, who had served as Jokowi's education and culture minister until the 2016 reshuffle, but who has now backed for the governorship by Prabowo's Gerindra and PKS. Finally, the outside candidate, backed by the Partai Demokrat and the three other main Muslim parties (PPP, PKB, and PAN), was Agus Harimurti Yudhoyono, son of the previous president.[5] The parties backing the two gubernatorial challengers were likely to be more or less those supporting Jokowi's 2019 presidential rival. If Ahok lost in Jakarta, it would provide early momentum for the campaign to unseat Jokowi himself.

The crowd that turned out in Jakarta on December 2 was the biggest the Indonesian capital had seen for many years. Somewhere between 500,000 and 750,000 protesters thronged the streets of central Jakarta,[6] converging on Medan Merdeka. Islam was very clearly the unifying factor here, and the whole thing had by this stage been dubbed the 212 Movement after the date of the demonstration. But researchers on the ground reported that many of the protesters did not appear particularly radical or indeed particularly sympathetic to the Islamism of the FPI.[7] Claims that Indonesia was, at this point, on the brink of some sort of "Islamic Revolution" are decidedly far-fetched.

But for Jokowi, inside the presidential palace, it was the tensest moment of his presidency to date. There were suggestions that political

---

[3] Greg Fealy, "Bigger than Ahok: explaining the 2 December mass rally," Indonesia at Melbourne, December 7, 2016, https://indonesiaatmelbourne.unimelb.edu.au/bigger-than-ahok-explaining-jakartas-2-december-mass-rally/ [accessed October 22, 2020].

[4] Ibid.

[5] Ahmad Ibrahim Almuttaqi, *Jokowi's Indonesia and the World* (Singapore: World Scientific Publishing, 2020), 62.

[6] Fealy, "Bigger than Ahok."

[7] Ibid.

agitators might be encouraging the protesters to storm the palace. There had also been vague rumors the previous month of a plotted military coup.[8] This had never been a very likely outcome, but almost two decades since Indonesia's embrace of democracy the possibility of such a rumor was itself shocking enough.

In the event, Jokowi did exactly what he had always tried to do at moments of conflict: he went on to the ground to meet the people on the other side; he went out into the December rain to join the protesters for Friday prayers.

Many of Jokowi's foreign critics were outraged by the sight of him sharing a platform with the leadership of the FPI. And it was an uncomfortable moment for many progressive Indonesians, too. But meeting face-to-face with potential antagonists, listening directly to their concerns, and engaging in dialogue has been absolutely central to Jokowi's ethos from the very start. As mayor of Surakarta, he had reached out to the street vendors instead of simply calling in the bulldozers. He had also engaged in dialogue with Surakarta's conservative Muslim groups over various cultural concerns.[9] Jokowi's engagement with the 212 Movement was not, then, any kind of aberration. It was exactly what he would have done whatever they were protesting about. It was also, in the moment, the most likely way to diffuse the tension, and in that respect it worked perfectly. At the end of the day, the gathering broke up peacefully, there was no repeat of the violence of November 4, and subsequently the wider street protest movement gradually fizzled out. Online agitation continued, however, and it was clear by this stage that it would be politically impossible for Jokowi to intercede on behalf of his former colleague.

In the February first round of the gubernatorial vote, Ahok still managed to take the largest share of the vote. But it was nothing like the landslide majority he might have expected six months earlier, and he was forced into an April runoff, which Anies Baswedan won solidly. The following month Ahok was found guilty of blasphemy and jailed for two years.[10]

....

[8] Almuttaqi, *Jokowi's Indonesia and the World*, 66.

[9] Rushda Majeed, "The City with a Short Fuse," September 11, 2012, https://foreignpolicy.com/2012/09/11/the-city-with-a-short-fuse/ [accessed October 22, 2020].

[10] "Jakarta governor Ahok found guilty of blasphemy," BBC, May 9, 2017, https://www.bbc.com/news/world-asia-39853280 [accessed October 22, 2020].

Handling political Islam has been a perennial challenge for Indonesia's leaders. A century ago, Sukarno recognized that an independence movement dominated by Islam would unlikely produce a unified nation, and both he and subsequent presidents have often sought to strike a balance between accommodating and sidelining the interests of political Islam. Of course, "political Islam" itself encompasses a wide gamut, from the mainstream Muslim parties committed to democracy to the tiny Islamist minority seeking to replace that democracy with a theocratic state.

In the early years of the Reformasi period, the Muslim parties appeared to be in the ascendancy at the polls. The larger nationalist parties tended to respond to this by colonizing some of the same territory, making policy allowances for those wishing for a greater role for Islam in public life, a strategy that appears to have been broadly effective at halting further increases in support for the Muslim parties (though it could also be argued that they have simply reached the natural limit of their demographic appeal). Handling the far more extreme Islamist minority requires a more delicate and fraught balance between accommodation and pushback, though there are certainly those who have been willing to exploit this constituency for political purposes.

Jokowi is, of course, a Muslim himself, like every other Indonesian president before him. He grew up in the committed but undogmatic tradition common to the vast majority of Javanese people in the mid-twentieth century. His mother's devout faith was well known and she imparted her meditative, prayerful relationship with Islam to her children. During his first presidential campaign, Jokowi had been happy to brush off the various outrageous slurs about his religious background in his customary *aku rapopo* manner. And he had not placed any particular emphasis on connecting with major Muslim organizations. But in the aftermath of the Ahok affair, he made a greater effort to signal engagement, particularly with the Nahdlatul Ulama (NU), Indonesia's largest Muslim organization. NU can, broadly, be said to represent an "indigenous" Muslim tradition in Indonesia, while the second largest organization, Muhammadiyah, has a more "international" outlook. In recent years, NU has made considerable effort to promote its idea of Islam Nusantara, a new term for the old reality of Islam embedded in Indonesia's unique cultural conditions, with tolerance a key facet. Jokowi had been approving of this move from the outset[11]

---

[11] Greg Fealy, "Nahdlatul Ulama and the politics trap," *New Mandala*, July 11, 2018, https://www.newmandala.org/nahdlatul-ulama-politics-trap/ [accessed October 22, 2020].

(NU formally adopted Islam Nusantara as a core concept in 2015), not least because it spoke to his own religious heritage. But he made a further effort to show his backing in the second half of his first term,[12] and also to show government support for NU more generally. In early 2017, the Ministry of Finance announced a partnership with NU, which has a long-established track record in community development), for a major scheme to provide grants to micro businesses.[13]

On another level, however, Jokowi signaled that he was willing to act decisively against extremist groups. In May it was announced that the government would ban Hizbut Tahrir Indonesia (HTI), the local branch of an international movement pushing for the establishment of a caliphate, which had been prominent in the anti-Ahok protests. This move had the support of NU and Muhammadiyah, which had both long been alarmed by HTI's infiltration of mosques and Islamic schools.[14] But HTI was a legally registered organization and the mechanism for banning such a group was cumbersome, involving various mandatory steps and judicial oversight. The government turned instead to the constitutional option for a president to issue a quick-fire Perppu, or Regulation in Lieu of Law. Though such regulations must be debated and carried or rejected by the DPR in its next sitting to permanently enter the statute book, they allow for rapid action in the moment. This particular Perppu enabled effectively instant banning of any organization deemed to have violated the pluralist principles of Pancasila. In July 2017, Hizbut Tahrir Indonesia was outlawed.[15]

Inevitably, many of the same people who had expressed distaste at Jokowi's engagement with the 212 Movement leaders in December now expressed concern at this seemingly draconian measure. For some outside observers, it was part of the president's alleged "authoritarian turn."[16] These were legitimate concerns, but it is important to recognize that any

---

[12] Thomas P. Power, "Jokowi's Authoritarian Turn and Indonesia's Democratic Decline," *Bulletin of Indonesian Economic Studies* 54, no. 3 (2018): 313.

[13] Galih Gumelar, "Gandeng PBNU, Pemerintah Salurkan Bantuan Investasi Rp1,5 T," CNN Indonesia, February 23, 2017, https://www.cnnindonesia.com/ekonomi/20170223183635-78-195737/gandeng-pbnu-pemerintah-salurkan-bantuan-investasi-rp15-t [accessed October 22, 2020].

[14] Sidney Jones, "Two decisions that leave Indonesia more polarised than ever," *The Interpreter*, May 10, 2017, https://www.lowyinstitute.org/the-interpreter/two-decisions-leave-indonesia-more-polarised-than-ever [accessed October 22, 2020].

[15] Matthew Busch, "Jokowi's Panicky Politics," *Foreign Affairs*, August 11, 2017, https://www.foreignaffairs.com/articles/indonesia/2017-08-11/jokowis-panicky-politics [accessed October 22, 2020].

[16] Power, "Jokowi's Authoritarian Turn."

such "turn" was reactive, itself prompted by thoroughly antidemocratic factors: the existence of groups committed to replacing pluralist democracy with theocracy; coup rumors; the deployment of mobs to unseat elected leaders; and a willingness to spread division and hatred for political ends.

It is also worth considering again Jokowi's origins as a politician. Despite the characteristics projected onto him by some of his supporters during his first presidential campaign, he was not himself from an activist or campaigning background. He was a businessman, who, after a successful two-decade-long career, had moved into politics wanting simply to get things done, to make tangible progress, to make concrete improvements to the lives of both the small-town business class and the *wong cilik*. And for all the challenges and frustrations of the presidency, he was undoubtedly still moving forward on those fronts. Despite all the fuss and all the column inches expended over the Ahok affair, the Perppu and other issues, in mid-2017 Jokowi's public approval ratings were still at 67 percent.[17] Most Indonesians were happy with what he was doing, with advances in health and education earning particular approval.

"Poor People Can't Get Sick"

Poor people are not allowed to get sick: this bitter proverb was commonplace amongst the residents of the Kali Anyar riverbank during Jokowi's childhood. For the pedicab drivers, hawkers, and manual laborers who made up the lowest level of Surakarta's working classes, sickness meant an inability to work, and an inability to work meant that there would be no food to eat. And it was not simply a matter of lost earnings: there were costs for treatment and medication, costs which poor people could seldom afford.[18]

Although Jokowi's family were by no means amongst the very poorest, he nonetheless has strong recollections of the money-related fear of health problems, within his own family and amongst the wider community. Amongst his siblings, only Jokowi was born in hospital; his three younger sisters were all born at home to avoid the cost of a hospital stay.[19] He grew up in the age of traditional medicine. This was not simply a matter of

---

[17] Cici Marlina Rahayu, "Survei SMRC: 67% Masyarakat Puas terhadap Kinerja Jokowi," *detikNews*, June 8, 2017, https://news.detik.com/berita/d-3524763/survei-smrc-67-masya-rakat-puas-terhadap-kinerja-jokowi [accessed October 22, 2020].

[18] Alberthiene Endah, *Jokowi Perjalanan Karya bagi Bangsa Menuju Cahaya* (Solo: Tiga Serang-kai, 2018), 30.

[19] Ibid

superstition; quack remedies and herbal potions were often the only afford-able option for families unable to meet the cost of conventional medicine.

"I remember, often poor people in my neighborhood had to endure pain in their bodies because they had to earn a living," Jokowi recalls.[20]

For decades, Indonesia's healthcare system has been deeply inadequate, fragmentary, badly funded, partly marketized, and with even public facil-ities requiring upfront payments from patients. Those who could afford it invariably turned to private hospitals, but even these often provided poor care. And a serious or long-term condition could prove financially ruin-ous. Indonesia abounds with stories of once relatively wealthy families forced to sell off land or property to cover spiraling medical bills. For poor people, meanwhile, there was every reason to avoid professional healthcare altogether when even relatively simple medication might cost as much as a month's supply of food.

Throughout Jokowi's political career, from his time as mayor of Sura-karta onwards, he has displayed an obvious commitment to improving access to healthcare.[21] This partly stems from his own childhood experi-ence when even his own mother would sometimes turn to herbal reme-dies to avoid the cost of medication. "I still remember how worried we felt when our parents or one of us were sick in the past," he says.[22] It also partly emerges from his *blusukan* approach to connecting with voters: for decades, a lack of access to affordable healthcare has been a top concern of Indonesians, and it is something that comes up over and over again when a politician speaks to people directly and asks about their worries.

Building a Universal Healthcare Coverage System

There have been moves towards providing comprehensive healthcare in the decades since the fall of the New Order. A universal healthcare coverage system was actually mandated by law as far back as 2004, but it took years to make progress putting it into action. In 2010, Susilo Bambang Yudhoyono's government was actually sued by a workers' rights group over its failure to implement the law.[23] One of the major challenges was consolidating the

---

[20] Ibid., 231.
[21] Ibid.
[22] Ibid.,232.
[23] Jeffrey Hutton, "Indonesia launches world's largest health insurance system," *The Christian Science Monitor*, March 10, 2014, https://www.csmonitor.com/World/Asia-Pacific/2014/0310/Indonesia-launches-world-s-largest-health-insurance-system [accessed October 22, 2020].

multiple existing insurance schemes for workers in different sectors, and for those living in poverty. The existence of these various schemes led to inevitable gaps in coverage. There was no coverage, for example, for the self-employed or those working in Indonesia's vast informal employment sector,[24] people who were often very close to poverty, but not quite in the extreme circumstances that qualified them for coverage under the existing Jamkesmas scheme.

The card-based health insurance scheme for all Jakarta residents regardless of income which Jokowi had launched as governor[25] was widely viewed as a sort of unofficial pilot for a consolidated national universal healthcare coverage system,[26] and in the final year of Susilo Bambang Yudhoyono's government, such a scheme was finally initiated. This "National Health Insurance" scheme (JKN; Jaminan Kesehatan Nasional) was administered by the Healthcare and Social Security Agency, BPJS Kesehatan.[27]

Coming into office, Jokowi was determined to expand on that existing program, with a particular emphasis on providing healthcare free at the point of delivery to all Indonesians of limited means, not simply those officially deemed to be in outright poverty. He swiftly launched the "Healthy Indonesia Card," generally known by the abbreviation KIS (Kartu Indonesia Sehat).[28] The earlier, similarly named Jakarta program had experienced some serious teething problems, with hospitals and public health centers in the capital struggling to cope with the initial demand. But the establishment of a principle of simplified universal healthcare was popular with voters and a nationwide equivalent was a key Jokowi campaign promise. Within fourteen days of his inauguration, he had launched the KIS scheme.

"There are still many poor people who are not accommodated when there is health commercialization as there is today. This is ironic, this is a slap in the face for us and our country. The state has the responsibility to protect," Jokowi had said during the run-up to his election.[29]

---

[24] The Economist Intelligence Unit, *Universal healthcare coverage in Indonesia*, January 2015, available at https://www.clearstate.com/wp-content/uploads/2016/12/Universal-health-care-coverage-in-Indonesia_One-year-on-WEB.pdf [accessed October 22, 2020].

[25] Wikku Adisasmito, *Sistem Kesehatan* (Depok: Rajawali Pers, 2016), 184.

[26] Ibid.

[27] https://bpjskesehatan.go.id/BPJS/index.php/post/read/2014/291/Ini-yang-Perlu-Anda-Ketahui-Soal-Kartu-Indonesia-Sehat [accessed July 29, 2019].

[28] Ibid.

[29] Agib Tanjung, "4 Cerita orang miskin 'dilarang' sakit," *Merdeka*, January 25, 2014, https://www.merdeka.com/peristiwa/4-cerita-orang-miskin-dilarang-sakit.html [accessed August

The wider BJPS Kesehatan program with which the new KIS scheme was combined functioned as a straightforward state-run health insurance model in which the monthly premium for poor recipients is covered by the Ministry of Health, with healthcare then provided free at the point of delivery at community health centers and hospitals, including inpatient stays in Class III wards (the cheapest class, with three or more beds).

Budget wrangling delayed the full launch of the KIS program until April 2015, but from that point the cards were distributed to those on low incomes,[30] with 92.4 million people across the country receiving health coverage at no direct personal cost by 2018,[31] rising to 96.8 million in 2019.

"If the people want to get health services, don't make it difficult for them. I only ask for that," Jokowi told one group of KIS recipients.[32]

By 2018, the overall membership of the BPJS Kesehatan-administered National Health Insurance scheme was 195.2 million, with an aim of achieving membership for every Indonesian.[33] Universal coverage was already in place in 200 cities nationwide, as well as four provinces, namely Jakarta, Gorontalo, West Papua, and Aceh.[34]

Universal healthcare coverage for Indonesia had become a realistic aspiration, something which garnered international praise. During a visit to Jakarta in 2018, managing director of the International Monetary Fund, Christine Lagarde, joined Jokowi on a *blusukan* visit to a Jakarta hospital and expressed surprise at the achievement in such a large country.[35]

For Jokowi, the KIS aspect of the wider health cover provision was a manifestation of one of the fundamental principles of Indonesian nationalism, namely, *gotong-royong*, mutual cooperation, as a means of achieving

3, 2019].

[30] Novy Lumanauw, "Govt Starts Distribution of Social Benefit Cards," *Jakarta Globe*, April 28, 2015, https://jakartaglobe.id/news/distribution-of-healthy-indonesia-and-smart-indonesia-cards-start-this-week/ [accessed September 24, 2020].

[31] Ibid.

[32] "Pelayanan Kesehatan Kepada Masyarakat Jangan Dipersulit," PresidenRI.go.id, http://presidenri.go.id/berita-aktual/pelayanan-kesehatan-kepada-masyarakat-jangan-dipersulit.html [accessed July 16, 2019].

[33] Devina Heriyanto, "Q&A: BPJS Kesehatan, health for all Indonesians," *The Jakarta Post*, April 7, 2018, https://www.thejakartapost.com/academia/2018/04/06/qa-bpjs-kesehatan-health-for-all-indonesians.html [accessed September 24, 2020].

[34] "Pemkot Cilegon dan BPJS Kesehatan Deklarasikan UHC," *Banten News*, https://www.bantennews.co.id/pemkot-cilegon-dan-bpjs-kesehatan-deklarasikan-uhc/ [accessed July 16, 2019].

[35] Desca Lidya Natalia, "IMF director lauds Indonesia's health care system," *Antara*, February 28, 2018, https://en.antaranews.com/news/114800/imf-director-lauds-indonesias-health-care-system [accessed September 24, 2020].

social justice. Access to healthcare was to be opened up fairly and equally for all people. The costs of providing care for the poorest was to be covered by the contributions of the better off, and also by the de facto contributions of all healthy people who place no demands on the system. Furthermore, the implementation of the program has required collaboration between multiple stakeholders, including cross-ministerial cooperation, taking in the Ministry of Health, Ministry of Finance, Ministry of Social Affairs, Ministry of Home Affairs, as well as cooperation with local governments and the many healthcare providers.

Inevitably with such a huge system, there have been a multitude of teething problems. Even the original, pre-Jokowi National Health Insurance scheme, without the KIS component and prior to the launch of the consolidated version, ran a deficit from the outset. By 2017, that deficit had reached Rp9 trillion, partly down to the huge overall running cost of the program, but also because of patchy collection of monthly premiums from those not qualifying for free assistance.[36] Once Jokowi's expanded scheme was launched, healthcare facilities sometimes struggled to cope with increased demand, just as had been the case in Jakarta. And efforts to bring private hospitals into the scheme at times ran into difficulties, with operators complaining of the slow reimbursement process and the practical difficulties of providing Class III wards to accommodate public patients.

More widely, the general standard and capacity of the Indonesian healthcare system clearly still requires serious improvement. Both quality and quantity of provision often lag behind other countries in the region. The National Development Planning Agency (Bappenas) states that Indonesia has only 0.13 specialist doctors and 0.52 general practitioners per 1,000 people, well below official targets of 0.28 and 1.12 respectively.[37] Hospital infrastructure is also lacking, with just 1.2 beds per 1,000 residents, well below the ratio in China (4.3) and even India (2.7).[38] These deficiencies would be starkly underscored by the global Covid-19 pandemic of 2020.

---

[36] Heriyanto, "Q&A: BPJS Kesehatan, health for all Indonesians."

[37] Tri Indah Oktavianti, "COVID-19 doctor tells Jokowi about shortage of healthcare workers in video call – National," *The Jakarta Post*, September 27, 2020, https://www.thejakartapost.com/news/2020/09/27/covid-19-doctor-tells-jokowi-about-shortage-of-healthcare-workers-in-video-call.html [accessed October 22, 2020].

[38] Nina A. Loasana and Marchio Irfan Gorbiano, "COVID-19 pandemic exposes problems in our health care, Jokowi says," *The Jakarta Post*, May 1, 2020, https://www.thejakartapost.com/news/2020/04/30/covid-19-pandemic-exposes-problems-in-our-health-care-jokowi-says.html [accessed October 22, 2020].

Nonetheless, the initial emphasis was on the wider principle of provision, and this was plainly a success: a framework had been put in place for universal healthcare coverage, provided without payment to the most needy and available all across Indonesia.

Beneficiaries of the Scheme

Amongst the beneficiaries of the KIS scheme was a 27-year-old woman from Garut in West Java named Fitri, who suffered from a painful ovarian condition.[39] After diagnosis by a local doctor, surgery was recommended, which required hospitalization in Bandung, the nearest large city. This was the sort of scenario which, in years past, could have pushed a low-income household into debt or forced them to sell land or valuables to cover treatment costs.

"An operation is not a small cost. For me it's very big," Fitri said. However, as a KIS recipient, the upfront costs of the treatment, including the post-op checkups, were fully covered.

Of course, the commitment to cover treatments such as Fitri's is one of the major challenges for the system, contributing to its persistent budgetary deficit. Long-term health problems place a particular burden on the system. During a forum with KIS recipients at the presidential palace in 2018, Jokowi noted one case in Central Java that had cost the Ministry of Health more than Rp1 billion.

"I saw this in Karanganyar, [a case of] haemophilia, [costing] more than Rp1 billion. Yes! [But] it is the government's duty; if it checks out, BPJS must pay; it must be paid," Jokowi said.[40]

To mitigate such costs, efforts have been made to enforce the payment of premiums through action by local governments right down to the village level. An additional emphasis has also been developed on preventative healthcare, with the point made that in the long term this may reduce the burdens on the system. Jokowi launched a program providing additional food assistance for pregnant women, toddlers, babies, and school-age children, and a campaign in remote and impoverished areas to prevent childhood stunting with better nutrition, clean water provision, and

---

[39] JokowiApp interview with Fitriani in Garut, March 12, 2019.

[40] "Jokowi: Jangan Hambat Pelayanan Kesehatan untuk Rakyat," Jpnn.com, https://www.jpnn.com/news/jokowi-jangan-hambat-pelayanan-kesehatan-untuk-rakyat [accessed July 16, 2019].

improved family awareness.[41] Stunting has long been a problem in Indonesia,[42] and recent editions of the Basic Health Research (Riskesdas) survey, which is carried out every five years, identified some degree of stunting in more than a third of Indonesian babies.

"We are reducing the stunting rate so that our children grow up to be a premium generation," Jokowi said in his State Address on August 16, 2019. "Pregnant women must eat nutritionally so that our children are clever, intelligent, able. We want our nation to be strong in the future so our children can compete with other countries."

The National Health Insurance scheme is also intended to cover checkups, particularly during pregnancy, as well as reactive treatments. One resident of Semarang, Budiati, explained how she had used her KIS card despite not initially understanding what it was for.

"In the beginning, someone delivered it in the mail to the house. After I opened the envelope, it turned out that it contained the KIS," she said.[43] Budiati said she had not heard of the program at that point, but asked the neighborhood head about it and learned that it would entitle her to free checkups at the local community health center (known as Puskesmas in Indonesia). Since then she has made regular use of the service, particularly during pregnancy, and has also used her KIS for other treatments.

"All the health checks have been without spending money, not even a thousand rupiah," she said.

Budiati is a member of the sort of community in which Jokowi grew up, the *wong cilik*, the little people for whom the cost of healthcare and the fear of illness or injury have long been a burden.

"The threat of illness is very frightening for people, especially the economically weak. The presence of the Healthy Indonesia Card makes them feel protected," Jokowi has said.[44]

The Transformative Power of Education

The Healthy Indonesia Card was not the only card-based social justice program that Jokowi launched within the first few weeks of his presidency. At the same time, he also launched the "Smart Indonesia Card," or KIP (Kartu

[41] Nursodik Gunarjo, *Nawacita Meretas Indonesia Maju* (Jakarta: Kominfo, 2016), 32–33.

[42] Ibid., 32.

[43] "Semua Pemeriksaan Tanpa Keluar Uang," PresidenRI.go.id, http://presidenri.go.id/berita-aktual/semua-pemeriksaan-tanpa-keluar-uang.html [accessed July 16, 2019].

[44] Setneg, *Laporan 4 Tahun Pemerintahan Jokowi-JK* (Jakarta: Setneg, 2018), 236.

Indonesia Pintar), aimed at ensuring access to education for children from impoverished backgrounds.

During Jokowi's own childhood, his parents had placed a firm emphasis on education as a route to a more prosperous future. "Go to school. Learn to be smart," his father had urged him.[45] Though quiet, he was always considered a relatively bright child and he did reasonably well at school,[46] though not quite as well as he might have liked.

All children in Indonesia are supposed to go through a minimum of twelve years of compulsory education. This begins with six years of elementary school (SD), followed by three years of junior high school (SMP), and a further three years at senior high school (SMA). The vast majority of children go through this system at state schools overseen by the Ministry of National Education, while a much smaller number attend private or semiprivate religious schools, most of which, but by no means all, have a Muslim ethos, under the Ministry of Religious Affairs, and a very small minority attend exclusive private and international schools. Within the state school system there has always been a certain hierarchy, with some schools attaining elite status through the perceived quality of their teaching and their exam results. So-called "National Plus" schools are those that demonstrably go beyond the minimum curriculum requirements. There is considerable competition for places in prestigious state high schools, with the more elite institutions typically demanding higher grades in the final exams at the end of the previous level for entry.

As a teenager, Jokowi set his heart on Surakarta's SMAN 1, the most prestigious of the city's public senior high schools. However, his final grades from the SMPN 1 junior high school were not high enough to gain him entry. This hit the teenager hard. Having been widely considered a bright boy, he felt humiliated by the failure to gain a place at the best school and locked himself away in his room.[47] In the end, with much parental encouragement, he took a place at the recently opened Development Preparatory Middle School (SMPP) No. 40. Despite the name, this school taught the senior high school curriculum, and was renamed SMAN 6 after Jokowi's time there, a name change that has resulted in some confusion, and a few online conspiracies, around his educational history.[48]

---

[45] Endah, *Jokowi Perjalanan Karya bagi Bangsa Menuju Cahaya*, 31.

[46] Domu D. Ambarita, *Jokowi Spirit Bantaran Kali Anyar* (Jakarta: Elex Media Komputindo, 2012), 18.

[47] Keen Achroni, *Jokowi Memimpin dengan Hati* (Yogyakarta: Ar-Ruzz Media, 2012), 42–43.

[48] "Profil SMAN 6 Surakarta, Almamater Presiden Jokowi," *Liputan6*, January 17, 2019, https://

Jokowi's mother continued to encourage his high school studies,[49] and he was ultimately able to take up a place at Gadjah Mada University, one of Indonesia's most prestigious higher education institutions. In 1985, he was amongst the five fastest students to graduate from his cohort in the forestry faculty.[50]

Throughout his life, Jokowi has retained a firm belief in the transformative power of education, the same belief that his parents impressed upon him as a child. "I have nothing but hope and belief that education will change our destiny," he says.[51]

Reducing the Drop-out Rate

Despite being notionally compulsory for twelve years, Indonesian schools have always suffered from a high drop-out rate, with poverty the major factor. In some cases, financial pressure forces children to leave school to work in support of their families; in other cases, a lack of cash to buy uniforms or study materials prompts parents to keep their children out of school. This was a regular phenomenon amongst Jokowi's childhood neighbors, and it remains a common problem today, even in the national capital.

Thirteen-year-old Fikhri Ramadhan from Cengkareng in West Jakarta is such a case. Although he should be in Class 7 at junior high school, he has been out of education since the age of ten because of financial pressures. He now spends his days selling fried snacks on the street to boost his family's income.[52] Likewise, nine-year-old Aldi from Manado, who should still be in elementary school, instead spends his days as a hawker in the North Sulawesi capital's Pasar 45 market.[53]

At the start of Jokowi's administration, nearly 70,000 school-age children had dropped out of education, mainly for economic reasons. This was despite a sustained annual increase in the national education budget during previous administrations, and a subsidy scheme, Bantuan Siswa

www.liputan6.com/news/read/3873010/profil-sman-6-surakarta-almamater-presiden-jokowi [accessed September 24, 2020].

[49] Achroni, *Jokowi Memimpin dengan Hati*, 43.

[50] Ambarita. *Jokowi Spirit Bantaran Kali Anyar*, 29.

[51] Endah, *Jokowi Perjalanan Karya bagi Bangsa Menuju Cahaya*, 34.

[52] Sherly Puspita, "Kisah Fikhri, Bocah Putus Sekolah Penjual Empek-empek," *Kompas*, August 15, 2017, https://megapolitan.kompas.com/read/2017/08/15/12094471/kisah-fikhri-bocah-putus-sekolah-penjual-empek-empek?page=all [accessed September 19, 2019].

[53] Handhika Dawangi, "Kisah Anak Putus Sekolah: Aldi Mengenyam Pendidikan hingga Kelas 2 SD," *Tribunnews*, https://manado.tribunnews.com/2017/09/06/kisah-anak-putus-sekolah-aldi-mengenyam-pendidikan-hingga-kelas-2-sd [accessed September 19, 2019].

Miskin (BSM; "Poor Student Assistance"), already in place to help children from impoverished backgrounds cover the incidental costs of schooling, such as transport, uniforms, and books. There was a simple flaw with this program, however. In Indonesia, the school year ends in May, at which point children move up a grade or move up to the next level of schooling. Entering the new academic year involves buying new uniforms, books, and so on. Typically, however, because of the sluggish bureaucratic process, the BSM funding was not disbursed until July or August, by which time the new school year was well underway, and those children unable to afford new books or uniforms had already dropped out.

This is the sort of thing to which Jokowi, with his managerial background and penchant for problem solving, responds enthusiastically: a difficulty with a fairly obvious solution which has gone unaddressed seemingly only because of incompetence or inertia. With the Smart Indonesia Card (KIP) program, he simply made the educational support funding directly available to its recipients, without the need to wait until the new school year was already underway.

KIP cards were provided to all students previously in receipt of BSM support, as well as those poor families already enrolled in other social support schemes. In the second year of Jokowi's presidency, the drop-out rate fell by approximately 30,000 children, with a further reduction of 7,000 the following year.[54] But efforts continued to reduce the drop-out rate further, with a continued expansion of the KIP program. A total of 7.9 million cards were distributed in 2014, rising to 18.7 million by 2018, with a budget allocation of Rp9.71 trillion that year.[55]

Human Resources: Developing the National Talent Pool

While Jokowi's idealistic view of the transformative personal value of education is a legacy of his parents and his own childhood experience, his background as a businessman also informs his approach. He tends to see improving both access to and the quality of Indonesia's education system in managerial terms, as a human resources issue. For Jokowi, a

---

[54] Dhita Seftiawan, "Jumlah Anak Putus Sekolah Menurun," *Pikiranrakyat*, October 25, 2018, https://www.pikiran-rakyat.com/pendidikan/pr-01302672/jumlah-anak-putus-sekolah-menurun-432186 [accessed July 7, 2019].

[55] "Number of Smart Indonesia Card recipients increases significantly," *Antara*, March 12, 2019, https://en.antaranews.com/news/122634/number-of-smart-indonesia-card-recipients-increases-significantly [accessed September 25, 2020].

better educated population means a greater HR talent pool for the nation. He believes that only high-quality human resources can accelerate national development, and he looks towards other more developed Asian countries such as Japan, South Korea, and China as models in this respect.

Around 60 percent of Indonesia's current population are productive young people. It is predicted that by 2040, that category will amount to around 195 million people.[56] Developing an economy that will provide useful roles for these millions of young people, and that will avoid chronic unemployment or underemployment, is a pressing need. But Jokowi has long been inclined to present Indonesia's demographics in a positive light.

"This is a strength, if we can manage it, if we can take advantage of its potential," he said in 2016.[57]

After the heavy focus on infrastructure during the first four years of his presidency, in the final year of his first term, Jokowi placed an explicit emphasis on human resources as a development priority,[58] with the idea that national infrastructure and national HR were essential and complementary components of development.[59]

During the MPR Annual Session on August 16, 2018, he stressed the idea that, in the end, human resources would determine the growth and survival of any country. Again, this is arguably an ethos that emerges from his own business background.

"Developing the Indonesian people is our investment to face the future, paving the way for a developed Indonesia," he said, going on to emphasize the idea of both healthcare and education investments as components of this approach. "We are preparing the Indonesian people to become a superior people from the womb to independent adulthood, as well as improving the welfare of themselves and their families."[60]

Delivering his speech on the draft 2019 State Budget during the same session, Jokowi outlined further increases to education expenditure:

"In 2019, the planned education budget is Rp487.9 trillion, an increase of 38.1 percent compared to the realized education budget in 2014 of around Rp353.4 trillion," he said.

[56] Adhitya Himawan, "Penduduk Usia Produktif Indonesia 2040 Diprediksi 195 Juta Orang," *Suara*, September 14, 2016, https://www.suara.com/bisnis/2016/09/14/073153/penduduk-usia-produktif-indonesia-2040-diprediksi-195-juta-orang [accessed July 8, 2019].

[57] Ibid.

[58] https://www.YouTube.com/watch?v=xBhvkpWg9hE [accessed July 9, 2019].

[59] Nurul Ulfatin and Teguh Triwiyanto, *Manajemen Sumber Daya Manusia Bidang Pendidikan* (Depok: Rajawali Pers, 2016), 2.

[60] Eko Sulistyo, *Konservatisme Politik Anti Jokowi* (Jakarta: Moka Media, 2019), 176.

Some of that funding was earmarked to increase the number of scholarship recipients through the Bidikmisi program, which supports access to higher education for students from disadvantaged backgrounds. Increased educational funding has also been targeted at vocational training, with a program to build an additional 1,407 practical workshop spaces across the network of vocational high schools (SMK), and provision of assistance for 3,000 vocational students. Further funding has gone to providing laboratory facilities to religious schools.[61] Jokowi had previously expressed a need to focus on vocational education in order to produce a skilled workforce at all levels of the job market.[62]

"Vocational high schools need a major overhaul, because more than 80 percent [of the staff] are standard teachers, such as civic education teachers, Indonesian language teachers, and religion teachers; [but] 80 percent should be skills teachers, teachers who can become trainers for our children to strengthen their skills," he said in 2017.[63]

During a convention in Sentul, Bogor, West Java, in February 2019, Jokowi launched a number of further card-based support programs to build on the KIS and KIP schemes: the Cheap Essential Food Card (KSM; Kartu Sembako Murah) to provide assistance with essential foodstuffs for disadvantaged families; the Smart Indonesia Card for Higher Education (KIPPT; Kartu Indonesia Pintar untuk Perguruan Tinggi); and the Pre-Employment Card for Vocational Education (KPKPV; Kartu Pra Kerja untuk Pendidikan Vokasi).

The aim of the KIPPT was to provide support, similar to that of the KIP, for students in higher education, while the KPKPV was aimed at vocational high school graduates to provide further training after finishing school.

Chasing Unicorns: The Potential of the Start-up Sector

The idea of a better educated population of young Indonesians is connected to a government focus on the potential of the tech industry and digital start-ups for the Indonesian economy.[64] Jokowi has expressed a desire to see more

[61] Yopi Makdori, "Jokowi Dorong Peningkatan Kerja Sama Australia dalam Pendidikan Vokasi," *Liputan6*, June 29, 2019, https://www.liputan6.com/news/read/4001040/jokowi-dorong-peningkatan-kerja-sama-australia-dalam-pendidikan-vokasi [accessed July 7, 2019].

[62] Erman Suparno, *Grand Strategy Manajemen Pembangunan Negara Bangsa* (Jakarta: Empowering Society Institute, 2009), 100.

[63] Ibid.

[64] https://web.facebook.com/dialog/send?app_id=1645337432347069&link=https%3A%2F%2Fwww.idntiidn.com%2Fbusiness%2Feconomy%2Findianamalia%2Fjokowi-

Indonesian start-ups attain "Unicorn" status (a Unicorn is a start-up with a valuation of more than US$1 billion). Currently, the country has produced four Unicorns, namely e-commerce companies Tokopedia and Bukalapak, travel booker Traveloka, and the iconic Gojek. Initially a ride-hailing app which transformed the Jakarta transport sector, Gojek is now a multi-faceted digital payment platform expanding rapidly into international markets. Opening the Ideafest 2018 technology convention in Jakarta, Jokowi expressed his hopes for more success stories: "In the last five or six years there have been four Unicorns. I want more than that," he said.[65]

That year, 2018, Indonesia's digital economy grew to an overall value of US$27 billion, a massive surge in a very short space of time, driven in particular by the expansion of the e-commerce sector. During a "National Online Shopping Day" promoted in December 2018, participating platforms recorded transactions worth a total Rp6.8 trillion, and Indonesia's e-commerce sector was identified as the fastest growing anywhere in the world.[66] Online travel companies also showed dramatic growth.

Under Jokowi, the Ministry of Communication and Informatics (Kominfo) has been seeking ways to encourage the development of start-ups. Indonesia's potential domestic market alone is enormous, the largest in Asia after China and India.[67] Prior to the start of the Covid-19 pandemic, the value of Indonesia's digital economy was expected to reach around US$130 billion in 2020, approximately 11 percent of gross domestic product. Clearly, however, this potential can be expanded further by improvements to both infrastructure and regulatory frameworks. Programs to improve broadband access are already underway,[68] and Jokowi has continually pressed for bureaucratic reform and internal deregulation, with a trimming of Indonesia's approximately 42,000 innovation-hindering regulations.[69] It was, after all, the frustrations of Surakarta's business community with bureaucracy and red tape that provided his first push towards politics, back in 2004.

---

masa-depan-ekonomi-indonesia-di-tangan-millennials [accessed July 27, 2019].

[65] Andina Librianty, "Jokowi: Pemerintah Akan Terus Dorong Kehadiran Startup Unicorn Baru," *Liputan6*, January 11, 2019, https://www.liputan6.com/tekno/read/3868252/jokowi-pemer-intah-akan-terus-dorong-kehadiran-startup-unicorn-baru [accessed July 15, 2019].

[66] "Not all bad in 2018: Indonesian economic review," *The Jakarta Post*, December 26, 2018, https://www.thejakartapost.com/news/2018/12/26/not-all-bad-in-2018-indonesian-econom-ic-review.html [accessed October 28, 2020].

[67] Librianty, "Jokowi: Pemerintah Akan Terus Dorong Kehadiran Startup Unicorn Baru."

[68] Setneg, *Laporan 4 Tahun Pemerintahan Jokowi-JK*, 31.

[69] Hasbullah, "Ini Isi Lengkap Pidato Visi Indonesia Presiden Terpilih Jokowi," *Times Indonesia*, July 14, 2019, https://www.timesindonesia.co.id/read/news/220379/ini-isi-lengkap-pidato-visi-indonesia-presiden-terpilih-jokowi [accessed July 15, 2019].

On a *blusukan* visit to an Indonesian village.

Chapter Eight

Pulang Kampung: Beyond the Cities

Going for Gold: Jokowi's Fourth Year in Office

In late November 2017, a month after Jokowi had marked the beginning of his fourth full year as president, Gunung Agung erupted. The 3,031-meter volcano that dominates Bali had been rumbling for several months. But the magmatic eruption that began on November 25 was something out of the ordinary. Flights were diverted, Bali's airport was closed, and tens of thousands of people were evacuated from their homes. It was the first of a series of violent natural events in the coming year, unusual in their frequency and severity even by Indonesia's geologically unstable standards. The tectonic rumbling of 2017–18 would serve as an ominous overture for the presidential election of 2019. Nonetheless, Jokowi would finish his fourth year in a relatively solid position.

At the start of 2018, he reshuffled his cabinet for the third time. This was likely to be the final chance to change the ministerial team ahead of the 2019 election: once the campaign period formally began towards the end of the year, the presidency would go into a sort of holding pattern, with no major formal changes. The January reshuffle was, on the face of it, a minor one. Minister of social affairs Khofifah Indar Parawansa had resigned to run for governor of East Java in upcoming regional elections. She was replaced by Golkar's Idrus Marham.[1] The cabinet was also

---

[1] Erin Cook, "What Does Indonesia's New Cabinet Reshuffle Mean for Jokowi's Future?" *The Diplomat*, January 27, 2018, https://thediplomat.com/2018/01/what-does-indonesias-new-cabinet-reshuffle-mean-for-jokowis-future/ [accessed October 26, 2020].

joined by formidable retired military man Moeldoko, who became the new presidential chief of staff. There were now three Golkar figures in the cabinet,[2] and Jokowi looked to have created a robust party-based foundation for his re-election campaign, consolidating the backing he would receive from Golkar ahead of time. Moeldoko, meanwhile, was understood to have had his own presidential ambitions, but the appointment placed him firmly within the Jokowi camp.

There were now three retired generals in the cabinet, the others being Wiranto and Luhut Binsar Pandjaitan. This fact attracted a certain amount of critical attention. But it is important to recognize that the military element was only one part of the multifaceted careers of Wiranto and Luhut, in particular. Wiranto was also the former leader of a political party (Hanura), while Luhut was a former ambassador, a former minister (in Abdurrahman Wahid's government), and also, since 2009, Jokowi's business partner in a furniture export venture.[3] They were arguably not appointed as former generals, or certainly not exclusively in that capacity. Nonetheless, a certain security emphasis in the government played well a few months later, in the aftermath of a major terrorist attack in Surabaya, East Java capital and Indonesia's second largest city.

On the morning of May 13, suicide bombers attacked three Surabaya churches, killing fifteen people as well as themselves. Shockingly, the attackers belonged to a single family and women and young children were amongst the bombers. The following day, another family attacked the city's police headquarters. These were the deadliest terrorist attacks in Indonesia in many years. After a spate of bombings in the early 2000s, security forces appeared to have successfully broken up local terrorist networks. There had been a smaller attack in Jakarta in early 2016, but the Surabaya bombings came as a major shock to a country in which many people felt the threat of terrorism had receded. The attackers were members of a local Islamic State-affiliated group, and concerns about IS-linked violence were heightened by the fact that just a few days earlier there had been a deadly riot led by convicted terrorists in a prison in Depok on the outskirts of Jakarta.

---

[2] Andrew Wong, "Indonesian leader's third cabinet reshuffle could have elections implications," CNBC, January 19, 2018, https://www.cnbc.com/2018/01/19/third-reshuffle-in-five-years-may-help-joko-widodo-secure-his-next-term-advisory-says.html [accessed October 26, 2020].

[3] Hasyim Widhiarto and Kusumari Ayuningtyas, "Furniture business propels Jokowi's path to prominence," The Jakarta Post, June 30, 2014, https://www.thejakartapost.com/news/2014/06/30/furniture-business-propels-jokowi-s-path-to-prominence.html [accessed October 26, 2020].

In the aftermath of the attacks, Jokowi moved swiftly to strengthen police powers. On May 25, the DPR voted through a new antiterrorism law, allowing for extended detention of suspected terrorists by police, and mandating an upgraded role for the military in counterterrorism.[4] Jokowi had been able to hurry the bill through the legislature having warned that he would resort once again to a Perppu, a Regulation in Lieu of Law, if parliamentarians stalled its progress.[5]

On June 27, millions of Indonesians went to the local polls to elect a total of 171 governors, mayors, and regents.[6] The results were a mixed picture. Although PDI-P did not do particularly well,[7] Jokowi had a wider and well-established supporting coalition by this stage, and taken as a whole his backers did reasonably well in the elections. In West Java, for example, a solid Prabowo stronghold in 2014, a decent majority of votes went to Jokowi-backing parties and candidates.[8] The president had reason to be reasonably confident as his next electoral battle approached. But first he had to choose a new running mate.

Jokowi would have been happy to continue with Jusuf Kalla as his vice president in a second term. The pair had had a solid working relationship throughout the previous four years. But Kalla had previously served as vice president to Susilo Bambang Yudhoyono in his first term, and the constitution placed a limit of two terms on any president or vice president. Naturally, in most cases that would mean two consecutive terms, so constitutional debate arose over whether Kalla might, in fact, still be eligible for the 2019–24 term. But in June, the Constitutional Court rejected petitions to review the regulation,[9] and Jokowi was faced with the challenge of finding a fresh partner for the 2019 race.

---

[4] Erwidia Maulia, "Indonesia passes tougher terror law after Surabaya attacks," *Nikkei Asia*, May 25, 2018, https://asia.nikkei.com/Politics/Indonesia-passes-tougher-terror-law-after-Surabaya-attacks [accessed October 26, 2020].

[5] Ahmad Ibrahim Almuttaqi, *Jokowi's Indonesia and the World* (Singapore: World Scientific Publishing, 2020), 105.

[6] Andhika Prasetia, "Ini 171 Daerah yang Gelar Pilkada Serentak 27 Juni 2018," *detikNews*, April 20, 2017, https://news.detik.com/berita/d-3479819/ini-171-daerah-yang-gelar-pilkada-serentak-27-juni-2018 [accessed October 26, 2020].

[7] Almuttaqi, *Jokowi's Indonesia and the World*, 100.

[8] Tasha Wibawa, "Joko Widodo faces challenges in 2019 Indonesia poll as blank ballots, child marriages spark regional dissatisfaction," ABC, July 7, 2018, https://www.abc.net.au/news/2018-07-08/indonesians-cast-blank-votes-in-crucial-local-elections/9943300 [accessed October 26, 2020].

[9] "Indonesia's Constitutional Court refuses to pave way for V-P Jusuf Kalla to seek third term," *The Straits Times*, June 29, 2018, https://www.straitstimes.com/asia/se-asia/indonesias-constitutional-court-refuses-to-pave-way-for-v-p-jusuf-kalla-to-seek-third-term [accessed October 26, 2020].

On the evening of August 9, 2018, just one day ahead of the deadline for submission of candidates to the Electoral Commission (KPU), the media gathered at the upmarket Plataran Restaurant in the Menteng District of central Jakarta. Jokowi appeared flanked by the leaders of the various parties backing his second run. The "Awesome Indonesia Coalition" of 2014 had been replaced by the more stolid-sounding Koalisi Indonesia Kerja (KIK), the "Working Indonesia Coalition." While the emphasis in 2014 had been on freshness and excitement, this time the aim was to stress Jokowi's continued focus on development and his record for getting things done. With Megawati seated to his right and Nasdem Party chair Surya Paloh on his left, Jokowi confirmed that he would himself be running again, to a ripple of applause. He then went on to explain "a very important decision" in a barrage of press photographers' flashbulbs. Having taken account of various advice and opinions, he said, he had decided with the approval of his coalition that "the one who will be accompanying me as the vice presidential candidate for the 2019–2024 period will be Professor Doctor Kyai Haji Ma'ruf Amin."[10]

The announcement was a genuine surprise. Many observers had expected that Jokowi would choose former justice and human rights minister and Constitutional Court judge Mahfud MD. And until the August 9 gathering there had never been any serious speculation around Ma'ruf Amin as a potential candidate.

Amin was leader of the Nahdlatul Ulama (NU) and also chair of Indonesia's main Islamic clerical body, the Majelis Ulama Indonesia, or MUI. He was from NU's more conservative side, and as MUI chair he had been central to the clerical condemnation of Ahok for blasphemy two years earlier. Some of Jokowi's more secular-minded supporters were disappointed by the decision, with some even threatening to boycott the election in protest. International media tended to refer to Amin as a "hard-line cleric."[11] But it was a carefully considered choice, one that bolstered the closeness Jokowi had signaled to NU in recent years, and that went a long way to neutralize the anticipated attacks on the allegedly weak Muslim credentials of his campaign. The move also reassured the leadership of the NU-linked PKB, one of Jokowi's key party backers. There had been recent

---

[10] "Resmi, Jokowi dan Ma'ruf Amin, Capres-Cawapres 2019," YouTube, https://www.youtube.com/watch?v=bAiAspanZxc [accessed 26 October 2020].

[11] Tasha Wibawa, "Why has Indonesian President Joko Widodo picked a hard-line cleric as his running mate?" ABC, August 17, 2018, https://www.abc.net.au/news/2018-08-18/joko-widodo-picks-a-hardline-muslim-cleric-as-his-running-mate/10117820 [accessed October 26, 2020].

rumors that they were considering pulling out of the arrangement,[12] but with a major NU figure running for vice president, they were now much more firmly wedded to the coalition.

There was another factor at play in Jokowi's choice. The role of the vice president is not, of itself, particularly powerful, but it can be seen as a stepping-stone to the presidency itself. No one, however, thought that Ma'ruf Amin had presidential ambitions. Despite a minor, and long-past parliamentary career, he was a cleric and academic first and foremost. He was also seventy-five years old. In terms of active party politics, he was an unthreatening figure, and by choosing him Jokowi had actually further consolidated his coalition. There could be no grumbling about favoritism or worries that he had already anointed a preferred successor.

Jokowi's vice presidential choice also scored him an early goal against his challenger. Once again, he would be running against Prabowo Subianto. But this time Prabowo's coalition looked much shakier at the outset. Like Jokowi, he had waited until very late in the day to confirm his running mate, Jakarta vice-governor Sandiaga Uno, a fellow Gerindra member. Although Sandiaga announced he would quit the party ahead of the campaign,[13] Prabowo had, in effect, announced a one-party ticket, which alarmed some other members of his coalition and prompted some angry accusations. His pairing also lacked obvious Islamic credentials, certainly in comparison to the Jokowi-Ma'ruf ticket. Jokowi looked to be entering the race with a solid advantage.

Nine days after the announcement of Ma'ruf as vice presidential candidate, the 18th Asian Games got underway in Jakarta. The opening ceremony was a lavish affair, beginning with a slick and humorous stunt. Huge screens in the Bung Karno Stadium in Jakarta showed prerecorded footage of Jokowi's motorcade stuck in traffic en route to the event, and the president apparently taking to a high-powered motorbike to complete the journey. The footage, with its heavy metal soundtrack, was perfectly choreographed with the arrival of a stunt rider in the stadium and the real Jokowi's appearance in the VIP box.

The games ran for two weeks, with events split between Jakarta and Palembang in South Sumatra. They were widely praised for their professional organization, and the hosts did well, taking thirty-one golds and

---

[12] Ibid.

[13] Kristian Erdianto, "Jadi Cawapres Prabowo, Sandiaga Keluar dari Gerindra," *Kompas*, August 9, 2018, https://nasional.kompas.com/read/2018/08/09/23573541/jadi-cawapres-prabowo-sandiaga-keluar-dari-gerindra [accessed October 26, 2020].

ending up fourth in the medal tables overall.[14] It was a rare non-political moment that captured nationwide attention and created a genuine atmosphere of enthusiastic unity. And Jokowi's own involvement helped to reboot the youth-appeal element of his personal brand. The only shadow was that cast by natural events elsewhere in Indonesia.

On August 5, a powerful earthquake had rocked Lombok, followed by a series of ferocious aftershocks throughout the month, with one on August 19 as powerful as the original quake. More than 500 people were killed and tens of thousands were left homeless. Jokowi skipped the closing ceremony of the Asian Games to visit an evacuation camp on the island. There was a certain amount of criticism from NGOs that the Indonesian authorities had not declared a national disaster, which, they claimed, would have allowed for the flow of foreign aid. But as cabinet secretary Pramono Anung pointed out, there were other factors under consideration, not least the long-term impact on the local tourist industry, especially in the Mandalika SEZ. "Once declared as a national disaster, tourists will be barred from entering the entire Lombok island, and that will cause even more losses," Pramono told reporters. "It could have an overwhelming effect that the public are not aware of."[15]

The Lombok earthquake paled into insignificance alongside another geological disaster the following month. On September 28, a huge 7.5-magnitude earthquake hit Central Sulawesi, triggering a tsunami which devastated the Palu region. Well over 4,000 people were killed. There was considerable criticism when it later emerged that offshore monitoring systems were not working at the time, and that the inadequate tsunami warnings issued had been based on modeling rather than live data.

The natural disasters brought a touch of tragedy to the final weeks of Jokowi's fourth full year in office. But more generally, he had good reason to feel confident and proud. The rupiah was still weak, largely because of high international oil prices and high interest rates in the USA. Indonesia's central bank raised its own interest rates six times across 2018, which helped to stabilize the currency. More generally, however, it had been a year of solid economic advances. The economy had expanded by 5.2 percent in the first three-quarters of the year. There had been excellent growth in information and communications and in the transport and storage

---

[14] Stephen Wright, "Asian Games stir Indonesia's pride, boost Jokowi's campaign,"AP, September 3, 2018, https://apnews.com/article/aab2cd47401947bea366f896240a4f70 [accessed October 27, 2020].

[15] "Govt Says Lombok Quake Not National Disaster," *Tempo*, August 20, 2018, https://en.tempo.co/read/920968/govt-says-lombok-quake-not-national-disaster [accessed October 27, 2020].

sectors.[16] But the major driver of domestic growth was infrastructure investment. Of the 223 "National Strategic Projects" that Jokowi's team had identified at the start of his presidency, 36 were already complete and around 100 others were already in progress.[17] In early October, a further 79 key infrastructure projects were unveiled, with state-owned enterprises actively encouraged to partner with private-sector investors to fund the developments.[18] After a somewhat slow start, the dramatic physical overhaul of the country that Jokowi had always planned was now fully underway.

But the transformation was not restricted to eye-catching mega-projects, the bridges and toll roads and ports. The third element of the Nawacita framework had called for the development of Indonesia from the "peripheries," which meant marginalized economic and social areas as well as outlying geographical regions. A national poverty rate of 11 percent at the start of Jokowi's presidency had fallen to 9 percent by the end of his first term, and by 2018 his policies were already having an impact in many villages and rural communities.

Going Back to the Villages

Though he grew up in an urban environment, as a child Jokowi had strong connections to his ancestral villages in the countryside north of Surakarta. His immediate family belonged a demographic that has been renewed in Indonesian cities decade after decade: those who make the move from the villages in search of a better life and who tend to retain strong rural links for at least a generation of two. Many city-born Indonesians still talk of *pulang kampung*, "going home to the village" during national holidays or for major family events.

Jokowi had spent the first forty days of his life in his mother's home place, Gumuk Rejo hamlet, Giriroto village.[19] Throughout his childhood, he often went to visit relatives there and in Kragan, Gondangrejo District,

[16] "Indonesia: Year in Review 2018," *Oxford Business Group*, January 29, 2019, https://oxfordbusinessgroup.com/news/indonesia-year-review-2018 [accessed October 27, 2020].

[17] "Indonesia's leader, Jokowi, is splurging on infrastructure," *The Economist*, May 5, 2018, https://www.economist.com/asia/2018/05/05/indonesias-leader-jokowi-is-splurging-on-infrastructure [accessed October 27, 2020].

[18] "Diversified financing to boost private investment in Indonesian infrastructure," *Oxford Business Group*, November 21, 2018, https://oxfordbusinessgroup.com/news/diversified-financing-boost-private-investment-indonesian-infrastructure [accessed October 27, 2020].

[19] Deden Gunawan and Ibad Durohman, "Kisah Mulyono Menjadi Joko Widodo," *detikNews*, January 14, 2017, https://news.detik.com/x/detail/investigasi/20170113/Kisah-Mulyono-Menjadi-Joko-Widodo/ [accessed September 11, 2020].

where his paternal grandfather, Wiryo Miharjo, was still serving as *lurah*, or headman. Jokowi was familiar from childhood with both the tight-knit nature of the Indonesian village community with its strong ethos of *gotong-royong* and also with the stifling lack of opportunity, the potholed roads, and the rudimentary infrastructure which had compelled his own father to leave in search of greater economic and social mobility, despite his being the son of the respected village leader.[20]

Nearly half of Indonesia's population still lives in rural areas, and there are 74,093 villages across the country. According to official data, in 2014 of these villages 20,432 were designated as underdeveloped, with the greatest concentration in that category (6,139) to be found in Papua. Typically, a village classified as "underdeveloped" has a range of limitations, including poor infrastructure, and a lack of access to public services.[21]

For farmers, poor road infrastructure hampers their ability to bring crops to market and leaves them open to the depredations of exploitative middlemen. Lack of irrigation infrastructure, meanwhile, limits productivity.[22] Village children may find it difficult to access education and hospitals and clinics may be out of reach. As a result, the productivity of villages and villagers is low. According to government statistics, in 2014 there were 17.7 million Indonesian villagers living in poverty.[23] All this fuels a continuing drift from villages to cities, the same journey undertaken by Jokowi's father in the late 1950s. Villages are left with an ever-increasing demographic imbalance, which hollows out their communities. The 2013 Agricultural Census found that 60.79 percent of Indonesian farmers were over forty-five years of age.

In an effort to mitigate these perennial problems, at the start of his first term as president, Jokowi allocated a "Village Fund" (Dana Desa) of Rp20.7 trillion to be disbursed to and managed by village communities. This was another aspect of his stated ethos of encouraging development from the periphery.[24] From year to year across his first term, the funding for villages increased. By 2019, a total of Rp257 trillion had been allocated.

---

[20] Wawan Mas'udi and Akhmad Ramdhon, *Jokowi: dari Bantaran Kalianyar ke Istana* (Jakarta: Gramedia Pustaka Utama, 2018), 67.

[21] "Indeks Pembangunan Desa 2014" and "Tantangan Pemenuhan Standar Pelayanan Minimum Desa 2015," 33.

[22] Ibid, 34.

[23] BPS, "Berita Resmi Statistik, Profil Kemiskinan di Indonesia Maret 2014," Berita Statistik Nomor 52/07/Th.XVII, July 1, 2014, 2.

[24] Humas, "Dana Desa, Pemerintahan Jokowi Wujudkan Kedaulatan Desa," Sekretariat Kabinet Republik Indonesia, https://setkab.go.id/dana-desa-pemerintahan-jokowi-wujud-kan-kedaulatan-desa/ [accessed May 3, 2019].

In front of thousands of participants at the April 2019 all-Indonesia National Gathering of Village Governments (Silaturahmi Nasional Pemerintah Desa) at the Bung Karno Stadium, venue for the Asian Games the previous year, Jokowi said, "The village is always in my thoughts and in my heart. Not because I come from a village; it's not just that. I think building villages means building Indonesia."

Since the 1970s there have been a series of interventions intended to better the condition of Indonesia's villages. But these have tended to be issued from the center and then administered by village authorities without any direct community input. Jokowi intended to revise this approach: villagers are generally well aware of what they need. They know the areas where roads need to be built. They know their own irrigation needs better than anyone, and their main aspiration is the obvious one: to increase their own productivity and standard of living.[25]

In implementing this, Jokowi once again picked up on work begun by the previous administration. A new 2014 law on villages provided a framework in which the village would no longer be the object of development, but its subject and spearhead.[26] Jokowi's Village Fund program used this framework, with development funds to be channeled directly from the national budget to village government accounts, to allow for local agency in their use according to unique local needs. Under the program, villagers are able to decide themselves through local meetings how to use their Village Fund allocation without being hampered by strictures from the subdistrict, district government, or provincial government levels.[27]

Umbul Ponggok: A Village Success Story

A classic example of proactive use of the Village Fund is Umbul Ponggok in the Klaten Regency of Central Java, a place which has found nationwide fame for its grassroots economic transformation.

Umbul Ponggok was once a poor community where most residents worked in agriculture or in local quarries. But change began with the

[25] Domu D. Ambarita, *Jokowi Spirit Bantaran Kali Anyar* (Jakarta: Elex Media Komputindo, 2012), 18–19.

[26] Ryan Dwiky Anggriawan, "Fakta-fakta Seputar Dana Desa yang Cair di Masa Jokowi," *Tempo*, February 22, 2019, https://nasional.tempo.co/read/1178318/fakta-fakta-seputar-dana-desa-yang-cair-di-masa-jokowi [accessed October 26, 2020].

[27] A. Mukhtar Hadisaputra, "Perencanaan Pembangunan Desa," *AFPM*, April 18, 2016, http://afpmidpwjatim.blogspot.com/2016/04/perencanaan-pembangunan-desa.html [accessed February 12, 2019].

election of a progressive new village head, Junaedi Mulyono, in 2006, at a time when Jokowi himself was still settling into his first year as mayor of Surakarta, twenty kilometers to the east. Mulyono began by systematically identifying the village's needs and economic weaknesses with the aid of students from Jokowi's own alma mater, UGM. He then set about encouraging villagers to sign up for a Village-owned Enterprise with the intention of turning Umbul Ponggok into a tourist destination.[28] A muddy pond was cleaned out and turned into a waterpark for visitors, and soon the place was attracting a steady stream of domestic tourists. Of the 700 households in the village, 430 put money into the project, and as investors they now receive a solid monthly income from its profits. In 2006, the annual village income was Rp80 million; by 2019, it had risen to Rp14 billion.[29]

Clearly, the village already had a progressive self-motivating attitude, and once it gained access to Jokowi's Village Fund it used it to continue its self-improvement, with better infrastructure, improved irrigation, and further tourism facilities. Scholarships for local children are provided from the Village Fund development proceeds,[30] which also cover the premiums for villagers' membership of the national health insurance scheme.[31]

Other villages in Indonesia have followed Umbul Ponggok's lead and used the Village Fund to develop tourist facilities. The residents of Pujon Kidul near Malang in East Java used a Village Fund investment of Rp60 mill to develop physical tourism infrastructure, targeted at the large domestic market which the wider Malang area already attracts.[32] It now receives a steady flow of vacationing families and Instagrammers from Surabaya and other big cities who come to enjoy the cool mountain landscapes.[33]

---

[28] Hendra Cipto, "Jokowi: Desa Ponggok Bisa Jadi Contoh, Pendapatannya Rp 14 Miliar Per Tahun," *Kompas*, December 22, 2018, https://makassar.kompas.com/read/2018/12/22/11423271/jokowi-desa-ponggok-bisa-jadi-contohpendapatannya-rp-14-miliarper-tahun [accessed May 3, 2019].

[29] Ainur Rohmah, "How a village pond became a quirky tourist attraction in Indonesia in the social media age," *South China Morning Post*, August 5, 2019, https://www.scmp.com/lifestyle/travel-leisure/article/3021430/how-village-pond-became-quirky-tourist-attraction [accessed September 28, 2020].

[30] Ibid.

[31] Anissa Dea Widiarini, "Kisah Pujon Kidul, Sukses Kelola Dana Desa Hingga Berhasil Tingkatkan PADes," *Kompas*, May 8, 2019, https://kilaskementerian.kompas.com/kemendes/read/2019/05/08/14433161/kisah-pujon-kidul-sukses-kelola-danadesahingga-berhasil-tingkatkan-pades [accessed August 23, 2019].

[32] www.sie.pujonkidul.desa.id/ [accessed February 15, 2019].

[33] Fitri Syarifah, "Dalam KIS, Jokowi Akan Ubah Istilah 'Rakyat Miskin,'" *Liputan6*, June 17, 2014, https://www.liputan6.com/health/read/2064398/dalam-kis-jokowi-akan-ubah-istilah-rakyat-miskin [accessed February 2, 2019].

Elsewhere, Segara Jaya, a fishing village in Bekasi Regency, West Java, has used the Village Fund to diversify its economy and make use of its natural surroundings, in particular its expanses of mangrove forest, as an ecotourism location. By attracting visitors, mainly domestic tourists from the Greater Jakarta area, the local community has been able to expand its long-established seaweed industry, creatively processing seaweed into superior food products for sale to sightseers instead of simply passing it on to buyers as a raw material. The local batik industry has also been boosted by direct access to the tourist market.[34]

In more remote regions, however, the Village Fund has often been used to meet much more basic needs. In Pasi Padangan on tiny Muna Island in Southeast Sulawesi, the residents have used the cash to address their most essential requirement for survival: water.[35] With no adequate springs on the island, the 500 members of this small fishing community previously had to collect their drinking water by boat from another village an hour away. However, the Village Fund has been used to install a desalination plant on the island to supply fresh water directly. The fund was also used to obtain generators, allowing villagers to refrigerate their catches ahead of transportation to market and to provide electrical lighting after dark.[36]

Elsewhere, as in Nggumbelaka village near Ende in Flores, East Nusa Tenggara,[37] Village Fund cash has been used to improve road access to allow ease of access to markets, thus boosting local incomes from agriculture. Similarly, in Gunung Makmur village in East Kalimantan,[38] Village Fund-supported transport infrastructure has allowed local farmers to reduce their reliance on exploitative middlemen to get their crops to market, while in Kaongkeongkea village in Southeast Sulawesi,[39] a Village Fund-supported road-building project intended to ease the transport of

---

[34] "Desa Pasi Padangan Menggunakan Dana Desa untuk Mengolah Air," available at https://inovasidesa.kemendesa.go.id/desa-pasi-padangan-dana-desa-untuk-penyulingan-air-laut-dan-listrik-desa/ [accessed August 24, 2019].

[35] https://inovasidesa.kemendesa.go.id/desa-nggumbelaka-gelorakan-hortikultura-dari-utara-ende/ [accessed July 1, 2019].

[36] Mas'udi and Ramdhon, *Jokowi: dari Bantaran Kalianyar ke Istana*, 88.

[37] "Desa Gunung Makmur dan Sebakung Jaya Adalan Kecamatan Babulu," *Vivaborneo*, http://www.vivaborneo.com/?p=37272 [accessed August 24, 2019].

[38] Sigiranus Marutho Bere, "Atraksi Kebudayaan di PLBN Motaain Akan Tarik Wisatawan Timor Leste," *Kompas*, October 6, 2018, https://travel.kompas.com/read/2018/10/06/100300827/atraksi-kebudayaan-di-plbn-motaain-akan-tarik-wisatawan-timor-leste?page=all [accessed August 10, 2019].

[39] Nursodik Gunarjo, *Nawacita Meretas Indonesia Maju* (Jakarta: Kominfo, 2016), 32.

local coffee crops also created an unexpected local tourism boom around a nearby waterfall.

For Jokowi, the Village Fund scheme has been both a necessary complement to the large-scale development programs, filling uniquely local gaps in nation- or islandwide energy, infrastructure, or welfare projects, and a means of empowering village communities, giving them the potential to emerge from the torpor which, many decades ago, compelled his own father to leave Kragan in search of a more dynamic existence in Surakarta. However, some of the developmental requirements of rural areas do demand direct interventions from the center, not least large-scale water supply solutions.

Rural Water Supplies: The Key to Food Security

Thinking back to his childhood, Jokowi still recalls the dramatic seasonal difference in the environment around his mother's home in Gumuk Rejo, Giriroto. During the rains, the crops thrived on the villagers' land and the scenery was dominated by green. But when the dry season began, the villagers stopped farming. The ricefields were left to go dry and soon became parched and cracked. The reason for this was simply that there was no water supply to irrigate the fields during the dry season, and without water, farming is impossible. The residents of Giriroto were able to cultivate only one crop a year and so had little chance to earn a decent living from their land.[40] They were not poor because they were lazy; they were poor because of structural poverty: they received no helping hand from the government to increase their earning potential.

Irrigation reservoirs at the village level are a less dramatic form of infrastructure than airports and toll roads. But they are essential to boosting prosperity in rural Indonesia. Despite the country's monsoon climate, water shortages have always been a part of rural life. The complex irrigations networks developed over many centuries in Java and Bali were designed to maintain a flow to the ricefields through the long dry months in the middle of the year. And *embung* (irrigation reservoirs) were constructed by local kings to support their subjects. The Dutch colonial authorities also built *embung* but these did not extend their reach to every farming community. Although the Cengklik Reservoir, built in the 1920s by the Dutch in cooperation with the Mangkunegaran Palace, Surakarta's

---

[40] Nawacita Institute, *Wujud Kerja Nyata* (Jakarta: Republika, 2017), 226.

junior royal house, was close to Giriroto,[41] its network did not extend to the fields around Jokowi's mother's village.

As part of a nationwide *embung*-building program, in 2018 the village finally got its own 1.3-hectare reservoir, with a capacity of 48,000 cubic meters. The water gathered here during the rainy season is stored to provide irrigation during the dry months, greatly extending the growing period for Giriroto's farmers.

The poorest regions of Indonesia are often also the driest. East Nusa Tenggara, for example, has patchy rainfall and none of the lush tropical conditions of Java. Rice agriculture is limited here, and maize and cassava are staple crops. To mitigate this, Jokowi's administration built seven new dams and dozens of smaller *embung* in the region during his first term. In the Rote Ndao Regency, which lies off the coast near Kupang in West Timor, a total of seventy-four *embung* were constructed. Jokowi made a visit to the village of Oelolot in Rote Ndao in January 2018 to see one of these new reservoirs.

"We saw earlier that around the *embung* the community have embraced it by making new ricefields, then planting them. Above [the reservoir] I saw maizefields [which require less water]; below I saw that the rice was starting to be planted," he said while speaking to villagers and visiting journalists.[42]

On the national level, Jokowi issued a special Presidential Instruction to accelerate the construction of *embung*, with a five-year target to build 1,053 across the country, of which 949 had been built by 2019. In poor and dry regions like Rote Ndao, where subsistence farming is still common, this was not simply a matter of improving agricultural incomes but of survival, which in turn is linked to the demands of Indonesia's 1945 Constitution, Article 33 Paragraph 3,[43] according to which the state is obliged to use natural resources maximally for the prosperity of the people and to strive for the fulfillment of food needs for the population.

---

[41] Mas'udi and Ramdhon, *Jokowi: dari Bantaran Kalianyar ke Istana*, 89.

[42] "Tinjau Embung Saina, Presiden Jokowi: Pemerintah Bangun 74 Embung di Rote Ndao," available at https://dinaspuprovntt.blogspot.com/2018/01/tinjau-embung-saina-presiden-jokowi.html; http://setkab.go.id/tinjau-embung-saina-presiden-jokowi-pemerintah-bangun-74-embung-di-rote-ndao/ [accessed May 30, 2019].

[43] Syahrir Ika, "Kedaulatan Pangan dan Kecukupan Pangan: Negara Wajib Mewujudkannya," *Kemenkeu*, https://www.kemenkeu.go.id/sites/default/files/2014_kajian_pprf_kedaulatan%20pangan%20dan%20kecukupan%20pangan.pdf.

Regreening the Forests in the Name of Poverty Elimination

One of the key events of Jokowi's childhood was his family's eviction from their rented home on the banks of the Kali Anyar. The experience informed his understanding of the adult world and of the relationship between the state and its citizens, which in turn went on to inform the "humanizing", dialogic approach he developed as mayor of Surakarta.[44] Practically speaking, the eviction arose from an issue has affected countless lives across Indonesia for decades: insecurity of land tenure. In urban areas, this might lead to an uncompensated eviction and demolition to make way for a new development; in rural areas, it can result in protracted clashes between entire communities and companies granted forestry, mining, or other development concessions.

Communities living on marginal agricultural land, or in the vast areas of forest that still cover parts of Indonesia, have often faced eviction from land they have worked on for decades.[45] Indeed, the land may have been cultivated by the same families for generations without them ever possessing proper legal title. According to data from the Consortium for Agrarian Reform, in 2016 there were at least 450 agrarian conflicts in Indonesia, involving a total area of 1.2 million hectares and 86,745 households. That number had increased from 252 conflicts in 2015.

The roots of such agrarian conflict can often be traced back to the Dutch colonial period, when areas of land traditionally held by local communities was requisitioned for commercial plantations or designated for forestry concessions. In some cases, these concessions were never taken up, but the designation remained in place into the era of Indonesia's independence, leaving the traditional occupants ever vulnerable. Under Sukarno, the process of nationalizing land portioned up by the previous colonial authorities sometimes entrenched this vulnerability. State companies and large private corporations were empowered to manage nationalized agrarian resources and used claims on plantation and forestry land, the boundaries of which had been drawn up in the colonial era. Again,

---

[44] Alberthiene Endah, *Jokowi Memimpin Kota Menyentuh Jakarta* (Solo: Metagraf, 2012), 108–22.

[45] Rasyid Ridha Saragih and Kiai Nur Aziz, "Perlawanan Petani Kendal: Kronologi Konflik Lahan Antara Warga Surokonto Wetan dan PT Perhutani Kab. Kendal, Jawa Tengah," https://daulathijau.wordpress.com/2016/04/07/perlawanan-petani-kendal-kronologi-konflik-lahan-antara-warga-surokonto-wetan-dan-pt-perhutani-kab-kendal-jawa-tengah/ [accessed February 17, 2019].

under Suharto the massive extraction of agrarian resources was an aspect of economic development,[46] and the task of that exploitation was often handed to large companies owned by cronies of the regime.

With his own childhood experience of insecurity brought about by lack of land title, and with his academic and professional background in forestry, Jokowi came to the presidency with a pledge to begin an ambitious process of agrarian reform in line with the Nawacita principle of developing Indonesia from the periphery.

Jokowi presented six programmatic outlines for agrarian reform: strengthening the regulatory framework and settling agrarian conflicts; arrangement of land control and ownership; legal certainty and legalization of rights to land; community empowerment in land use; allocation of forest resources for community management; and the institution for implementing central and regional agrarian reform. One aspect of this was a push to speed up the issuing of land certificates by the National Land Agency (BPN) from around 500,000 a year in 2016 to 5 million by 2017.

"I worked out that if only 500,000 certificates a year [were issued], while 80 million were still lacking, it means that you would have to wait 160 years. Can you wait 160 years or not? Waiting 160 years means there will be more disputes," said Jokowi during an event to distribute land ownership certification to thousands of East Kalimantan residents in Samarinda in October 2018.[47]

Another dramatic manifestation of agrarian reform was a highly ambitious pledge to turn over 12.7 million hectares of state forestry land to communities by 2019.[48] This target was met with skepticism by some critics. However, other commentators lauded its ambition, even if it were to fall short. In the event, only around a third of this amount was made over to communities during Jokowi's first term, but as Delia Catacutan of the World Agroforestry Center has noted, "In the bigger scheme of things, the 4.2 million hectares of licensed land presents significant progress given

[46] Lilis Mulyani, "Kritik atas Penanganan Konflik Agraria di Indonesia," University of Melbourne, 344–45, available at https://www.researchgate.net/publication/263619338_Kritik_atas_Penanganan_Konflik_Agraria di_Indonesia [accessed April 5, 2019].

[47] Pebriansyah Ariefana, "Jokowi Sebut Butuh 160 Tahun Selesaikan Masalah Sertifikat Tanah," *Suara*, October 26, 2018, https://www.suara.com/news/2018/10/26/053000/jokowi-sebut-butuh-160-tahun-selesaikan-masalah-sertifikat-tanah [accessed July 5, 2019].

[48] *Strategi Nasional Pelaksanaan Reforma Agraria 2016–2019*, available at kpa.or.id/publikasi/baca/buku/57/Strategi_Nasional_Pelaksanaan_Reforma_Agraria_2016_-_2019/.

the tumultuous land conflict in Indonesia."[49] No overall target was set for the entirety of Jokowi's second term, and further progress was initially hampered by the Covid-19 pandemic. But annual targets continue to be set and the program is ongoing.

The Community Forest Program

Rural communities living at the edge of forests in Indonesia are typically deeply impoverished. The land is rarely particularly productive compared to the long-established agricultural landscapes of Java and other developed rural areas. The persistent poverty, in turn, exacerbates environmental damage: for example, 58.87 percent of households around forest areas use firewood as their main source of fuel.[50] In 2007, the Central Statistics Agency (BPS) released a report that 5.5 million people were classified as poor around forest areas.[51] Other data suggested a higher number of around 10 million.

In 2017, Jokowi issued Presidential Regulation No. 88 as a form of commitment to recognizing community rights over land in forest areas and mitigating such poverty through the establishment of community forests.

"The spirit of agrarian reform and social forestry is how land and forests, which are part of Indonesia's natural resources, can be accessed by the people and can bring economic justice and prosperity to the people," he said during the signing of the regulation.

The Community Forest Program breaks down into various categories, including Village Forest, where a community can apply for a 35-year permit to manage protected forest areas, with the possibility of a further 35-year extension; Community Forests, where a similar arrangement is provided to organized farmers' groups, and Customary Forests (Hutan Adat), which is an arrangement specifically designed for indigenous peoples in places such as Kalimantan. In the first three years of his administration, Jokowi legalized thirty-three Customary Forests in an effort to prevent agrarian conflicts between indigenous communities and commercial interests.[52]

---

[49] Harry Jacques, "Indonesia inches forward on community forest goal, hobbled by pandemic," *Reuters*, August 6, 2020, https://www.reuters.com/article/us-indonesia-forests-communities-trfn-idUSKCN252194 [accessed September 28, 2020].

[50] BPS, *Ringkasan Eksekutif Survei Rumah Tangga di Sekitar Kawasan Hutan 2014* (Jakarta: Subdirektorat Statistik Kehutanan BPS, 2016), 23.

[51] Myrna A. Safitri, *Menuju Kepastian dan Keadilan Tenurial* (Jakarta: Epistima Institute, 2011), 35.

[52] Ibid., 35–43

With his own Javanese rural background, Jokowi has a particular understanding of the sensitivities around the control of land. In Javanese culture, as in other Indonesian traditions, land is considered an heirloom, to be protected at all costs. As the Javanese proverb has it, *Sadumuk bathuk, sanyari bumi, ditohi pati* (One touch on the forehead or one inch of land: defend it to the death).

Telukjambe in Karawang, around fifty kilometers east of Jakarta, was the scene of one of Indonesia's many long-standing conflicts over land. In this case, the clash was with a developer, PT Pertiwi Lestari, and members of the Telukjambe Bersatu Farmers Union over a 791-hectare area of forest land which had long been regarded as belonging to the local community but which the company had obtained for development. The issues dated from 2012, and there were a series of clashes in 2016 and 2017 over the issue, with local farmers protesting and alleging harassment by the police and the company.[53]

"Our houses were demolished, our agricultural land was destroyed and 64 of our children dropped out of school for eight months," said Maman Nuryaman, chairman of Telukjambe Bersatu Farmers Union. Between 600 and 800 residents, who had occupied the land since 1962, were affected. Following a protest outside the presidential palace in Jakarta, Jokowi met with their representatives and promised to facilitate a settlement. He then assigned the Ministry of Agrarian Affairs and Spatial Planning and the National Land Agency to find a solution. In the end, the villagers received an allocation of alternative land nearby, with full certification for their individual plots.

Another community impacted by land issues is that of Sanca village in Gantar District, Indramayu, a coastal regency east of Jakarta. One local resident, Dasuki, lives at the edge of a forest area but had long felt an anxiety when using the forest for gain, aware of the potential illegality of his actions.[54] However, he has now legally been granted land to work for thirty-five years through the Social Forestry Program. Other Sanca residents have also benefited. Zainal Abidin, a 41-year-old farmer from the hamlet, said he had been able to obtain legal certification for a plot of forest land without having to go through intermediaries or brokers and without having to make any illegal payments. He and Dasuki are among

---

[53] "PT Pertiwi Lestari Bantah Memburu Petani Karawang," *Tempo*, October 19, 2016, https://nasional.tempo.co/read/813358/pt-pertiwi-lestari-bantah-memburu-petani-karawang/full&view=ok [accessed September 28, 2020].

[54] Abdul Rohim, interview with Dasuki, farmer in Indramayu, December 12, 2018.

the members of 217 local families who are now legally working on 350 hectares of forest.[55]

As well as land conflicts, forest fires have been a major issue in Indonesia for decades. Beyond the serious environmental impact of destroying large areas of tree cover, the haze created by massive blazes in Sumatra and Kalimantan leads to clashes with the governments of neighboring countries which suffer from the resultant fog because of prevailing wind directions. While some fires are accidental or sparked by natural causes, many are lit deliberately to clear land for cultivation.

For Jokowi, the Community Forest Program has a potential role in reducing the problematic burning of Indonesia's forests. Communities with a secure sense of ownership of surrounding forests tend to have an interest in preserving them. An example of this can be seen in Tebing Siring village in the Tanah Laut Regency of South Kalimantan. For decades the people living around the forest had used the land at its edge to plant rubber and timber trees and to grow rice, chillies, pumpkins, maize, and other crops. They did not, however, have any legal title to the land and permits were very difficult to obtain. Their efforts to cultivate the forest were thus considered illegal. In 2017, however, under Jokowi's Social Forestry Decree, they finally received official license to control over 400 hectares of land managed by two local farmers' groups. Having gained this security, the community has shifted away from exploiting the land with fast-growing crops planted on land cleared by burning and has begun instead to invest time in more sustainable forest management. There have been no fires in the area in recent years. This, in turn, has contributed to wider efforts to slow the pace of deforestation. According to the Ministry of Environment and Forestry, the annual deforestation rate fell from 1.09 million hectares the year Jokowi became president to 480,000 hectares in 2017.[56]

---

[55] Abdul Rohim, interviews with Sanca village residents, Zainal Abidin, Suparlan, and Tariza, December 12, 2018.

[56] Hugh Biggar, "Forest protection efforts earn Indonesia millions," *Landscape News*, March 25, 2019, https://news.globallandscapesforum.org/33544/forest-protection-efforts-earn-indonesia-millions/ [accessed October 29, 2020].

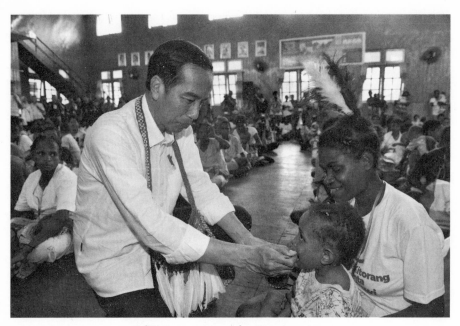

Jokowi on a visit to the Asmat region,
launching a childhood nutrition program.

Chapter Nine

Nation Building: Jokowi and Papua

The Final Stretch: Into the Fifth Year

As Jokowi began his fifth full year as president, Indonesia was already on an election footing. The campaign period had officially begun on September 23 with a pledge from both candidates for an election that would be "safe, orderly, peaceful, honourable and free from hoaxes, SARA [ethnic, religious, racial or inter-group] politicization and vote buying."[1] The election itself was scheduled for April 17, and it would take up much of the political energy of the coming six months.

But there was a still a country to run in the meantime, and by this stage Jokowi's infrastructure drive was going at full tilt. Over the course of the year, government expenditure reached 99.2 percent of the total allocated budget, at US$155 billion,[2] with lavish spending on development projects. In March, a month before the election, Jokowi would formally open the Jakarta Metro, a project which he had broken the ground on as the city's governor. The first 15.7-kilometer line had thirteen stops and had been built with Japanese investment, and as it opened to passengers construction

---

[1] Karina M. Tehusijarana, "Election campaign kicks off with peace pledge," *The Jakarta Post*, September 23, 2018, https://www.thejakartapost.com/news/2018/09/23/election-campaign-kicks-off-with-peace-pledge.html [accessed October 28, 2020].

[2] Muhammad Zulfikar Rakhmat, "Indonesia Is Spending Big on Infrastructure," *Fair Observer*, February 25, 2019, https://www.fairobserver.com/region/asia_pacific/indonesia-election-joko-jokowi-widodo-indonesian-world-news-32480/ [accessed October 28, 2020].

work on a second line got underway.[3] After decades of delay, Jakarta had finally joined the other major regional capitals as an Asian megacity with a modern MRT.

There were other notable development successes too. In 2018, for the first time, Indonesia hit its target for house building. At the outset of his presidency, Jokowi had identified a lack of modern housing stock and an inability of the construction industry to keep pace with the growing population. He had set a target of one million new homes to be built each year. The Ministry of Public Works and Public Housing recorded that 1,132, 621 units were built in 2018, with half of the overall construction costs met through government grants and mortgage schemes, and 70 percent of the new homes intended for low-income families.[4]

Elsewhere, 2018's notable run of tragedies continued, with a fatal air crash in late October and yet another natural disaster on December 22 when the collapse of the Anak Krakatau volcano in the Sunda Strait triggered a tsunami which killed more than four hundred people on the westernmost coast of Java. But the dominant media story was, by this stage, the election, and worryingly, despite the candidates' opening pledge, there were already indications that the dirty underbelly of the 2014 campaign would be making another showing.

Media analysts recorded a 61 percent upsurge in fake news stories circulating online between December 2018 and January 2019. More than half of them were political in nature. Of course, there had been many false stories about Jokowi circulating in 2014, but analysts now identified an alarming trend for fake news intended to undermine the perceived legitimacy of the electoral process itself.[5] The authorities did their best to stem the tide of deliberate misinformation, and in October and November 2018 more than a dozen people were arrested for spreading fake news online.[6] But it was clear that things would get rough on the way to the polls, and

---

[3] "Indonesia's first metro opens in gridlocked Jakarta," *Global Construction Review*, March 25, 2019, https://www.globalconstructionreview.com/news/indonesias-first-metro-opens-grid-locked-jakarta/ [accessed October 28, 2020].

[4] "Indonesia hits million-home target for first time in 2018," *Global Construction Review*, January 9, 2019, https://www.globalconstructionreview.com/news/indonesia-hits-million-home-target-for-first-time-2018/ [accessed October 28, 2020].

[5] Kate Lamb, "Fake news spikes in Indonesia ahead of elections," *The Guardian*, March 20, 2019, https://www.theguardian.com/world/2019/mar/20/fake-news-spikes-in-indonesia-ahead-of-elections [accessed October 28, 2020].

[6] "Indonesian Police Intensify Crackdown on Fake News," *VOA News*, November 21, 2020, https://www.voanews.com/east-asia-pacific/indonesian-police-intensify-crackdown-fake-news [accessed October 28, 2020].

this time around Jokowi appeared somewhat less relaxed, less inclined to take the casual *aku Rapopo* approach to attacks and insults. An online hashtag, "#2019GantiPresiden" ("2019, Change the President"), propagated by PKS public relations chief Mardani Ali Sera,[7] had been developed as the foundation of an orchestrated campaign, and the slogan had begun to appear on T-shirts. "How can wearing a T-shirt change the president? It can't!" Jokowi said at one campaign event.[8]

The slogan also appeared on December 2 during a restaging of the massive 212 Movement protest against Ahok two years earlier. The same contingent of white-clad demonstrators descended again on Lapangan Merdeka. Jokowi did not meet with the leaders on this occasion, though Prabowo spoke briefly to the crowd, with uncharacteristic restraint, for active electioneering had been forbidden in Jakarta's vast central space by the KPU (the Electoral Commission).[9] Attendance at the 2018 protest was reportedly actually higher than it had been for the original 2016 version.[10] But it was peaceful, and as an organized movement 212 had clearly lost its earlier momentum. It no longer had internal unity and no longer had a single-issue catalyst. Jokowi's canny choice of running mate had also made it harder to frame him as some sort of "anti-Islam" figure. But still, the protest indicated that enduring tensions would be a feature of the campaign.

The day before the so-called "212 Reunion," a series of much smaller protests took place at a number of locations around Indonesia over a very different matter: they were organized in support of a long-running secessionist movement in Papua, Indonesia's easternmost region.[11]

Papua would be in the news again before the end of the year. The very next day separatists there killed members of a road crew working on a

---

[7] Gibran Maulana Ibrahim, "Jokowi Sindir Kaus #2019GantiPresiden, Ini Respons PKS," *detikNews*, April 7, 2018, https://news.detik.com/berita/d-3958976/jokowi-sindir-kaus-2019gantipresiden-ini-respons-pks [accessed October 28, 2020].

[8] Ray Jordan, "Jokowi Sindir #2019GantiPresiden: Masak Kaus Bisa Ganti Presiden?" *detikNews*, April 7, 2018, https://news.detik.com/berita/d-3958859/jokowi-sindir-2019ganti-presiden-masak-kaus-bisa-ganti-presiden [accessed October 28, 2020].

[9] "'212 Reunion' Rally Shows Waning Opposition Support, but Jokowi Better Watch His Back," *Jakarta Globe*, December 2, 2018, https://jakartaglobe.id/news/212-reunion-rally-shows-waning-opposition-support-jokowi-better-watch-back/ [accessed October 28, 2020].

[10] Francis Chan, "Identity politics rears its head again in Indonesia," *The Straits Times*, December 8, 2020, https://www.straitstimes.com/asia/se-asia/identity-politics-rears-its-head-again-in-indonesia [accessed October 28, 2020].

[11] Arnold Belau and Wahyoe Boediwardhana, "537 Papuan arrested before and after Dec. 1 rallies in various cities," *The Jakarta Post*, December 2, 2018, https://www.thejakartapost.com/news/2018/12/02/537-papuan-arrested-before-and-after-dec-1-rallies-in-various-cities.html [accessed October 28, 2020].

major highway project. On December 21, meanwhile, Jokowi announced that Indonesia had finally taken on majority ownership, after a lengthy and convoluted process, of the Grasberg Mine in Papua's Central Highlands. One of the largest copper and gold mines on earth, Grasberg had been controlled by US-based Freeport-McMoRan Inc. But the US$3.85 billion deal finalized in late 2018 signed over a 51.23 percent share to Indonesia (itself divided between state-owned company Inalum and the Papua provincial government),[12] seen as a key symbolic and practical step towards the economic independence mandated by the Nawacita framework.

Papua, as the demonstrations and attacks at the start of the month had indicated, is one of Indonesia's most fraught regions. It is also a place towards which Jokowi had frequently turned his attention during the course of his presidency. The region, which comprises the western half of the island of New Guinea and its outlying islands, is split into two provinces, Papua and West Papua. Confusingly, both names are at times used to discuss the whole region. In this chapter, when not discussing a specific province, "Papua" refers to the two provinces as a geographical whole.

Papua: A Colonial Legacy

In the late 1950s and early 1960s, hundreds of children born all over Indonesia were given variations of a particular name: Irianto, Iriandi, Iryanto, or Iriawan for boys; Irianti, Iryanti, Irianingsih, Iriantiningsih, or Iriana for girls. This bout of themed naming was an expression of the nationalist discourse of the day. "Irian" was the term used in Indonesia at the time for the western half of the huge island of New Guinea, still held by the Netherlands, long after they had given up their claim to the rest of the archipelago.

Sukarno had made the handing over of Papua (as Irian is now known) an essential cause, representing the completion of an unfinished anticolonial revolution. Under heavy international pressure, in 1962 the Dutch finally handed the territory over to a United Nations Temporary Executive Authority (UNTEA), which then transferred it provisionally to Indonesia the following year on the grounds that an "act of free choice" (of unspecified form) would be conducted to confirm the inhabitants' wishes. This condition was judged to have been met, controversially, after a vote by a gathering

---

[12] Stefanno Reinard Sulaiman, "Indonesia officially controls 51.23 percent of Freeport shares: Jokowi," *The Jakarta Post*, December 21, 2018, https://www.thejakartapost.com/news/2018/12/21/indonesia-officially-controls-51-percent-of-freeport-shares-jokowi.html [accessed October 28, 2020].

of around a thousand selected community leaders in 1969, after which the UN General Assembly formally recognized Papua as part of Indonesia. Throughout this period, patriotic Indonesian parents named their children in honor of the country's newest province.[13] One of those children, born in 1963, was Iriana, who would grow up to become Indonesia's First Lady.

Critical international commentaries on conflict in Papua often talk of "Indonesian colonialism" but seldom acknowledge the actual roots of the situation there in Dutch colonial actions. Though isolated and far from the historical centers of Java and Sumatra, coastal and offshore regions of Papua have been tied into archipelago trade networks for centuries. The northern coastal regions, in particular, had old links with neighboring Maluku, and the Sultanate of Tidore claimed sovereignty there, sovereignty which was acknowledged and then assumed by the ascendant Dutch. The Dutch established their own first Papuan outpost in 1828, but only made concrete steps to realize their notional claim to the region at the end of the nineteenth century,[14] and paid little serious attention to it even beyond that point. Throughout this period, however, Papua was regarded as an undifferentiated and integral part of the Dutch East Indies.[15] And naturally, for those fighting to replace the Dutch East Indies with an independent nation, it was regarded as an undifferentiated and integral part of Indonesia. Of course, many local Papuans had no awareness of either territorial concept, but the same could have been said of many other people in remote areas of Indonesia at the time.

From the 1920s onwards, the nationalist movement used the phrase "from Sabang to Merauke" to describe the independent nation they were striving to create,[16] mentioning its extreme poles, the first in northernmost Sumatra, the second in easternmost Papua. Nothing changed until the period of the Indonesian Revolution. Having been ousted by the Japanese during World War II, the Dutch initially fought to re-establish their colony in its entirety and then to resist the establishment of an independent unitary Indonesian republic, insisting instead on a federation over which they would retain a degree of influence. In 1949, very late in the day, the

---

[13] In 2003, the province, originally known as Irian Jaya, was divided into two parts, now known as Papua and West Papua.

[14] M. C. Ricklefs, *A History of Modern Indonesia since c.1200*, 3rd edn (London: Palgrave, 2001), 178.

[15] Robert Cribb and Colin Brown, *Modern Indonesia: A History Since 1945* (London: Longman, 1945), 24.

[16] C. L. M. Penders, *The West New Guinea Debacle: Dutch Decolonisation and Indonesia, 1945–1962* (Adelaide: Crawford House, 2002), 137.

Dutch side unilaterally amended the Linggadjati Agreement which formed the basis of their acknowledgment of Indonesian independence, to state that Papua was now no longer a part of the Dutch East Indies and was to be retained as a colony by Holland. The move was driven by conservative, procolonial Dutch parties who, as one historian puts it, "after losing their fight in Indonesia, and with their national pride deeply hurt, still insisted on extracting their colonial pound of flesh in the form of a Dutch West New Guinea."[17] The move outraged the Indonesian leadership, but was grudgingly accepted on the United Nations-brokered proviso that the transfer of Papua be dealt with in the coming year. In the event, the Dutch held on to the region for a further twelve years in the face of mounting international pressure.

Having ignored the place for decades, Holland now began to invest heavily in Papua. There had been aspirations since the 1920s to develop the region as a settler colony, occupied by mixed-race Indo-Europeans and other Asia-based Dutch citizens, and as a "tropical Netherlands" to "absorb Holland's own excess population,"[18] an idea which certainly took no account of the local inhabitants. This plan was maintained by some in the 1940s and 1950s. But with international opinion tending to favor Indonesia by this stage, the long-term sustainability of a Dutch colony in a postcolonial world looked unlikely, so the Dutch authorities began working to encourage a proto-national identity in Papua. The acting Dutch Resident, Jan Pieter Karel van Eechoud, was already pushing as early as 1949 for the replacement of the long-established Malay lingua franca (the official Indonesian language) with Dutch to create a greater disparity between Papuan people and the rest of the archipelago, and to quash any emerging sense of Indonesian identity there.[19] Deliberate antiIndonesian campaigning by the Dutch in Papua continued throughout the 1950s,[20] culminating in the establishment of a quasi-legislative council in 1961,[21] in response to which Indonesia launched a series of military incursions. No less than the US president, JFK, was by this stage pushing for a solution in Indonesia's favor,[22] and the following year the UN-brokered transfer finally took place. But in their belated departure, the Dutch had bequeathed to

---

[17] Ibid., 49.
[18] Ibid., 57.
[19] Ibid., 103.
[20] Cribb and Brown, *Modern Indonesia*, 161.
[21] Ibid., 86.
[22] Ricklefs, *A History of Modern Indonesia*, 326.

Indonesia a territory deliberately kindled for conflict, much as the Japanese had done to the Dutch with Indonesia itself two decades earlier.

During the Japanese occupation of World War II, there had been early traces of a "national Papuan consciousness,"mainly in reaction to Japanese oppression.[23] But in the aftermath, some educated Papuans were also involved in the Indonesian anticolonial movement.[24] It seems very reasonable to argue that had the region been transferred to independent Indonesian governance at the same time as the rest of the former Dutch East Indies, Papua's subsequent history would have been a much happier one and its relationship with the rest of Indonesia would have been far less complicated. It is in Papua that the Indonesian state has unquestionably been responsible for some of its worst human rights violations over the last fifty years. But it is essential to recognize the situation there for what it is at base: a bitter legacy of European colonialism and, in its deliberate engineering by the Dutch authorities, one of the most egregious of the many such legacies around the world.

Given that a commitment to Papua as an integral part of Indonesia is non-negotiable for any Indonesian government, the authorities tend to find themselves in a "damned if you do, damned if you don't" position in the eyes of international critics. Should the place receive little attention or investment from the central government, as has been the case in the past, then the accusation will be of arrogant neglect. But if the Indonesian government puts money into Papua, develops its economy and its infrastructure, builds schools, markets, roads, then the claim will be "colonialism". For Jokowi, however, the latter path was the only possible option and the only approach that could bring material benefits to the people of the region. It is an approach he pursued energetically throughout his first term.

A New Dawn

Shortly before dawn on January 1, 2016, Jokowi, barefooted, dressed in a loose white shirt and a checked sarong, crossed the white sand beach at Waiwo in the Raja Ampat archipelago at the western end of Papua, and walked out to the end of a wooden jetty to watch the first sunrise of the new year. The overnight stay at the Waiwo Dive Resort was part of his third trip to Papua since his inauguration, and just one of many to come. The

---

[23] Penders, *The West New Guinea Debacle*, 89.
[24] Ibid., 136–37

decision to welcome 2016 in Indonesia's easternmost region was intended to send a clear message, according to then cabinet secretary Pramono Anung, "that developments not only take place in Jakarta."[25]

During a visit to New Zealand in 2018, Jokowi met with a group of students and other Indonesian expats based in Wellington. One Papuan member of the audience, Fransiscus Orlando, asked the president what motivated his frequent visits to the region.[26] Jokowi has, in fact, visited Papua more times than any previous Indonesian president.

"My visits to Papua were first triggered by curiosity about the area," Jokowi explained. "As leader, I wanted to see the condition of the people and infrastructure there, not just based on reports. This is because eastern Indonesia has been forgotten for too long; it hasn't received enough attention or improvement."[27]

He went on to tell an anecdote about a *blusukan* trip he had made to Nduga, a remote regency in Papua's Central Highlands. The trip was made against the advice of police and military leaders, as this has long been an unsettled area. Nonetheless, he made the visit accompanied by the First Lady, traveling by helicopter as there was no road access at the time. On arrival at the regency capital, Jokowi was shocked by its apparent desertion.

"There was no one there, not a single person!" he said. But according to regency head, Yairus Gwijangge, Nduga had 129,000 inhabitants, living scattered in remote settlements in the surrounding forest. The president asked to be taken to the busiest place in the regency and local officials drove him to a nearby market.

"I was shocked when we got there; there were at most 60 people, not 60,000; just 60!" Jokowi was also told by the regent that there was not a single meter of surfaced road in the entire Nduga Regency, and that the overland trip from Wamena, the largest settlement in the highlands with good airlinks to coastal cities, took at least four days through the forest. Having seen these conditions on the ground, Jokowi ordered the acceleration of work on a road link from Nduga to Wamena.[28]

---

[25] Reza Aditya, "Jokowi Celebrates New Year's Eve in Papua Despite Shooting," *Tempo*, December 28, 2015, https://en.tempo.co/read/731269/jokowi-celebrates-new-years-eve-in-papua-despite-shooting [accessed October 29, 2020].

[26] Discussion with students in New Zealand, available at https://www.youtube.com/watch?v=7xvyl82mnUM [accessed October 29, 2020].

[27] Ibid.

[28] Fikri Faqih, "Di tanah Irian, Jokowi cerita sejarah nama sang istri Iriana," *Merdeka*, June 5, 2014, https://www.merdeka.com/peristiwa/di-tanah-irian-jokowi-cerita-sejarah-nama-sang-istri-iriana.html [accessed July 17, 2019].

It was the experience of seeing Papua on the ground that drove his development focus there, he told the Wellington audience, and a desire to gain first-hand experience of the reality and to check on progress which impelled his frequent return visits.[29]

During his first term, Jokowi oversaw a massive investment in infrastructure in Papua, most significantly the 4,600-kilometer Trans-Papua Highway, stretching from Sorong in the west to the eastern border. The highway is intended to connect to other new provincial roads, boosting economic activity across the vast and sparsely populated region.

"We hope that with the completion of this Trans-Papua road the mobility of goods, mobility of people, logistics, deliveries will be faster and will ultimately reduce transportation logistics costs. I think we're moving in that direction," Jokowi said in 2018.[30]

As well as road building, a project was launched to rehabilitate fifteen small and medium-sized ports throughout Papua, to expand four existing airports, and to build two new airports. The aim is to level out the patchy development across Papua, which ranges from conditions comparable to western Indonesia in the larger coastal towns, to a near-total absence of state infrastructure in some remote inland areas.[31]

For many decades, Indonesia's human rights record in Papua has been severely tarnished,[32] and it remains a place of seemingly intractable problems when it comes to nation building.[33] Jokowi has acknowledged that his government has yet to overcome the issue of human rights violations. However, he sees an emphasis on infrastructure improvements in Papua as a strategy for reducing inequality and delivering more equitable development in the spirit of his wider "Indonesia-centric" approach of building from the periphery.[34] Improved infrastructure, the theory goes, reduces the isolation of Papuan regions, allowing residents to conduct trade between districts, obtain access to better healthcare and education, cheaper energy, and so on, things which are themselves crucial aspects of human rights.

---

[29] Ibid.

[30] "Jalan Trans Papua Akan Pangkas Waktu Tempuh dan Biaya Logistik," *Beritatrans*, November 17, 2018, http://beritatrans.com/2018/11/17/jalan-trans-papua-akan-pangkas-waktu-tempuh-dan-biaya-logistik/ [accessed July 19, 2019].

[31] Jacobus Perviddya Solossa, *Otonomi Khusus Papua Mengangkat Martabat Rakyat Papua di Dalam NKRI* (Jakarta: Pustaka Sinar Harapan, 2006), 79.

[32] Ibid., 97–101.

[33] Eko Sulistyo, *Konservatisme Politik Anti Jokowi* (Jakarta: Moka Media, 2019), 203.

[34] Iwan Supriyatna, "Presiden Jokowi: Ketimpangan Nduga dan Jawa Ibarat Bumi dan Langit," *Suara*, March 11, 2019, https://www.suara.com/bisnis/2019/03/11/054052/presiden-jokowi-ketimpangan-nduga-dan-jawa-ibarat-bumi-dan-langit [accessed July 17, 2019].

But developing infrastructure in Papua is more challenging, and more costly, than in any other Indonesian region. The first challenge is the low baseline, a near total absence of existing infrastructure when compared to other parts of the country. The mountainous, thickly forested, sparsely populated terrain is another major practical challenge. And, finally, there are the security concerns of an area where armed separatist groups are still active. Nonetheless, Jokowi has frequently restated a commitment to development in Papua.

Beyond the context of the belated Dutch departure and their late efforts to foster a divergent identity there, a major contributing factor that has prompted some indigenous Papuans to take up arms against the Indonesian state has arguably been the vast gap between Papua and other regions in Indonesia in terms of development.[35] The one progressive option to address Papua's problems from an Indonesian nationalist perspective is working to reduce the sense of marginalization in the area through development.[36] This approach appeared to have had some initial success. In August 2017, Kris Nussy (also known as Corinus Sireri), the separatist commander in the East Yapen District (part of a large island regency in Cenderawasih Bay off the north coast of the Papuan mainland), surrendered along with his 77-man unit, handing over weapons to the local military unit and declaring his allegiance to Indonesia,

"We are tired of fighting in the forest, but achieving nothing," Nussy said, going on to request assistance from the authorities to buy outboard motors and forestry equipment which would allow him and his men to earn a living in their home villages.[37]

Building Bridges

When discussing the challenges of development in Papua, Jokowi has repeatedly described how difficult the terrain is for Trans-Papua Highway construction workers. In places, the route traverses mountains over 3,000 meters above sea level, as on the 278-kilometer stretch from Wamena to Mamugu. These conditions demand solutions very different from the relatively straightforward road-building projects in Java and Sumatra.

---

[35] Muridan S. Widjojo et al., *Papua Road Map: Negotiating the Past, Improving the Present and Securing the Future* (Jakarta: Obor Indonesia, 2009), 16–17.

[36] Basuki Hadimuljono, *Infrastruktur Meningkatkan Daya Saing* (Jakarta: Kementerian PUPR, 2017), 95–103.

[37] Widjojo et al., *Papua Road Map*, 136.

"We're only able to carry heavy equipment there using helicopters, the asphalt is also carried in using helicopters," Jokowi has said.[38]

The cost of building a single kilometer of unsurfaced road in Papua requires a minimum of Rp1 billion, with further funding of Rp1–2 billion rupiah to surface it with asphalt depending on the location.[39] These costs alone have put off previous administrations from tackling infrastructure in the region. The security situation, meanwhile, brings extra costs to development projects in some areas, costs which at times have included human lives.

As well as the highway spanning the entire region, Jokowi's development drive in Papua has involved various smaller individual projects aimed at building connectivity and raising economic potential. Jayapura, the Papuan capital, and the neighboring Muara Tami District are separated by Youtefa Bay. The journey by land around the edge of the bay typically takes more than two hours, and for many years boats were the fastest way to make the trip. To create a better link to the city for Muara Tami's 18,000 residents, Jokowi ordered the acceleration of the Holtekamp Bridge project.[40] This 732-meter bridge, spanning the inner part of the bay, has reduced the journey time to around an hour, which, amongst other things, opens up access to a number of tourism destinations in Muara Tami,[41] and reduces the distance to the Papua New Guinea frontier at Skouw.

"I am here, in the land of Papua. Let's roll up our sleeves together, because Papua is Indonesia, because we are one country. The sun always rises from the east, and Papua is the light in eastern Indonesia," Jokowi said during an inspection of the Holtekamp Bridge.[42]

The bridge was a joint project of the Ministry of Public Works and Public Housing, the Papua Provincial Government, and the Jayapura City Government, representing an investment of Rp1.7 trillion. The Provincial Government was in charge of funding the construction of an approach road from the direction of Holtekamp. Meanwhile, the City Government

---

[38] Solossa, *Otonomi Khusus Papua*, 226.

[39] "Jokowi: Bangun Jalan di Papua Berat, Pekerjanya Bertaruh Nyawa," *Kumparan News*, December 5, 2018, https://kumparan.com/kumparannews/jokowi-bangun-jalan-di-papua-berat-pekerjanya-bertaruh-nyawa-1543989233307330546 [accessed July 18, 2019].

[40] Hadimuljono, *Infrastruktur Meningkatkan Daya Saing*, 97.

[41] Afif Farhan, "Jokowi, Pembangunan dan Kekayaan Indonesia," *detikTravel*, April 13, 2018, https://travel.detik.com/travel-news/d-3970080/jokowi-pembangunan-dan-kekayaan-indonesia [accessed July 16, 2019].

[42] Hadimuljono, *Infrastruktur Meningkatkan Daya Saing*, 97.

built an approach road from the direction of Hamadi. The bridge has two main spans with a length of 112.5 meters and a height of 20 meters. Its construction is linked to medium-term planning for the development of Jayapura, pushing the growth of the city eastwards instead of encroaching on the forested hills to the west.

Although Jayapura is a relatively modern and cosmopolitan city of around quarter of a million people, aspects of the bridge project underscored the challenges of development in such a remote region. The two middle spans, weighing 2,000 tons, had to be shipped 3,200 kilometers from their construction site in Surabaya, the longest shipment of intact suspension bridge spans ever made.

Papua has also been the scene of some of Jokowi's most flamboyant exercises in *blusukan*, including a trip by dirt bike along a partially completed section of the Trans-Papua Highway in 2019. It was a carefully considered event, intended to convey the idea of a committed state presence in Papua, with the president himself on the ground there. This was a far cry from his earliest impromptu *blusukan* as mayor of Surakarta, hustling civil servants out to visit local slums, and the security preparations were considerable. Riding a KLX Kawasaki trail bike over the unsurfaced roadbed, Jokowi inspected the Wamena-Mamugu I segment of the project, traveling around seven kilometers along its length with journalists and security forces in tow.

"If you're on a dirt bike, you can clearly see the difficulty," he said during one stop. "We're just trying to see things in the field, just traveling it. Try to imagine building it!"[43]

The initial stage of the road construction, breaking the unsurfaced line of its route, has been overseen by the Indonesian military, with the Ministry of Public Works and Public Housing then stepping in to lay the asphalt. By the time of Jokowi's dirt bike trip, the full length of the route was passable to traffic, thought not all had been surfaced. Around half of the thirty-five new bridges required had also been built.

"We are trying out roads that are asphalt and roads that have not been paved so that people throughout the country know how difficult it is to build roads in Papua. It's not just difficult; it's very difficult," Jokowi said.

---

[43] Available at https://youtu.be/xibrSgbJx0w [accessed July 19, 2019].

The Cost of Nation Building

On paper, the cost of Jokowi's development projects in Papua is enormous, with a relatively minimal immediately quantifiable return. The entire population of the two Papuan provinces is similar to that of Depok, just one part of the Great Jakarta metropolitan area. Much of the heavy equipment used on the Papua road projects effectively becomes single-use: the cost of airlifting diggers and graders deep into the highlands means that it is often too expensive to fly them back out when the work is finished. The Indonesian Directorate General of Highways alone has allocated annual funds of more than Rp2 trillion to road projects in Papua, around 5 percent of the entire national road-building budget.

But the cost to the national coffers will ultimately greatly reduce the cost of living for ordinary Papuans. For years the prices of commodities and goods for the people of Papua were extremely high compared to other parts of Indonesia.[44] This was largely due to inadequate transportation infrastructure. Distribution was hampered by poor or non-existent roads and a lack of scheduled transportation.[45] In the inland and mountainous areas, the only way to transport basic consumer goods was often by air, and generally by small propeller aircraft at that. Even getting those goods to Papua's ports in the first place involved long journeys and high costs.

One attempt to mitigate this was Jokowi's stated aim to develop an archipelago-spanning "Sea Highway."[46] During a debate in Jakarta as part of his first presidential campaign, Jokowi drew attention to the weaknesses in Indonesia's internal maritime networks: "When it comes to sending goods from Java to Papua or from Java to Europe, it is more expensive to send them to Papua because there are no ships traveling [on that route]," he said.[47] The proposed Sea Highway was the simple concept of strengthening shipping lanes focused on Eastern Indonesia. As well as improving the supply chain to Papua and other eastern regions, this would also facilitate commercial access from South Pacific states. The project involves the development of two large commercial ports on the route, namely, Kuala Tanjung

---

[44] Summa Riella Rusdianti and Cahyo Pamungkas, eds., *Updating Papua Road Map, Proses Perdamaian, Politik Kaum Muda, dan Diaspora Papua* (Jakarta: Yayasan Pustaka Obor Indonesia, 2017), 12.

[45] Akhmad Sujadi, *Tol Laut Jokowi Denyut Ekonomi NKRI* (Jakarta: Balai Pustaka, 2019), v.

[46] Estu Suryowati, "Kirim Barang ke Papua Lebih Mahal Ketimbang ke Eropa," *Kompas,* June 15, 2014, https://money.kompas.com/read/2014/06/15/2141527/Kirim.Barang.ke.Papua.Lebih.Mahal.Ketimbang.ke.Eropa [accessed July 19, 2019].

[47] Sujadi, *Tol Laut Jokowi Denyut Ekonomi NKRI,* ix.

in North Sumatra and Bitung in North Sulawesi.[48] The ultimate goal is to reduce the price disparity between western and eastern Indonesia, directly improving people's welfare and enhancing regional economic growth.[49]

Explaining the concept during his first presidential campaign in 2014, Jokowi stressed the need to improve Indonesia's internal networks to level out price disparities: "Why must there be a Sea Highway? Because cement in Java costs Rp56,000, while in Papua it can be Rp1.2 million, Rp1 million or Rp500,000. If we build this Sea Highway, with deep seaports in Sumatra, Kalimantan, Java and Papua, this will provide a sense of justice, because cement prices will be the same. Unlike today, it is very different because infrastructure is not built on the basis of maritime affairs," he said.[50]

Since 2014, east–west connectivity has advanced, which, coupled with improved road access, has already brought prices down in Papua. A 40-kilogram sack of cement in the Puncak Jaya Regency of the Central Highlands can now be obtained for Rp500,000, down from a previous price of Rp2 million. The price of petrol, which previously reached Rp100,000 per liter in remote parts of Papua, is now standardized nationwide.[51]

Jokowi's commitment to ongoing investment in Papua was reaffirmed at the end of his first term. In 2019, he confirmed the allocation of Rp20.97 trillion in the State Budget for Papua and West Papua, along with Aceh, a province at the opposite end of the country, but with certain parallels in the form of past separatism, challenging geographical conditions, and local complaints of historical central government neglect. Like the Papuan provinces, Aceh operates under Special Autonomy arrangements. Additional funding for the three provinces was confirmed in 2019 at Rp5.850 trillion for Papua, Rp2.507 trillion for West Papua, and Rp8.357 trillion for Aceh, with further support provided under the Additional Infrastructure Fund in the Framework of Special Autonomy, all amounting to a huge financial commitment to development at Indonesia's most troubled peripheries.

Speaking at a student conference in late 2018, Jokowi made the point that it would be illogical to view the massive investments in Papua as attempts at vote-buying for his own coming second presidential campaign.

"If I just wanted political capital, I'd just build in Java, because 60

---

[48] Suryowati, "Kirim Barang ke Papua Lebih Mahal Ketimbang ke Eropa."

[49] "Laporan Implementasi Konsep Tol Laut 2015," Direktorat Transportasi, http://nusantara-initiative.com/wp-content/uploads/2016/02/150915-Buku-Tol-Laut-bappenas.pdf [accessed June 7, 2019].

[50] Suryowati, "Kirim Barang ke Papua Lebih Mahal Ketimbang ke Eropa."

[51] Sulistyo, *Konservatisme Politik Anti Jokowi*, 200.

percent of the Indonesian population is in Java; in politics the [loudest] voice is in Java, so I'd benefit if I continuously built in Java," he said. "[But] I'm willing to take the risk. To repeat [the point]: if you want a quick political and economic return, build here; 60 percent of the population is in Java. How many people is that? There are nearly 150 million in Java. But we have to think about the unity of Indonesia, have to think about social justice for all the Indonesian people."[52]

Plainly, there is still some way to go. In 2017, the Inclusive Development Index ranking released by the World Economic Forum ranked Indonesia 22nd out of 79 developing countries in terms of equitable development, well below Thailand and Malaysia, which are ranked 12th and 16th. But this is in no small part a legacy of the historic imbalances in development and the heavy focus on Java for many decades.

While the long-overdue but deeply unpopular reduction of national fuel subsidies was one of Jokowi's most challenging early tasks as president, in Papua he put in place policies designed to reduce the cost of petrol for residents: the One Price Fuel policy, fixing a national standard per liter retail price (initially set at Rp6,450) for premium petrol. Previously, per liter prices in parts of Papua were as high as Rp100,000.

"If it's Rp60,000, that's already 10 times more [than the standard price elsewhere]. I've asked the State-Owned Enterprises Minister; I've asked for the price of petrol in Papua, especially in the Central Highlands and in Wamena, to be the same price as in Java," said Jokowi.[53]

This was a costly undertaking for state fuel company Pertamina.[54] According to the company, the cost of shipping fuel even within Papua, from Timika to Wamena, amounts to Rp54,000 per liter. From Wamena, the capital of Jayawijaya Regency, onward distribution to outlying places such as Yahukimo can only be carried out by small aircraft. The overall cost of fuel distribution to isolated Indonesian regions amounts to Rp800 billion.[55] But the One Price Fuel policy now mandates that at official

---

[52] Andhika Prasetia, "Jokowi: Kalau Hitungan Politisi, Pembangunan Hanya di Jawa," *detikNews*, December 7, 2018, https://news.detik.com/berita/d-4333804/jokowi-kalau-hitungan-politisi-pembangunan-hanya-di-jawa [accessed July 19, 2019].

[53] "Presiden Jokowi Jelaskan Manfaat Pembangunan Infrastruktur," Ministry of Finance, https://www.kemenkeu.go.id/publikasi/berita/presiden-jokowi-jelaskan-manfaat-pembangunan-infrastruktur/ [accessed May 1, 2019].

[54] "Jokowi Minta Menteri Terkait Kebut Penerangan Listrik di Papua," *Papua Today*, December 21, 2017, https://papuatoday.id/2017/12/21/jokowi-minta-menteri-terkait-kebut-penerang-an-listrik-di-papua/ [accessed July 19, 2019].

[55] Ibid.

outlets even in the remotest of places, a liter of premium costs the same as it would at a filling station in Jakarta.

"This is not a matter of profit and loss. This is a matter of social justice for all Indonesian people. The Rp800 billion is down to finding cross-subsidies; that's Pertamina's business. But what I want is justice for all Indonesian people, so that the current price in all districts is Rp6,450 per liter for premium," Jokowi said at the launch of the program in 2016 during a visit to Papua to inaugurate the new Goliat Dekai Airport at Yahukimo.[56]

The reallocation of several of Indonesia's large oilfields from foreign companies to Pertamina, in particular the Rokan Block in Sumatra and the Mahakam Block in Kalimantan, was one element of the potential cross-subsidization required to offset the cost of the One Fuel Price policy, while ongoing road building within Papua is itself reducing the distribution costs.

The policy has had a rapid impact for Papua residents and residents of other outlying areas, including parts of Kalimantan and East Nusa Tenggara, previously burdened with unequal fuel prices. One resident of the isolated Intan Jaya Regency of Papua, named Aprianus, explained the financial benefits of the change: "In the past, fuel in Intan Jaya was very difficult, in the past one liter was expensive, Rp50,000. But now one liter of fuel is Rp6,450," he said.[57]

Responding to criticisms of the cost of the program, Jokowi has pointed out that he previously removed the cripplingly expensive national fuel subsidy in the face of popular protests. "Previously, when fuel subsidies were costing Rp300 trillion, there was silence. Now, with Rp800 billion there's a fuss," he said during the inauguration of a new fuel terminal in Pontianak in 2017, a terminal intended to improve supplies to isolated areas of West Kalimantan, another region which had previously been hit by unequal fuel pricing.[58]

As well as suffering from unequal fuel pricing, electrification in Papua has lagged far behind most other parts of Indonesia, unsurprising in such a vast, geographically rugged and sparsely populated region. But under Jokowi's development drive, efforts have been made to improve the supply

---

[56] "Presiden Jokowi Canangkan Satu Harga BBM di Papua," Liputan1.com, diakses pada 4 Juli 2019, https://www.liputan1.com/2016/10/18/presiden-jokowi-canangkan-satu-harga-bbm-papua/.

[57] "BBM Satu Harga," *Infonawacita*, https://infonawacita.com/satu-tahun-kebijakanbbm-satu-hargaberjalan-masyarakat-papua-berterimakasih-padajokowi/ [accessed July 4, 2019].

[58] "BBM Satu Harga," *Publikreport*, https://www.publikreport.com/jokowikebijakan-bbm-satu-harga-habiskan-biaya-rp-800-miliar/ [accessed July 4, 2019].

by building a number of power plants and applying the latest technology.[59]

"The electricity must not go out again, it must illuminate the community. In Papua we keep speeding up so that all villages must be electrified, so that every night the lights can be bright and the children can learn well. This is our commitment to Papua," Jokowi said in 2017.[60]

A program to roll out micro hydro power plants has been launched as an alternative to a comprehensive region-wide grid, a near impossibility given Papua's geography. One such plant is located at Warabiyai Sausapor, Tambraw, West Papua. According to data from the Ministry of Energy and Mineral Resources, it can produce 1.6 megawatts, providing power to 3,000 households in the area. Similar micro hydro plants have been built elsewhere in Papua. As an interim lighting solution for very remote communities, energy-efficient solar lights have been distributed in large numbers; a total of 29,155 have gone to households in the mountainous Lanny Jaya Regency, for example.[61]

Rony Wanimbo, a Lanny Jaya resident, explains the difference made by this one simple piece of technology: "Now our children can learn well. Their eyes no longer hurt, and they don't cough from the smoke of the fire. We also use these lights for deliberation, gathering with residents for discussions. Because it can be removed, we can also use it as a flashlight."[62]

In 2013, the electrification rate for villages in Papua stood at 30.48 percent. According to government figures, by 2018 the rate had reached 72.04 percent.[63] For Jokowi, this is a further manifestation of periphery-based development as a move towards nationwide social justice.

Elusive Peace

On December 1, 2018 a group of employees of PT Istaka Karya, working on the Trans-Papua Highway in the Nduga, the remote regency which Jokowi had previously visited by helicopter, as he had told the students in New Zealand, were kidnapped by armed men and taken into the nearby forest. The following day, as the "212 Reunion" protest was getting underway

[59] Ibid.

[60] "Presiden Jokowi Akan Sediakan Pembangkit Listrik Di Pedalaman Tanah Papua," *Papua Today*, https://www.papua.us/2017/05/presiden-jokowi-akan-sediakan.html [accessed July 19, 2019].

[61] Available at https://www.YouTube.com/watch?v=fXSxCTebzLI [accessed July 19, 2019].

[62] Setneg, *Laporan 4 Tahun Pemerintahan Jokowi-JK* (Jakarta: Setneg, 2018), 102.

[63] Sulistyo, *Konservatisme Politik Anti Jokowi*, 206.

2,500 kilometers away in Jakarta, the hostages were brought to a hilltop and shot.[64] At least nineteen were killed, though several members of the group survived by playing dead and then fleeing to a nearby army post.[65] An Indonesian soldier was also killed in the aftermath of the initial attack.

The West Papua Liberation Army claimed responsibility for the killings. A few months earlier, the same group had kidnapped teachers and medical staff in the Nduga area.[66] Roadwork was temporarily halted and a joint police-military security operation in pursuit of the attackers was launched, which, inevitably, saw many local residents fleeing their homes to the safety of temporary camps and enduring serious hardships in the process. But Jokowi insisted that the wider road project would not be affected. "This has fueled our determination to continue our great task of developing the land of Papua," he said.[67]

Sporadic violence has continued since 2018,[68] including street protests and attacks by armed groups. Given the deep roots of conflict in Papua, it will likely be a long while before an ultimate settlement is reached. In the meantime, there will doubtless be more protests against perceived inequality and more attacks on manifestations of the Indonesian state. But a continued emphasis on equitable development there, on the reduction of the cost of living and the advancement of economic opportunities, may, over time, gradually help to overcome the sad legacy of the region's history.

Jokowi once said, "Our homeland stretches from west to east. There are tens of thousands of islands that span the oceans, natural beauty, natural wealth, and amazing cultural diversity. With very challenging geographical conditions, the country continues to struggle and will continue to fight, so that equitable development can be carried out, from Sabang to Merauke."[69]

[64] "Lokasi Jembatan Trans Papua yang Pekerjanya Ditembak Mati oleh KKB," *Kumparan News*, December 4, 2018, https://kumparan.com/kumparannews/lokasi-jembatan-trans-papua-yang-pekerjanya-ditembak-mati-oleh-kkb-1543907954515593566 [accessed July 19, 2019].

[65] John Roy Purba, "Pura-pura Mati, Jimmi Selamat dari Pembantaian KKB di Nduga Papua," *Kompas*, December 5, 2018, https://regional.kompas.com/read/2018/12/05/08475511/pura-pura-mati-jimmi-selamat-dari-pembantaian-kkb-di-nduga-papua [accessed October 29, 2020].

[66] Mackenzie Smith, "West Papua Liberation Army claims responsibility for Papua killings," RNZ, December 5, 2020, https://www.rnz.co.nz/international/pacific-news/377548/west-papua-liberation-army-claims-responsibility-for-papua-killings https://www.bbc.com/news/world-asia-49806182#:~:text=A%20new%20wave%20of%20violence,were%20trapped%20inside%20burning%20buildings [accessed October 29, 2020].

[67] Setneg, *Laporan 4 Tahun Pemerintahan Jokowi-JK*, 100.

[68] "West Papua: Day of violence sees at least 27 dead," BBC, September 24, 2019 [accessed October 29, 2020].

[69] Sulistyo, *Konservatisme Politik Anti Jokowi*, 404.

Jokowi with Retno Marsudi at an ASEAN summit in 2019.

Chapter Ten

Jokowi and the World: Foreign Policy and International Relations

J okowi's long journey from the banks of the Kali Anyar has provided him with a wealth of relevant experience for leading Indonesia. The fairly humble family background; the still-strong link to the ancestral village; the conventional public education; then the taste of life as a relatively lowly employee of a state-owned company giving way to entrepreneurship with a very modest start-point: these were experiences that set him apart from the country's traditional political elite and which gave him a personal narrative thoroughly comprehensible to millions of ordinary Indonesians. His background had demonstrably informed his approach running Surakarta and Jakarta, and to great effect. But there was one area where his various predecessors, and the political elite more generally, seemed at first glance to be better qualified: the field of foreign affairs.

Those who have entered politics from the senior ranks of the military often arrive with extensive international officer training under their belt, and much experience of overseas deployments and joint training exercises with the militaries of neighboring countries. Jokowi's predecessor, Susilo Bambang Yudhoyono, is an excellent example of this. And since the 1960s, technocratic cabinet appointees and those who occupy Jakarta's high-level interface between business and politics tend to come laden with American postgraduate degrees. Jakarta governor Anies Baswedan, 2019 vice presidential challenger Sandiaga Uno, current state-owned enterprises minister Erick Thohir, and many others before them all fit this mold. Jokowi, meanwhile, has a bachelor's degree in a thoroughly practical field from a domestic university. He came to the presidency unaccustomed to foreign seminar rooms, and his spoken English, while more than adequate for entertaining international visitors, is certainly not fluent. Susilo Bambang Yudhoyono was perfectly at ease giving in-depth interviews, complete with abstract discussions, in English with foreign journalists; indeed, he seemed to relish it. But Jokowi typically relies on a translator for any extended encounter with the overseas media.[1] This leads to a certain opaqueness in international perceptions, a sometimes inadequate layer of mediation which fails properly to convey a sense of his character, and certainly any sense of how he might appear to other Indonesians.

There is also, it must be said, a tendency for international commentaries on Indonesia to be framed by the economic or geopolitical priorities of the countries from which they emanate, priorities which may be of minimal significance to the people of Indonesia or their government. At its worst, this discourse might be caricatured as "what Indonesia needs to do for Australia/the US," and it sometimes contains at least a suggestion of deeply anachronistic conceptions in which a compliant "Third World" is expected to take its instructions from "the West." But it is worth bearing in mind both what "foreign policy" actually is, and the specific nature of Indonesia's long-established and consistently maintained approach to the wider world as an impartial, non-aligned state.

The Indonesian Foreign Policy Tradition

According to Christopher Hill's formulation, "foreign policy is the hinge of domestic and international politics," the point at which internal and external impetuses intersect and determine a course of action.[2] But clearly, any strong state, governed with the interests of its own people to the fore, will tend to privilege the internal factors. Padelford and Lincoln describe the foreign policy of any country as "the overall result of the process by which a state translates its broadly conceived goals and interests into specific courses of action."[3] Plainly, national self-interest is the driving factor. Indeed, the nineteenth-century Prussian statesman Otto Von Bismarck put it most explicitly: "The extension of domestic policy is foreign policy."

---

[1] See, for example, Jokowi's 2016 BBC interview, available at https://www.youtube.com/watch?v=nnrX68k-EyI [accessed November 16, 2020].
[2] Cited in Alieu S. Bojang, "The Study of Foreign Policy in International Relations," *Journal of Political Sciences & Public Affairs* 6, no. 4 (2018): 2.
[3] Ibid.

The objectives of foreign policy are generally classified into three tiers, namely, the main objective (the main goals that must be achieved at all times, and which typically include sovereignty, autonomy, national interests, and territorial integrity); intermediate objectives (for example, foreign aid and so on, requiring cooperation with other countries); and long-term goals (for example, political or ideological visions in the international sphere).[4] The specifics of this are, of course, determined by the particular practical needs and ideological standpoint of a given country,[5] its domestic conditions,[6] policy-making networks,[7] and general character.[8] In Indonesia's case, this is all expressed in a very simple formula which has underpinned its for decades: *bebas-aktif*, "free and active."

Beyond this starting point, Indonesian is implemented based on principles that refer to the fourth paragraph of the Preamble of the 1945 Constitution: "to form a Government of the State of Indonesia that shall protect the whole people of Indonesia and the entire homeland of Indonesia, and in order to advance general prosperity, to develop the nation's intellectual life, and to contribute to the implementation of a world order based on freedom, lasting peace and social justice." Within this paragraph, there are several elements that constitute a mandate for the implementation of, namely, protecting the entire Indonesian nation and its people; promoting the common good; and helping to implement world order based on freedom, peace, and social justice. This constitutional mandate has always formed the ideological spirit of Indonesia's, which has also, typically, striven not to interfere in the domestic affairs of other nations.[9]

The "free and active" doctrine emerges from this in turn, as an approach which begins with the national interest. Firmly embedded in Indonesian foreign policy thinking for decades, it is rooted in the tradition of non-alignment pioneered by Sukarno in the 1950s. At its most basic,

---

[4] Kalevi Holsti, *International Politics: A Framework for Analysis*, 3rd edn (Englewood Cliffs, NJ: Prentice Hall, 1997).

[5] Mubeen Adnan, "Foreign Policy and Domestic Constraints: A Conceptual Account," *A Research Journal of South Asian Studies* 29, no. 2 (2014): 657.

[6] Fitrianidan Vido Chandra Panduwinata, *Analisis Kinerja Kementerian Luar Negeri Indonesia (2015–2018)* (CSIS Working Paper Series: WPSINT-3/2018), 32.

[7] Thomas Risse-Kappen, "Public Opinion, Domestic Structure, and Foreign Policy in Liberal Democracies," *World Politics* 43, no. 4 (1991).

[8] Rizal Sukma, *Islam in Indonesian Foreign Policy: Domestic Weakness and the Dilemma of Dual Identity* (London: Taylor and Francis, 2003); and James M. McCormick, ed., *The Domestic Sources of American Foreign Policy: Insights and Evidence* (Maryland: Rowman & Littlefield, 2012).

[9] Holsti, *International Politics*.

the "free and active" approach sees the country typically avoiding formal military or security alliances.

"Free and active" also has two essential emphases.[10] First, it dictates that Indonesia's foreign policy aims to maintain national identity. Secondly, it aims to educate the nation, improve people's welfare, and participate in maintaining world peace and order, in line with the Preamble to the 1945 Constitution. Although the latter aspiration can be seen as an external one, foreign policy is also intended to support the achievement of the first two ideals, which are more internal in nature: it is only through increasing national prosperity that participation in the maintenance of world peace be carried out. What is more, with the fulfillment of all these ideals, the goal of total independence will become meaningful and the sovereignty of the Indonesian nation and state will be achieved. This established Indonesian political philosophy can be identified as the underpinning of the formulation of the Jokowi government's vision and mission for foreign relations during his first term, namely, "the realization of an Indonesia that is sovereign, independent, and has an identity based on *gotong-royong* [mutual cooperation]."[11]

Jokowi's Nawacita vision, although largely directed at domestic issues, was also adapted to form the pillars of foreign policy, particularly those related to the security, stability, and independence of the Indonesian economy. The national objectives contained in Nawacita were translated into foreign policy directions through the National Medium-Term Development Plan (RPJMN) formulated by the Ministry of National Development Planning and the National Development Planning Agency (Bappenas). This acted as a policy guide for the Ministry of Foreign Affairs to formulate a framework for Indonesia's foreign policy activities in the 2014–2019 period, as outlined in its own Strategic Plan (Renstra).[12]

---

[10] Mangadar Situmorang, *Orientasi Kebijakan Politik Luar Negeri Indonesia di bawah Pemerintahan Jokowi-JK*, paper presented during a seminar on Networking Activities organized by the Secretariat of the Vice President, Hotel Grand Serela, Hegarmanah, Bandung, September 15, 2014.

[11] *Visi, Misi, dan Program Pemerintahan Jokowi & JK 2014–2019*.

[12] Panduwinata, *Analisis Kinerja Kementerian Luar Negeri Indonesia*, 2–3.

Expectations of Jokowi's Foreign Policy Approach

International perceptions of Indonesia's foreign policy, and indeed of its political culture as a whole, are inevitably heavily determined by its leader of the moment. Susilo Bambang Yudhoyono, with his polished presentation skills and penchant for the international summit and conference circuit, did an excellent job of promoting Indonesia's image internationally. His approach was typified as "a million friends and zero enemies,"[13] and he proved highly effective as a diplomatic presence. This, coupled with the period of solid economic growth that he oversaw, readily comprehensible as a simple statistic, fostered a generally favorable international perception of Indonesia during his presidency. But this international view failed to acknowledge the frustrated progress and considerable disaffection at home in the same period. Under Jokowi, meanwhile, the inverse has been true. A perception of a low-profile and inward-looking approach to foreign affairs when compared to SBY's record, has sometimes manifested as critical foreign commentaries of Jokowi's Indonesia, commentaries which may overlook or belittle the remarkable domestic developmental achievements of his first term and his ever-robust approval ratings even in the face of various upheavals and controversies.

The idea that Jokowi would be a more inward-looking president than SBY was already established before he won the 2014 election. Approaching the presidency without Fort Benning officer training certificates or a Harvard MBA, he would have little interest in or aptitude for international matters, or so the reasoning went. But this reading failed to acknowledge that Jokowi did, in fact, enter politics with considerable international experience, though it was experience with a very specific focus pertaining to his business background.

Jokowi had attended his first international expos in the early 1990s, a rising thirty-something entrepreneur without the glossy polish provided by an exclusive overseas education, but with a ready knack for informal personal engagement and a solid sense of what sold on the international market, and how to sell it. Through the final years of the New Order and into the Reformasi period, he totted up plenty of air miles, at first within Southeast Asia and then further afield in Europe and the Middle East. He also got well used to welcoming foreign would-be buyers in Surakarta,

---

[13] Ahmed Ibrahim Almuttaqi, *Jokowi's Indonesia and the World* (Singapore: World Scientific Publishing, 2020).

showing them around his workshop and deploying the best of Indonesian hospitality and charm. Of course, this international experience all came with a very clear and explicit focus: it was intended to generate sales, to advance his company, and later, as Asmindo's Surakarta chairman, to advance the local furniture industry more generally.

This formative understanding of interactions with the world beyond Indonesia did play into his ideas about foreign policy when he became president, with a distinct sharpening of focus towards tangible economic benefits rather than general prestige or goodwill. During one of the televised debates of the 2014 campaign, Jokowi raised the idea that Indonesia's ambassadors could act primarily as salespeople, devoting 80 percent of their time to marketing Indonesian products.[14] He reiterated this same idea in 2020.[15] In the first two years of his presidency, he also questioned the purpose of some of Indonesia's international activities. "Do not let us join international organizations just for formalities," he said, arguing that such memberships should be firmly based instead on the national interest, on what Indonesia got out of them, especially economically.[16] This thinking was, of course, very much that of the successful Surakarta businessman. But it was also in line with the wider established principles of Indonesian foreign policy based on the 1945 Constitution and the "free and active" doctrine.[17] Jokowi also brought at least one new grand concept with an international component to the table: his aspiration to develop Indonesia's potential as a "global maritime fulcrum," again, a business-minded concept.[18]

More broadly, however, Jokowi's approach to foreign policy has actually been consistent with that of his predecessor. His government has maintained many of the same individual approaches taken by SBY, even if Jokowi himself is less directly engaged, less obviously enthused by the role of president-as-diplomat. He is the leader of a nation of more than quarter of a billion people, after all, with a very long domestic to-do list; the bulk of his personal attention goes elsewhere.

---

[14] Ibid., xxiv.

[15] Hanni Sofia and Suwanti, "President Jokowi urges ambassadors to boost economic diplomacy," *Antara*, January 10, 2020, https://en.antaranews.com/news/139456/president-jokowi-urges-ambassadors-to-boost-economic-diplomacy [accessed November 15, 2020].

[16] Almuttaqi, *Jokowi's Indonesia and the World*, 83.

[17] *UU RI Nomor 37 Tahun 1999 tentang Hubungan Luar Negeri*, Bab. I, Pasal 2.

[18] CFP Luhulima, "Revisiting Jokowi's global maritime fulcrum," *The Jakarta Post*, April 30, 2019, https://www.thejakartapost.com/academia/2019/04/30/revisiting-jokowis-global-maritime-fulcrum.html [accessed November 15, 2020].

Jokowi in hard hat and customary untucked white shirt on the ground during a *blusukan* site visit to Kalimantan.

Jokowi, flanked by his deputy Jusuf Kalla, delivering his 2014 presidential victory speech aboard a traditional *pinisi* schooner at Jakarta's Sunda Kelapa harbor.

Jokowi reading the presidential oath during his inauguration on October 20, 2014.

Crowds throng Jakarta's streets on Jokowi's inauguration day.

Indonesia's first and second directly elected presidents stand side by side during Jokowi's inauguration.

The Kabinet Kerja, Jokowi's first-term "Working Cabinet," on the steps of the presidential palace.

Finance Minister Sri Mulyani Indrawati, a highly respected figure internationally, once rated by Forbes as amongst the world's most powerful women.

Luhut Binsar Panjaitan, cabinet stalwart and long-time Jokowi ally in business and politics, with then US Secretary of Defense Jim Mattis in 2017.

Jokowi's accomplished
foreign minister, Retno
L. P. Marsudi.

Jokowi in 2016 with then chief of the Indonesian Encryption Agency, Djoko
Setiadi, while Jusuf Kalla and Megawati look on. Djoko Setiadi became head of
the new National Cyber and Encryption Agency in 2018.

Road building has become a Jokowi trademark, with massive toll road projects, such as this intersection on the Cimanggis-Cibitung Toll Road on the outskirts of Jakarta.

With recent tourism investment and infrastructure upgrades, Labuan Bajo in East Nusa Tenggara has gone from sleepy fishing port with low-level backpacker traffic to major tourism center, attracting a large number of affluent domestic tourists as well as international travelers.

The Mandalika Special Economic Zone in southern Lombok is one of the Jokowi government's "Ten New Balis." For decades, tourism development in Lombok had remained stagnant despite the obvious potential.

The Sidrap wind farm in
South Sulawesi is one of
the first major projects in a
new push for renewable
energy in Indonesia.

Jokowi takes in the first sunrise of 2016 at the Waiwo jetty in the Raja Ampat archipelago at the western end of Papua.

Infrastructure projects have not been limited to massive road, seaport, and airport developments. Other programs have funded smaller construction projects to aid local connectivity, such as this bridge linking two communities near Sidoarjo in East Java.

Jokowi on a dirt bike touring an incomplete section of the Trans-Papua Highway, one of the most challenging of Indonesia's current infrastructure projects for political, security, and logistical reasons.

The Holtekamp Bridge, a major infrastructure project in Papua, connecting the regional capital, Jayapura, with the neighboring Muara Tami District. Jokowi's administration has invested massively in Papua.

Labuan Bajo, gateway to the Komodo National Park in East Nusa Tenggara, shown here, is one of the places identified and boosted by investment for tourism under the "Ten New Balis" program.

TOP Jokowi flicks the switch on a newly installed electricity connection provided free to underprivileged households in Bekasi in 2019, while the beneficiary, householder and shopkeeper Eni Nurbaini, looks on.

ABOVE Foreign Minister Retno Marsudi exchanges a cooperation agreement with her then Australian counterpart, Julie Bishop, during a visit to Australia in 2018, as Jokowi and then Australian Prime Minister Malcolm Turnbull look on.

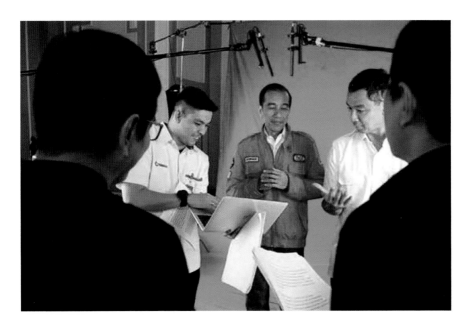

TOP Jokowi with Darmawan Prasodjo on his left, author of this book, during the image-capture process for the Holojokowi project for the 2019 election campaign.

ABOVE Shooting the hologram.

LEFT The finished Holojokowi project, ready for roll-out on the campaign trail.

BELOW The hologram in action during the 2019 presidential election campaign.

LEFT Jokowi and his running mate, Ma'ruf Amin, during the 2019 presidential election campaign.

BELOW The challengers, Prabowo Subianto with his running mate, Sandiaga Uno, a successful businessman and vice governor of Jakarta.

SURAT SUARA PEMILIHAN UMUM

2019
PEMILIHAN UMUM

PRESIDEN DAN WAKIL PRESIDEN REPUBLIK INDONESIA TAHUN 2019

A 2019 ballot paper.

A polling station in Kalimantan on the day of the 2019 presidential election.

Jokowi on the ground during a visit to East Nusa Tenggara.

Prabowo Subianto in his new role as defense minister, meeting with his US counterpart, Mark Esper, in Bangkok in late 2019.

Indonesia's parliamentary complex in Central Jakarta, with the iconic Nusantara Building with its distinctive wing-shaped roof in the background.

The Indonesian parliament, the Dewan Perwakilan Rakyat (People's Representative Council), in session.

Jokowi delivering his first address, virtually, to the United Nations General Assembly in September 2020. He called for global cooperation to ensure equal access to all Covid-19 vaccines.

Jokowi, the family man, with Iriana and their children and grandchildren.

Jokowi with other ASEAN leaders and the Korean president during the 2019 ASEAN-Republic of Korea Summit.

The same summit in 2020, held virtually due to Covid-19 restrictions.

The Kabinet Indonesia Maju, Jokowi's second-term
"Forward Indonesia Cabinet."

Jokowi, the president, at work.

Appointing a Foreign Minister

Coming into office with an agenda solidly focused on domestic issues, Jokowi needed to choose a foreign minister who could effectively be left to get on with the job. Some argued for retaining the man already in the post, Susilo Bambang Yudhoyono's slick foreign affairs chief Marty Natalegawa.[19] But while there is something to be said for continuity, this might inadvertently have signaled a particular disinterest in the foreign policy field, confirming the pre-emptive critique of various pundits. Instead, Jokowi chose another thoroughly qualified candidate, who also happened to be Indonesia's first female foreign minister.

Retno Marsudi was already a Ministry of Foreign Affairs veteran by 2014. Hailing from Semarang on the north coast of Java, she had first developed an interest in diplomacy as a teenager, and had gone on to study international relations at Gadjah Mada University where she was a contemporary of Jokowi. Her first foreign posting was to Canberra in 1990. Various roles in Europe followed before she was appointed Indonesia's ambassador to Norway and Iceland in 2005. By the time she got the call to join Jokowi's Working Cabinet, she was two years into another ambassadorial posting, this time to the Netherlands. She proved to be a highly competent foreign minister, and was one of the few ministers to retain her post in the new Forward Indonesia Cabinet after Jokowi's re-election in 2019.

Jokowi's preference has always been for a collaborative foreign policy that provides concrete benefits for the Indonesian people, in line with the stated aims of his administration to create national security, maintain territorial sovereignty, sustain economic independence by securing maritime resources, and reflect Indonesia's personality as an archipelago and its identity as a maritime country. The mission was formulated in the 2015–19 Ministry of Foreign Affairs Strategic Plan. This framework was branded with the slogan "Diplomacy for the People" and it laid out a stated vision for "The realization of diplomacy to strengthen the national identity as a maritime nation for the benefit of the people."

The Strategic Plan outlined three key missions, three aims, and eight strategic objectives for the Ministry of Foreign Affairs during Jokowi's first term. The three missions were strengthening Indonesia's leadership as a maritime country on the international stage; ensuring high-quality diplomatic representation; and strengthening the primacy of the Ministry

---

[19] Almuttaqi, *Jokowi's Indonesia and the World*, 9.

of Foreign Affairs as the executor of foreign relations. Foreign policy was also informed by the Nawacita framework and the National Medium Term Development Plan (RPJMN), which contained five relevant pillars: security and peace; economic diplomacy; protection of Indonesian citizens and interests overseas; ASEAN cooperation; and maritime diplomacy.[20]

During Jokowi's first term, these five pillars served for focus and guidance of foreign policy activities, and the country gradually increased its diplomatic footprint, opening new diplomatic relationships with three countries in 2016, namely, Chad, the Central African Republic, and Equatorial Guinea. This brought Indonesia's tally of diplomatic relationships to 190 of the 193 UN member states. In that same year, Jokowi recorded 55 bilateral and international meetings. The vice president recorded 13 separate meetings, while Retno Marsudi held a total of 302 bilateral and international meetings and the deputy minister of foreign affairs, Abdurrahman Mohammad Fachir, held 35.

Meanwhile, the Ministry of Foreign Affairs continued handling its multitude of routine tasks and problems. Amongst the issues that are permanently in the in-tray of the ministry is that of protecting Indonesian citizens abroad. A good deal of popular attention at home is given to the stories of Indonesian migrant workers, 75 percent of whom are women.[21] For decades, large numbers of young Indonesian women, typically from poor rural backgrounds, have been recruited to work as maids, cleaners, and nannies overseas, particularly in neighboring Southeast Asian countries as well as Hong Kong and the Middle East. Stories of the hardships and abuse that some of them face often emerge in the Indonesian media, and sometimes compel government intervention. Currently, Indonesia will only allow the recruitment of migrants if the destination country has regulations protecting such workers or has a bilateral cooperation agreement with Indonesia. The Ministry of Foreign Affairs has collaborated with other ministries to build online networks of communication to allow

---

[20] Kementerian Luar Negeri, "Pernyataan Pers Tahunan Menteri Luar Negeri Republik Indonesia YM Retno L. P. Marsudi Tahun 2015"; "Pernyataan Pers Tahunan Menteri Luar Negeri Republik Indonesia YM Retno L. P. Marsudi Tahun 2016"; "Pernyataan Pers Tahunan Menteri Luar Negeri Republik Indonesia YM Retno L. P. Marsudi Tahun 2017"; "Pernyataan Pers Tahunan Menteri Luar Negeri Republik Indonesia YM Retno L. P. Marsudi Tahun 2018."

[21] ICRC, Statistics on Labor Migration within the Asia-Pacific Region (2013), available at http://www.ifrc.org/Global/Documents/Asia-pacific/201505/Map_Infographic.pdf [accessed November 17, 2020]; and World Bank, Indonesia's Global Workers: Juggling Opportunities & Risks (Jakarta: November 2017), available at http://pubdocs.worldbank.org/en/357131511778676366/Indonesias-Global-Workers-Juggling-Opportunities-Risks.pdf [accessed November 17, 2020].

migrant workers to connect with diplomatic services and to provide assistance to any who find themselves in trouble, assistance which may include legal aid support.

In terms of protecting Indonesian citizens abroad more generally, in the 2014–19 period the Ministry of Foreign Affairs succeeded in freeing 25 Indonesians who were held hostage by the Abu Sayyaf group in the Southern Philippines. Four Indonesian citizens who had been held hostage in Somalia for 4.5 years were also released. The Indonesian authorities also succeeded in resolving 11,065 legal cases involving Indonesian citizens abroad, and deployed diplomatic pressure to exempt 71 Indonesian citizens from the death penalty in other countries. Jokowi's government was also able to rescue 399 victims of human trafficking and to repatriate 41,569 Indonesian citizens in difficulties abroad. Indonesian diplomats also worked to return funds amounting to more than Rp92 billion to Indonesians abroad through Islamic victim compensation (*diyat*) and other means. A total of 512 Indonesian sailors in trouble overseas also received assistance.[22]

Indonesia has also demonstrated its leadership in environmental issues by ratifying the Paris Agreement in November 2016. It was elected as a member of the Paris Committee on Capacity Building (PCCB) for climate change mitigation and adaptation. Indonesia also hosted the Habitat III Conference PrepCom meeting in Surabaya in July 2016. Its initiative on global cooperation in reef management was accepted through the UN Sustainable Coral Reefs Management resolution.[23]

Apart from all that, one area of foreign policy in which the president himself is particularly interested is economic diplomacy, which he has encouraged since the start of his time in office, and which is emphasized in the 14 Economic Policy Packages that have been issued by his government. The Ministry of Foreign Affairs is part of the Working Group I which handles Economic Policy Campaigns and Dissemination at the Task Force for the Acceleration and Effectiveness of the Implementation of Economic Policy (PEPKE). During 2016, 149 bilateral and multilateral economic agreements were agreed. That same year, 125 countries participated in the 2016 Trade Expo Indonesia which recorded transactions of US$974.76 million and saw the signing of 31 trade contracts worth a further US$200 million. For Jokowi, all of this represented an entirely familiar process, that

---

[22] "Pernyataan Pers Tahunan Menteri Luar Negeri Republik Indonesia YM Retno L. P. Marsudi Tahun 2017."
[23] Ibid.

which he had first engaged in as a young entrepreneur. But now it was an entire country rather than one small furniture company that was looking to sign contracts and strike international deals.

The Promotion of Peace

Indonesia's generally low profile on the circuits of international politics means that its long track record in the promotion of global peace is often overlooked. In fact, Indonesia is the eighth largest contributor of peace-keeping forces to conflict areas globally. Jokowi quietly maintained this tradition throughout his first term. In 2016, there were 2,731 Indonesian personnel serving on nine UN missions;[24] four years later, there were 2,847 Indonesian peacekeepers deployed around the globe. Elsewhere in the 2014–2019 period, a diplomatic emphasis was maintained on global peace and stability. On Indonesia's initiative, it was agreed to form a Contact Group on Peace and Reconciliation at the Organisation of Islamic Coop-eration to help resolve long-term tensions between Iran and Saudi Arabia.

As the world's largest Muslim-majority state, Indonesia has always been a strong proponent of Palestinian independence and sovereignty, a stance that has been consistently maintained under Jokowi. In March 2016, Jakarta hosted an Organisation of Islamic Cooperation Extraordinary Summit on Palestine and Al-Quds Al-Sharif (Jerusalem), which produced the "Jakarta Declaration" in support of Palestinian independence. Later that year, Indonesia's cooperation with the Arab League was strengthened through the signing of a Memorandum of Cooperation to advance eco-nomic cooperation, democracy, good governance, and interfaith dialogue.

Indonesia also maintained a firm line rejecting the status of Jerusalem as the capital of Israel. And it has made a number of practical gestures for the benefit of Palestinians. In 2016, Retno Marsudi inaugurated a new honorary Indonesian consulate in Ramallah, headed by a Palestinian businesswoman, and in 2018 the government agreed to exempt Palestinian dates and olive oil, key agricultural export products, from Indonesian import tariffs.

In another area of conflict, Indonesia has had a steady presence in efforts towards the reconciliation of hostile groups in Afghanistan. Indo-nesia was one of a number of countries invited to attend the 2020 Geneva Conference on Afghanistan. Jokowi also hosted a trilateral meeting with

---

[24] "Pernyataan Pers Tahunan Menteri Luar Negeri Republik Indonesia YM Retno L. P. Marsudi Tahun 2017," Jakarta, January 10, 2017.

Afghanistan and Pakistan in Bogor in 2018, aimed at fostering peace and reducing extremism and violence in the region. Indonesia agreed to provide scholarships for police training, support for infrastructure development, and encouragement for the empowerment of women in Afghanistan. In 2019, meanwhile, Retno Marsudi signed an agreement to build a clinic in Kabul at the Indonesian Islamic Center there, a wider project originally launched in collaboration with Nahdlatul Ulama in 2016.[25]

Elsewhere, Indonesia also took a firm stance on the actions of North Korea, with the Ministry of Foreign Affairs formally issuing a statement over nuclear testing: "The Indonesian Government deeply regrets the nuclear test carried out by the Democratic People's Republic of Korea on 9 September 2016, which is not in line with the spirit of creating peace and stability in the region and the world."[26] The vibrations of the test had actually been detected within Indonesia by the Meteorology, Climatology, and Geophysical Agency (BMKG). It was a violation of both the Test Ban Treaty (CTBT) and UN Security Council resolutions 1718 (2006), 1874 (2009), and 2087 (2013), and led to heightened tensions in a region not far beyond Indonesia's own doorstep.

Also in the wider region, during Jokowi's first term Indonesia continued diplomatic efforts, begun during Marty Natalegawa's time as foreign minister, to resolve tensions over Myanmar's treatment of the Muslim minority Rohingya population in Rakhine State, an issue that had attracted much public attention in Indonesia and led to a number of protests in support of the Rohingya Muslims. Rather than simply issuing condemnations of Myanmar's actions, as a fellow ASEAN member state Indonesia's approach to this issue has been dialogic, based on offers of resolution assistance and immediate and longer-term cooperation, albeit with a firm emphasis on the importance of inclusive development, respect for human rights, and protection of all communities. Various communications and meetings were held by Indonesia, including with the then state counselor of Myanmar, Aung San Suu Kyi, chairman of the Rakhine Advisory Commission, Kofi Annan, and senior Bangladeshi representatives, as well as various other stakeholders in Jakarta, Yangon, and Dhaka.[27]

---

[25] Marguerite Afra Sapiie, "Foreign Ministry, NU to open Islamic Center in Afghanistan," *The Jakarta Post*, May 12, 2016, https://www.thejakartapost.com/news/2016/05/12/foreign-ministry-nu-to-open-islamic-center-in-afghanistan.html [accessed November 17, 2020].

[26] Media broadcast, Kementerian Luar Negeri, Saturday, September 10, 2016.

[27] "Pernyataan Pers Tahunan Menteri Luar Negeri Republik Indonesia YM Retno L. P. Marsudi Tahun 2017."

ASEAN and the South China Sea

Indonesia's most immediate foreign policy imperatives often relate to its membership of the regional ASEAN grouping, the ten-member Association of Southeast Asian Nations. ASEAN has a firm priority position at the regional level of Indonesian foreign policy. There are three main priorities in ASEAN cooperation for Indonesia, namely, security, economic growth, and social cooperation in the region. As the largest country in the grouping, geographically and economically, it plays an essential role.

For ASEAN and the wider region, the key flashpoint is the South China Sea, an area that is disputed by many countries and in which Indonesia also has its own stake. The countries directly involved in territorial disputes there are China, Taiwan, Vietnam, the Philippines, Brunei Darussalam, and Malaysia, with conflict particularly focused on control of the Paracel and Spratly islands. The underlying causes of conflict in this maritime region are various. The South China Sea contains enormous natural resources, including oil and gas deposits. It is also a vital crossing route for international shipping, connecting European, American, and Asian trade routes, and of general strategic importance in an area of rapid economic development.[28]

Indonesia's own territorial waters extend to the southernmost fringes of the South China Sea, but in terms of the disputes there it is a non-claimant state, and it maintains a position of pushing for peaceful resolution to the conflict, encouraging ASEAN and China to complete the proposed Code of Conduct in the South China Sea. At the same time, Indonesia has been mindful of its own proximity to the disputes, specifically in the waters around the remote Natuna Archipelago. Based on the 1957 Djuanda Declaration, which formally integrated the entirety of Indonesia's maritime and land territories, and the 1982 Sea Law Convention, the country's outermost maritime frontiers were registered with the United Nations in 2009. There is a degree of overlap in the Natuna area with the claims of Malaysia and Vietnam, but this has been the focus of ongoing and generally low-stakes diplomatic discussion. However, China's highly contentious "nine-dash line" demarcating its sweeping claims to the South China Sea does, in its southern extremity, overlap Indonesia's Exclusive Economic Zone (EEZ). This area is particularly sensitive because of the issue of persistent incursions by foreign fishing vessels, including some from China. At the start of

---

[28] Muhar Junef, "Sengketa Wilayah Maritim di Laut Tiongkok Selatan," *Jurnal Penelitian Hukum De Jure* 18 (2018).

Jokowi's first term, the Indonesian authorities pursued a high-profile policy of impounding and sinking vessels caught fishing illegally in its waters. But the problem has not been entirely resolved, and though Indonesia seeks to avoid getting sucked into the vortex of the South China Sea dispute by insisting on its non-claimant status, in May 2020 it felt compelled to submit diplomatic correspondence to the UN reiterating its position over the outer maritime reaches of its Exclusive Economic Zone.[29]

In the field of border diplomacy, Indonesia maintains a position of encouraging all parties to respect international law, and its own diplomatic wrangles with Vietnam and Malaysia have progressed during Jokowi's presidency. Throughout 2016, the Ministry of Foreign Affairs held 20 meetings regarding maritime boundaries and 16 meetings regarding land boundaries.[30] One of the main achievements in this area during that period was the ratification of the Indonesia-Singapore Maritime Boundary Agreement on December 15, 2016.[31] There was also agreement on the draft MOU for the 20th Survey and Demarcation between Indonesia and Malaysia for the land boundary of North Kalimantan and Sabah; and completion of the final phase of two unresolved segments on the land boundary of Indonesia and Timor Leste. Negotiations on maritime boundaries continued through 2017 with Vietnam, Thailand, India, and Palau. The ratification of the determination of the Indonesia-Philippines EEZ boundary also took place that year.

In 2017, Indonesia became chair and host of the meeting of heads of state members of the Indian Ocean Rim Association (IORA). This organization, along with the East Asia Summit (EAS), together with diplomatic resolution of territorial disputes, were identified as vital to realizing the potential of Indonesia as a "global maritime fulcrum" connecting the Asia-Pacific region and the Indian Ocean.

Indonesia at the United Nations

The middle of 2018 was marked by a notable achievement for Indonesia's diplomacy: the country's selection as a Non-Permanent Member of the UN

---

[29] Viet Hoang, "The Code of Conduct for the South China Sea: A Long and Bumpy Road," *The Diplomat*, September 28, 2020, https://thediplomat.com/2020/09/the-code-of-conduct-for-the-south-china-sea-a-long-and-bumpy-road/ [accessed November 16, 2020].

[30] "Pernyataan Pers Tahunan Menteri Luar Negeri Republik Indonesia YM Retno L. P. Marsudi Tahun 2017."

[31] Ibid.

Security Council, a reflection of its solid, if low-key, standing in international diplomatic circles, and in particular its strong record of contributing peacekeeping personnel to UN operations.

The role of Indonesia's peacekeeping forces, known as the Garuda Contingent, began with the deployment of its first mission to Egypt in 1957. A 559-strong infantry contingent served there as part of the United Nations Emergency Force (UNEF) in Sinai. The Garuda Contingent also dispatched at battalion level in Congo twice in the 1960s, and returned to Egypt for two further tours in the 1970s (Garuda VI, 1973–1974; and Garuda VIII, 1974–1979). Indonesian forces also served as peacekeepers in Cambodia from 1992 to 1994, and in Bosnia in 1995. More recently, the Garuda XXIII Contingent as part of UNIFIL completed a long deployment in Lebanon (2006–2015). And currently, Indonesian troops are serving on eight UN peacekeeping missions, namely, UNIFIL (Lebanon), UNAMID (Darfur, Sudan), MINUSCA (Central African Republic), MONUSCO (Democratic Republic of the Congo), MINUSMA (Mali), MINURSO (Western Sahara), UNMISS (South Sudan), and UNISFA (Abyei, Sudan).

Indonesia's participation in UN Peacekeeping operations is, like all of its foreign policy engagements, based on the Preamble of the 1945 Constitution as well as the Law on Foreign Relations No. 37 of 1999, Law no. 34 of 2004 concerning the Indonesian National Army, Law no. 2 of 2002 concerning the Indonesian National Police, and Law no. 3 of 2002 concerning National Defense, as well as the UN Charter.

The most recent stint as a Non-Permanent Member of the UN Security Council ran for two years, from January 1, 2019 to December 31, 2020. This was the fourth time that Indonesia had been elected to the Security Council. Previously, it held the position 1973–1974, 1995–1996, and 2007–2008. In its most recent election in June 2018, Indonesia received 144 votes from the 193 UN member states, roundly winning over the other Asia-Pacific candidate, the Maldives. Here, again, during Jokowi's first term was a solid signal of foreign policy continuity, a maintenance of Indonesia's well-established position in the wider world, and its long traditions of engagement.

The author, Darmawan Prasodjo (right), discussing the Hologram project with the president during preparations for the 2019 election.

Chapter Eleven

Hologram President: Fighting a Hi-Tech Election

March 2019, a month out from the presidential election, on a narrow road above a ravine in the foggy hills of the East Priangan region of West Java. This is not one of the imposing new toll roads that have spread their web across Indonesia over the last five years, nor even one of the upgraded or repaired regional roads. It is a minor back route between villages, not designed for the two five-ton trucks inching along it. And with the rain of the late wet season sheeting down, it is little surprise that one of the trucks eventually gets stuck in the mud on a broken stretch of the road. Gears crunch, wheels spin, but the truck is hopelessly bogged.

Eight people gather in the rain beside the trucks, but it is clear that they cannot free the trapped vehicle without assistance. Two members of the team set off down the road on foot to look for help in the nearest village, four kilometers away. Another makes a worried phone call to Jakarta. They are on a tight schedule and need to be in Cikajang, south of Garut, within a few hours. But the trucks are not carrying vital emergency supplies; they are loaded with hi-tech audio-visual equipment. They are delivering a message, a message from the president of Indonesia.

Holojokowi: Taking the President to the People

Jokowi's team have long been aware of a certain conundrum. The president's easy-going personal charm is well-attested, and associates have long commented that whenever voters have the chance to meet Jokowi face-to-face they are almost invariably won over. But this quality does not transfer particularly well to the podium at large rallies or the stage at formal events. In Surakarta, and even in Jakarta, Jokowi's frequent informal *blusukan* had allowed him to connect directly with significant numbers of his voters. But given the vast scale of the Indonesian nation and its enormous population, his *blusukan* as president could only ever bring him into direct contact with a tiny proportion of citizens. And the heightened security and more complex choreography involved has inevitably eroded the open informality which had been possible in his earlier roles.

During the 2019 election, Jokowi would, once again, be going head to head with Prabowo, a man with indisputable rhetorical flair and considerable on-stage charisma. What was more, the challenger was paired this time with Sandiaga Uno, another notably slick public performer. This was an election in which personality and, more to the point, projection of that personality, would matter. How, then, could they bring "the real Jokowi" directly to as many of people with the power to return him to office as possible? The solution was obvious: if there was more than one Jokowi, then he could cover more ground, get onto the stump in more villages and small towns. And so, the idea of "Holojokowi" came about.

In 2018, a research and design team was put together headed by the author of this book, Darmawan Prasodjo, to create a hologram system for use during the upcoming presidential election. This would not be the first time that a politician had used a hologram for campaign purposes. Both India's Narendra Modi and Turkey's Recep Tayyip Erdoğan have used holograms in recent years.[1] But the previous examples have tended to be either impractical one-offs or produced at astronomical expense. The aim in this instance was to produce a practical device that could carry a "virtual Jokowi" to as many locations as possible. The challenge was to create a hologram mechanism that was portable, robust enough to survive frequent assemblage and dismantlement, and yet light and compact enough to be

---

[1] "President's hologram hits Indonesia's election campaign trail," *The Guardian*, March 28, 2019, https://www.theguardian.com/world/2019/mar/28/president-hologram-indonesia-election-campaign-joko-widodo [accessed November 12, 2020].

carried by trucks that could traverse the narrow village lanes and winding rural back roads. After much trial and error, a design was created involving a single sheet of reflective glass and instrumentation integrated into the body of a medium-sized truck. But a serious problem was identified with the prototype: it took around eight hours to install and make ready for a performance, which would seriously hamper plans for multiple screenings across a wide area. This issue was ultimately solved by the addition of semi-automated hydraulic systems to hoist the heavy components into place; the reflective glass alone weighed 300 kilograms. The final model could be fully installed by a five-person team in just an hour and a half.

Once the prototype was perfected, a total of ten such customized trucks were hurriedly created, each to be paired with a second customized truck to carry the generator needed to power the equipment and to provide space for the crew who would run the performances. These eight-person operating teams were put together and given extensive training, including preparation for going into the field in heavily opposition-favoring areas during what was widely predicted to be a tense and volatile campaign.

Next, attention turned to the image capture process. In early 2019, Jokowi shot the greenscreen footage which would be used to generate the hologram. The designers were eager to capture as authentic as possible a sense of the man himself, with something of the humor, emotion, and sincerity often remarked upon during his more informal *blusukan*. Dressed in sneakers, blue jeans, and his trademark untucked white shirt, Jokowi talked about the Healthy Indonesia and Smart Indonesia Cards and other social welfare programs, and about his infrastructure and development policies. He also directly addressed the various false rumors that were already circulating, some reheated from the 2014 campaign, others cooked up afresh, disputing his religion and ethnic background, alleging that he was a closet communist and claiming various ludicrous planned second-term policies, such as banning all Muslim prayer. The performance was deliberately designed to be given interactively in front of a live audience, with pauses built in for crowd responses. Ma'ruf Amin also recorded a segment, in which he directly addressed the misappropriation of religious discourse for political purposes. Illustrative footage was put together to accompany the holograms on large screens.

The ten individual teams rolled out of Jakarta in March 2019, with the election campaign at its height, and with the storm clouds of the wet season still frequently darkening the sky. A total of 98 individual locations had been identified for hologram performances, to be completed in a three-week timeframe. Sometimes an individual team had to conduct three showings in a single day. The campaign covered Banten Province, as well as Jakarta and parts of Central Java. But the main emphasis was on West Java, with a particular focus on nineteen districts and cities in the Bogor-Bekasi, East Priangan, and West Priangan areas. These were known strongholds of support for Jokowi's opponent, places where it was felt that direct contact with the president might make a material difference. The individual locations for hologram shows were determined through micro-targeting analysis, with a particular emphasis on "hotspots" where anti-Jokowi rhetoric was known to be particularly pronounced and where fake news stories were particularly prevalent. The fact that the small operating teams would be traveling deep into opposition party- and Prabowo-supporting communities sometimes made for fraught experiences. The teams had to deal with intransigent anti-Jokowi local officials and with security concerns in particularly hostile areas.

The teams also faced the practical challenges of moving through remote rural areas during the wet season, as was the case when the hologram truck got bogged down on a mountain road en route to Cikajang. After a lengthy wait, the two team members who had headed off in the rain to seek help from the nearest village returned with an enthusiastic army of volunteers. The locals put their shoulders to the trapped truck, and with a unified heave were able to free it and send the team on their way, with just enough time to reach their next scheduled show. It was a classic and deeply traditional example of *gotong-royong*, with village-style massed strength saving the day for state-of-the-art campaigning technology, neatly encapsulating the complex and contrasting logistics of electioneering in contemporary Indonesia.

The teams on the ground documented thoroughly positive responses wherever they went, with crowds enthusiastically responding to the call-and-response elements of the hologram president's delivery and giving warm feedback in the aftermath. But a key question remains, of course: did the hologram work?

The "Holojokowi" campaign certainly attracted considerable media attention, with extensive broadcast and print coverage, and also a number of international reports, including in *The Guardian* and *The Straits Times*. This in itself had campaign value, helping to reboot the quirky, youthful, innovative element of Jokowi's 2014 appeal, and also bolstering his emerging emphasis on human resources and the digital economy. The hologram project had, after all, been conceived, designed, built, and operated by a youthful all-Indonesian team. But did it have any impact on the ground in the target areas?

When final vote analysis was conducted, it was apparent that Jokowi had still trailed Prabowo in the nineteen West Java regencies and cities where the hologram campaign was conducted. Even when the analysis was narrowed to the level of village or subdistrict, Jokowi still lost in most target areas. But when the analysis was taken down still further, to the level of individual polling stations, it was found that at those stations located closest to the precise locations of the hologram performances, Jokowi had generally outperformed his rival by a significant margin. Clearly, then, the hologram campaign had had an impact. It might not have been as widespread as hoped, but it had been a productive pilot for future hi-tech electioneering in a vast nation. And it demonstrated that wherever Indonesians came into direct contact with Jokowi, whether in the flesh or merely in hologram form, they tended to favor him at the ballot box.

Election Themes and Undertones

The elections of April 17, 2019 were a democratic exercise on a vast scale. Some 192.8 million people were eligible to vote. As usual in Indonesia, polling day was designated a national holiday and scheduled for a Wednesday, a move intended to maximize participation, the reasoning being that if a poll was held at the beginning or end of a week, many people would be tempted to take advantage of the resultant long weekend for a holiday or a return to a home village instead of voting. Ballots would be cast at 800,000 polling stations scattered across the country from Sabang to Merauke. And not only would Indonesians be electing their president and vice president, they would also be voting for DPR and DPD members as well as members of some provincial and regency legislatures. Over 20,000 elected positions were up for grabs, and some six million election workers were hired to run the process. While some concerns were raised at the possibility of problems with the logistics of such a huge operation, long-term observers expressed few serious doubts about Indonesia's capacity to organize such a massive election.[2] The logistical mechanism of democracy is something that the country has always done well.

---

[2] "Guide to the 2019 Indonesian Elections: Path to the Presidency," The Australia-Indonesia Centre, September 20, 2018, https://australiaindonesiacenre.org/culture/politics/guide-to-the-2019-indonesian-elections-path-to-the-presidency/ [accessed November 12, 2020].

What was more troubling was the undertone of the presidential race itself. If the 2014 campaign had routinely been described as "divisive," that word was yet more apt in 2019. But as ever in Indonesian politics, a glance at the rival candidates' "vision and mission" statements, or at their various policy pronouncements revealed little sense of fundamental division. Both Jokowi and Prabowo had firmly positioned themselves once more in the traditional nationalist camp. Jokowi's team placed a heavy emphasis on the obvious developmental successes of his first term, the roads, the ports, the bridges, and on his deservedly popular social justice programs, such as the Healthy Indonesia Card and the various educational subsidy schemes. The message was of progress made and momentum gained, but with more work to be done in a second term. There was also a new emphasis, in line with Jokowi's pronouncements during the second half of his first term, on improving Indonesia's human capital, and on providing opportunities for small businesses. These emphases were outlined in a 38-page mission statement, issued in early December. As in 2014, it began with an aim to develop a sovereign, independent Indonesia with characteristics based on *gotong-royong*. The title of this program for a second term was Indonesia Maju, "Forward Indonesia."

Prabowo, meanwhile, went for a strong economic emphasis. The rupiah was still weak at the time and had passed the 15,000-to-the-dollar mark, which stirred up bad memories of the currency meltdown at the end of the Suharto era. In truth, the 2019 situation was very different: this time, the rupiah's fall was matched by most other relevant currencies, including those of Indonesia's neighbors. It was really only a decline relative to a dollar on the rise against virtually everything else, and the Indonesian economy as a whole was doing well. But still, the rupiah-dollar rate had potent historical resonances and the capacity to prompt popular anxiety. Prabowo plugged into this. He promised tax cuts and argued for the reduction of dependence on foreign investments in firm line with conventional Indonesian economic nationalism. There was a hint of the divisiveness in this last point: it spoke to popular resentment at the scale of recent investment from China in the Indonesian economy, resentment tangled up with old domestic ethnic prejudices. Religion also remained a factor, bubbling beneath the surface of the campaign discourse.

Jokowi's choice of Ma'ruf Amin as running mate had sent a clear message about the religious credentials of his government, and PKB was joined in his supporting coalition by two other Muslim parties, PPP and PBB. But in some ways Amin's vice presidential candidacy had simply served, in terms of voting allegiance, to separate the traditionalist Nahdlatul Ulama base from the rest of the political-Islam constituency and it was that other, non-NU section that generally accommodated the more determinedly Islamist and avowedly sectarian elements. The crowds at some of Prabowo's rallies featured a clearly identifiable Islamist component,[3] with continuities from the anti-Ahok movement of two years earlier.

The Millennial Factor

In the wider jostling for position, the youth vote had been identified as a key to electoral success. There would be five million first-time voters in 2019, and as much as 40 percent of the entire electorate had been classified as "millennial." In 2014, Jokowi very clearly had the edge when it came to that demographic. His style, existing profile, and outsider status gained him almost automatic support from many younger voters. But this time around he was fighting from a position of incumbency, a position which never lends itself to youth cred, despite efforts to woo fashionistas with some sharp PDI-P-branded clothes and accessories,[4] and despite the interest generated by innovative campaigning such as the hologram. Jokowi's running mate was a septuagenarian cleric, hardly the most obvious figure to connect with the youth vote. Prabowo, meanwhile, was paired with the preternaturally youthful and famously good-looking Sandiaga Uno, who strove to work up his appeal to millennials throughout the campaign. Jokowi's choice of Erick Thohir as his campaign chief was at least in part driven by the need to create a counterbalance to Sandiaga. Thohir was likewise a billionaire businessman with a youthful edge and obvious media savvy, and indeed a contemporary and long-time friend of Sandiaga.[5] His business interests included foreign sports teams, and he had headed the organization of the hugely successful 2018 Asian Games.[6]

---

[3] "Cheat Sheet: All You Need to Know About Indonesia's Elections," *Vice*, April 16, 2019, https://www.vice.com/en/article/mb8j43/cheat-sheet-all-you-need-to-know-about-indonesia-presidential-election-2019 [accessed November 12, 2020].

[4] "In fashion," *The Jakarta Post*, September 21, 2018, https://www.thejakartapost.com/news/2018/09/21/in-fashion.html [accessed November 12, 2020].

[5] Kevin Evans, *Guide to the 2019 Indonesia Elections* (Melbourne: The Australia-Indonesia Centre, 2019).

[6] "Indonesia president picks Asian Games chief to run re-election campaign," Reuters, September 7, 2018, https://www.reuters.com/article/us-indonesia-politcs/indonesia-president-picks-asian-games-chief-to-run-re-election-campaign-idUSKCN1LN1N9 [accessed November 13, 2020].

In 2014, and in his previous pre-presidential election campaigns, Jokowi had been confident of his own capacity, part intuitive and personality-based, part drawn from his own businessman's understanding of branding and marketing, to pitch himself to voters. But now he was calling in the big guns.

But the millennial vote, obsessive focus of many a campaign strategist, was a new and amorphous element of the Indonesian political scene, one that defied simple targeting. From generation to generation in Indonesia, "the Youth" (*Pemuda* in Indonesian) have played a central role in driving political discourse and forcing change. The earliest complete formula of Indonesian nationalism was the "Youth Pledge" way back in 1928. It was the restive Pemuda who compelled the middle-aged Sukarno to act and issue the unilateral proclamation of Independence in 1945, and it was the Pemuda who were in the vanguard of revolutionary action in the years that followed. Half a century later, another Pemuda generation, in the form of fiercely committed student activists and protesters, helped to precipitate the fall of Suharto. But as a demographic, millennials are far more amorphous and clearly not representative of any particular "movement." Most are committed users of the internet and social media, but their political engagement is typically understood to be low, as in many other parts of the world. Indeed, in the run-up to the 2019 election, Indonesia's millennials were characterized by one researcher as "conspicuous consumers, digital natives, and politically apathetic."[7] Recent surveys have suggested that only 2.1 percent of this generation in Indonesia use the internet for seeking news and that just 2.3 percent of them have a declared interest in discussion of politics and social issues.[8] Unsurprisingly, then, as polling day approached, some were wondering whether the millennials would bother to vote at all.

There was also more talk ahead of the 2019 election of a possibly significant golput wave than there had been for many years. Golput, short for *golongan putih*, or "white group," refers to the practice of deliberately marking an empty section of a ballot paper instead of piercing the designated box of one of the candidates (in Indonesia, ballots are punctured rather than marked with pen or pencil). The phenomenon, and the name, dates back to 1971 and the very first New Order election.[9] Golput persisted

---

[7] Budi Irawanto, "Young and Faithless: Wooing Millennials in Indonesia's 2019 Presidential Election," *ISEAS Perspective 2019*, no. 1 (2019): 2.

[8] Ibid., 3.

[9] Dwight Y. King, trans., *The White Book on the 1992 General Election in Indonesia* (Singapore: Equinox Publishing, 2010), 9.

as a deliberate form of low-key political protest throughout the New Order era. Now, in 2019, some young Indonesians were saying that they would embrace the practice anew to express their dissatisfaction with the political choices on offer.[10]

Some of those young people claiming that they would deliberately reject both candidates were from the liberal sector of the educated middle classes. They expressed disappointment over human rights and environmental issues in the previous five years. There were also committed secularists amongst them, who had expressed distaste at Jokowi's pairing with Ma'ruf Amin. Such people would almost certainly have been Jokowi voters in 2014, and it was generally assumed that any golput trend in 2019 would be to the president's disadvantage.[11] But, in the event, willful abstentions were not a major factor in the election.

For all the cynicism of a relatively small number of disillusioned students, on the ground in the run-up to the vote, it was obvious that many middle-class Indonesians from religious and ethnic minority backgrounds were genuinely alarmed by the sectarian undertones of the campaign, far more so than in any previous election, and at the same time fiercely committed to a second Jokowi victory. In the end, he took fully 97 percent of the country's entire non-Muslim vote as well as commanding significant loyalty from NU affiliates.[12]

The 2019 election had a curious quality. For all the talk of divisiveness, and for all the genuine anxieties about the outcome that some Indonesians clearly felt, at the surface it often seemed rather dull.[13] The public tone from both candidates was generally relatively measured. And with both men campaigning on essentially nationalist platforms, the five televised debates held between January and April at times seemed decidedly nebulous, though Jokowi did score one hit on his opponent during the second debate, on infrastructure, energy, agriculture, food, and environment, when Prabowo appeared confused about the meaning of "unicorn" in the

---

[10] Kate Walton, "'Golput': Why a number of Indonesians will not be voting," Aljazeera, April 9, 2019, https://www.aljazeera.com/news/2019/04/09/golput-why-a-number-of-indonesians-will-not-be-voting/ [accessed November 12, 2020].

[11] Ibid.

[12] "NU, non-Muslim voters held 'key role' in Jokowi's win," *The Jakarta Post*, July 25, 2019, https://www.thejakartapost.com/news/2019/07/25/nu-non-muslim-voters-held-key-role-jokowi-s-win.html [accessed November 12, 2020].

[13] Ahmad Ibrahim Almuttaqi, *Jokowi's Indonesia and the World* (Singapore: World Scientific Publishing, 2020), 155.

sense of a billion-dollar start-up.[14] The moment generated a flurry of viral online unicorn memes. These were harmlessly humorous. But elsewhere in Indonesia's seething online world, far removed from the staid and respectable television appearances and even the boisterous campaign rallies, the election was showing its darker side.

Fighting Fake News

In the first year of Jokowi's presidency, there were an estimated 55 million smartphone users in Indonesia.[15] Market analysts were expecting that number to have almost doubled by the time he stood for re-election, a forecast which appears to have been accurate, for in 2019 there were 104 million WhatsApp users in the country. There were also 126 million active Facebook users and around 143 million Indonesians were believed to have direct internet access.[16] It was online that much of the driving energy of the election campaign was to be found.

In 2014, Jokowi's team had a strong grasp of the significance of social media and had used it deftly to connect with voters. But 2019 was another world. The candidates still maintained their various official social media channels, with dedicated strategists on the central staff. But beyond the formal, KPU-registered campaign teams lay a shadowy zone of subcontracted influencers and coordinators working to push legitimate viral stories.[17] And somewhere beyond that, in the darkest corners of the political internet, were the untraceable sources of fake news.

The phenomenon of online hoaxes was already well-established in Indonesia beyond the world of electoral politics. Fake stories, from relatively

[14] Erwin Renaldi and Tracey Shelton, "Unicorns become an unexpected symbol of Indonesia's second presidential debate," ABC, February 17, 2019, https://www.abc.net.au/news/2019-02-18/joko-widodo-indonesia-presidential-debate-prabowo-subianto/10820310 [accessed November 12, 2020].

[15] "Indonesia is the 3rd-Largest Smartphone Market in the Asia Pacific," *Indonesia Investments*, April 30, 2016, https://www.indonesia-investments.com/news/todays-headlines/indonesia-is-the-3rd-largest-smartphone-market-in-the-asia-pacific/item6777? [accessed November 13, 2020].

[16] Adi Renaldi, "Indonesia's 2019 Election Is Keeping Fake News Fact Checkers Way Too Busy," *Vice*, December 19, 2018, https://www.vice.com/en/article/59v43d/indonesia-fake-news-presidential-election-jokowi-prabowo-hoax-season [accessed November 13, 2020].

[17] Adi Renaldi, "'This Is Pure Business. It Has Nothing to Do With Personal Politics': Inside the Hoax Industry," *Vice*, December 21, 2018, https://www.vice.com/en/article/pa58g7/inside-indonesia-hoax-black-campaign-industry-presidential-elections-jokowi-prabowo [accessed November 13, 2020].

harmless false rumors about celebrities to incendiary hoaxes intended to prompt sectarian unrest, had been circulating on social media for years. A 2017 survey found that well over half of respondents reported encountering online fake news at least once a day. Disturbingly, 91.8 percent of those respondents who said they had encountered fake news reported having seen false stories relating to politics, and 88.6 percent had received fake stories relating to SARA (ethnic, religious, racial, or inter-group) issues.[18] In the run-up to the 2019 election, there was a major surge in the volume of false stores specifically relating to politics.[19] Mafindo, a small NGO that works to counteract fake news by publishing carefully researched corrections, reported that around 80 percent of the fake stories they challenged in the early stages of the election period were targeted at Jokowi's administration.[20]

Some of the rumors that had circulated in 2014, and which had never really gone away, had received a new boost: stories that Jokowi was a secret Christian, of Chinese descent, a communist. Added to these were allegations that had emerged out of the anti-Ahok protests and their aftermath, not least that he was engaged in a vendetta against the *ulema* (Muslim clerics) despite having the nation's most senior *ulema* as his running mate. Amongst the fake news which sought to undermine the legitimacy of the vote itself, meanwhile, were widely shared claims that Chinese nationals employed on various infrastructure projects had been allowed to vote, and that containers loaded with ballots precast for Jokowi had been shipped into Jakarta from China.[21]

Prabowo and Sandiaga were by no means entirely immune to online fake news,[22] but Jokowi certainly bore the brunt of it. Mafindo's dedicated team did their best to counter falsehoods; highly reputable news publications such as *Tempo* and *Kompas* ran their own fact-checking operations; and the government itself acted to challenge false narratives. But with fake stories pinging from smartphone to smartphone all across the country, it

---

[18] "Hasil Survey Wabah HOAX Nasional 2017," February 13, 2017, *Mastel*, https://mastel.id/hasil-survey-wabah-hoax-nasional-2017/ [accessed November 13, 2020].

[19] Kate Lamb, "Fake news spikes in Indonesia ahead of elections," *The Guardian*, March 20, 2019, https://www.theguardian.com/world/2019/mar/20/fake-news-spikes-in-indonesia-ahead-of-elections [accessed October 28, 2020].

[20] Adi Renaldi, "Indonesia's 2019 Election Is Keeping Fake News Fact Checkers Way Too Busy."

[21] "What's at stake in Indonesia's general election 2019," *South China Morning Post*, April 12, 2019, available at https://www.youtube.com/watch?v=tZSjVPpJVmI [accessed November 13, 2020].

[22] "Fake news shoots up by 61 percent in lead up to election," *AustraliaIndonesia.com*, March 22, 2019, https://australiaindonesia.com/politics/indonesian-media-in-brief-fake-news-shoots-up-by-61-percent-in-lead-up-to-election/ [accessed November 13, 2020].

was impossible to stem the flood. For many Indonesians, it was the sheer volume of falsehoods at large that gave the 2019 election a particularly unpleasant flavor.

Counting the Ballots

Indonesia's vast geographical scale and enormous population makes the tallying of votes a mammoth undertaking, one which typically takes around a month to complete. The KPU (Election Commission) set a date of May 22 for the release of official results. However, Indonesia also has a polished quick count system, in which independent KPU-endorsed polling companies tally a representative sample of ballots as soon as the polls close. Quick count results are usually available by the morning after the vote, and though they have no constitutional standing, they have an excellent track record for accuracy, with their margin of error seldom exceeding a single point. By the morning of April 18, the quick counts were projecting a resounding victory for Jokowi, in the region of 55 percent. Turnout had been exceptional, around 80 percent, up by more than 10 points on 2014. Clearly Jokowi's supporters had not turned away in apathy after all; and clearly the fear of a widespread golput factor had been unfounded.

But in events prefiguring the 2020 US presidential election, Prabowo simply refused to accept the result. He made no fewer than three declarations of victory on the day following the vote, alleging "massive irregularities" and claiming that his own pollsters had projected a landslide victory of 62 percent in his favor.[23] Just as in the US the following year, there was little credible evidence of irregularities, and when Prabowo's supporters submitted official complaints to BAWASLU, the election supervisory agency, they were dismissed out of hand by the commissioners. The only evidence that had been provided to support the allegations had come in the form of online news links.[24]

The KPU released the official results one day ahead of schedule, in the early hours of 21 May. This was a deliberate move in anticipation of

[23] Tassia Sipahutar, "Indonesia Is a Country Divided as Both Candidates Claim Victory," *BloombergQuint*, April 24, 2019, https://www.bloombergquint.com/politics/indonesia-presidential-election-results [accessed November 13, 2020].

[24] Wahyudi Soeriaatmadja, "Indonesia's election watchdog throws out petitions claiming election fraud," *The Straits Times*, May 20, 2019, https://www.straitstimes.com/asia/se-asia/indonesias-election-watchdog-throws-out-petitions-claiming-election-fraud [accessed November 13, 2020].

potentially violent protests by disgruntled Prabowo supporters. Although security forces had been deployed in advance, violence still broke out in Jakarta the following evening and several people were killed. As for the results themselves, the quick counts had, as usual, been accurate: Jokowi had taken 55.5 percent of the vote. It was a solid vindication of the approach he had taken over the previous five years, and it gave him a clear mandate to pursue his agenda to 2024. His government got swiftly back to business. Prabowo, meanwhile, was still refusing to accept defeat. He took a case to the Constitutional Court, claiming various data errors and voter list irregularities (and having downgraded the scale of his own purported victory to 52 percent).[25] On June 27, the court unanimously rejected the challenge, stating that no credible evidence of electoral fraud had been provided, a conclusion with which independent election observers and virtually all serious analysts and journalists concurred.[26]

Nawacita Volume II and a New Cabinet

There had been talk throughout the long campaign period of a "Nawacita Volume II," a continuation of the original nine-point Nawacita framework to guide the direction of a second Jokowi term. The Indonesia Maju campaign document had identified a further nine missions for the second term, with human development placed to the fore. The other missions were economic competitiveness; development equality and sustainability; a focus on arts, culture, and national characteristics with a renewed call for a "mental revolution" to foster social harmony; the rule of law; security and defense; improved bureaucracy; and better synergy between regional and national governments.[27]

But after the election, Jokowi distilled these visions further. On the evening of July 14, 2019, with the outcome of the vote confirmed and the last legal challenge rejected, Jokowi gave a speech at the Sentul International

---

[25] Nur Asyiqin Mohamad Salleh, "Prabowo's suit to start a day later than planned," *The Straits Times*, June 15, 2019, https://www.straitstimes.com/asia/se-asia/prabowos-suit-to-start-a-day-later-than-planned [accessed November 13, 2020].

[26] Marguerite Afra Sapiie, "Court rejects Prabowo's vote-rigging claims," *The Jakarta Post*, June 27, 2019, https://www.thejakartapost.com/news/2019/06/27/breaking-court-rejects-prabowos-vote-rigging-claims.html [accessed November 13, 2020].

[27] Devina Heriyanto, "Here are Jokowi-Ma'ruf's nine 'missions' for 2019's presidential poll," *The Jakarta Post*, December 4, 2020, https://www.thejakartapost.com/news/2018/12/04/here-are-jokowi-marufs-nine-missions-for-2019s-presidential-poll.html [accessed November 25, 2020].

Convention Center in Bogor, outlining the vision for the coming five years. Most of the audience had followed Jokowi's sartorial lead, and the hall was a sea of untucked white shirts with top buttons undone. The president spoke from a podium backed by Iriana and his family members, Ma'ruf, and other senior officials. He began by firmly placing Indonesia in a global context:

> We must realize, we must all realize, that we now live in a global environment that is very dynamic—very dynamic! We know the characteristics of global phenomena, full of change, full of speed, full of risk, full of complexity and full of surprises, which are often far beyond our calculations, often far beyond our formulations.[28]

These were remarkably prescient comments given what was to come just six months later. But, of course, global pandemics did not feature in the July 14 speech. Instead, Jokowi went on to identify five key priorities that would underpin the coming term. These were clear and sharp, more so, indeed, than the nine points of the Indonesia Maju document or of Nawacita itself.

The first priority was a continued focus on infrastructure. There would be more toll roads, ports, airports, and railways. And the large infrastructure projects would be integrated with lesser works at the level of ricefields, irrigation reservoirs, and fishery ponds. The second priority, already extensively flagged during the election campaign and during the last years of the first term, was human resources.

"Developing human resources will be the key for Indonesia going forward," Jokowi said. This priority would begin with further efforts to improve childhood health in all communities, through improvements to educational standards and opportunities, to the development of high-level talent and expertise.

The third priority was to encourage investment. "Don't let there be anyone who's allergic to investment," Jokowi said, in a subtle reference to the xenophobia-tinged discourse of the recent election; "[because] it is by this means that employment opportunities will be expanded as widely as possible." Fourth, and connected to the idea of improving the investment climate, Jokowi restated a theme that had been part of his approach since

---

[28] "Pidato Lengkap Visi Indonesia Jokowi," *Kompas*, July 15, 2019, https://nasional.kompas.com/read/2019/07/15/06204541/pidato-lengkap-visi-indonesia-jokowi?page=all [accessed November 14, 2020].

his very first term as mayor in Surakarta: the streamlining of bureaucracy. "If there are institutions that are useless and have problems, I assure you, I will dissolve them!" he said. The final priority was a simple practical demand that state expenditure should be focused and on target.

Jokowi wound up with a forceful call for renewed optimism and a notably explicit underscoring of the principle of "unity in diversity" and national integrity: "Only by being united will we become a strong and respected country in the world! Pancasila ideology is the only national ideology that every citizen must be a part of [...]. There [should be] no more Indonesians who do not respect other religions, members of other groups, other ethnicities.

"This isn't about me, or you," Jokowi said in his final lines. "Nor is it about us, or them. It's not about West or East. Nor is it South or North. Now is not the time to think about all that. But it is the time to think about our nation together. Never hesitate to move forward, because we can do it if we are united!"[29]

It was, by any standards, a strong speech. Jokowi's formal oratorical skills had improved over the years and he looked confident, assured, and thoroughly presidential at the podium. And he delivered his words with a sense of conviction. After the fierce divisions and sectarian undercurrents of the election, and indeed of the previous few years more generally, the president was issuing a strong call for people to come together, to reunite. And there were already clues that he might be preparing to practice what he preached in the most improbable of ways.

The day before giving the speech, Jokowi had taken a trip on the glossy new Jakarta MRT, and he had a friendly companion along with him for the ride. It was none other than his erstwhile opponent, the man who just a couple of weeks earlier had seen his final challenge to the legitimacy of the election dismissed by the courts: Prabowo Subianto. In a carefully staged moment, the pair had come together at Lebak Bulus MRT station, with hearty handshakes and broad smiles, then boarded a Senayan-bound train. At the other end of the 18-minute ride, the pair spoke to the press. Prabowo formally congratulated Jokowi on his re-election, while Jokowi described the moment as "an encounter with a friend."[30]

---

[29] Ibid.

[30] Linda Yulisman, "Jokowi and Prabowo meet for first time since presidential election – at MRT station," *The Straits Times*, July 13, 2019, https://www.straitstimes.com/asia/se-asia/jokowi-and-prabowo-meet-for-first-time-since-presidential-election-at-mrt-station [accessed November 14, 2020].

On October 23, 2019, three days after his second inauguration, Jokowi announced the full line-up for his new Kabinet Indonesia Maju, the "Forward Indonesia Cabinet." As ever, it featured a mix of political appointees and technocrats. Some of the key figures from the previous cabinet retained their posts, not least Sri Mulyani in the Ministry of Finance and Retno Marsudi who kept the Foreign Affairs portfolio. But other high-profile ministers from the first term were out. The popular businesswoman Susi Pudjiastuti was replaced as minister of maritime affairs and fisheries by Edhy Prabowo who, significantly, was a senior Gerindra member. Wiranto was also out of the cabinet. Two weeks earlier, he had been seriously injured in a knife attack by an Islamic State-linked militant during a visit to Banten Province. He was still recovering from his wounds when the new cabinet was announced, but he would later be appointed to head the Presidential Advisory Council.

Amongst the twenty-three fresh ministerial faces were several chosen with Jokowi's vision for new economic impetus and an imaginative approach to developing Indonesia's human resource potential in mind. Fresh from his campaign-organizing success, Erick Thohir took the State-Owned Enterprises portfolio. And one of the more eye-catching appointments was the new minister of education and culture. As had been widely rumored for several months, Jokowi had given this job to 35-year-old Nadiem Makarim, the co-founder of Indonesia's best-known "unicorn," the all-conquering Gojek ride-hailing app. He came to the cabinet promising innovations and fresh thinking in the education sector.

But it was another cabinet appointment that stirred up the most conversation, garnered the most headlines, and prompted the most surprise: Jokowi's new minister of defense was to be Prabowo Subianto.

Reconciliation and Gotong-royong

Why did he do it? Why did Jokowi proceed with an appointment which on the face of it, and particularly to foreign observers, seemed just as unlikely as Joe Biden appointing Donald Trump as his secretary of commerce in 2021 (and, it must be said, as unlikely as Donald Trump accepting the offer)? The answer comes in several parts.

The first point to note is a very simple one, which was largely ignored or dismissed in the deluge of excited commentary that followed the October 23 announcement. Revealing Prabowo's new role on the steps of the presidential palace, Jokowi had said, "I believe I don't have to tell him about his job, he knows more than I do." This was in no way a meaningless comment: Prabowo really was very well-qualified to head the ministry of defense, and indeed for a senior ministerial role more generally, especially one with a notable international and diplomatic component. Prabowo is highly educated, with diverse international experience, and unlike Jokowi, a very fluent speaker of English and several other languages. And away from the campaign trail his persona is less that of a rabble-rousing demagogue than of measured competence. His controversial military background will always raise eyebrows and prompt fierce criticism from some quarters. But from a simple HR perspective, his appointment made good sense. Here, as ever, it is important to remember that Jokowi was, and is a small-town businessman first and foremost, rather than a born politician. In the furniture trade, he had employed Korean supervisors and French designers and had sought quality control guidance from Germany, choices determined entirely by the goal of achieving his desired outcome: the best product. Prabowo, as Jokowi pointed out to reporters after the announcement, had excellent qualifications for the job.[31]

Jokowi also told the reporters that he felt that "If it's good for the country and the nation, why not?"[32] He did not expand on what precisely he meant by this, but clearly there was need for reconciliation after all the political viciousness of the last few years. Jokowi, with his Javanese sense of the value of social and personal harmony, had been deeply unsettled by the sectarian currents of popular opposition movements and by the sheer coarseness of the attacks on his presidency. They had pushed him some way beyond the casual *Aku rapopo* pose of earlier years. Bringing Prabowo into the fold was an obvious way to drain the poison from the political discourse. Some supporters on both sides might have found themselves wondering exactly why they had been engaged in such a ferocious battle just a few months earlier, and members of the activist and reform movements certainly found the move hard to stomach. But there were many other Indonesians, especially in the Javanese heartlands, who recognized the principle of reconciliation, of the ending of enmities, of *lamun sira sekti, aja mateni* ("winning without defeating").

The other obvious question is why did Prabowo himself choose to

---

[31] Marguerite Afra Sapiie and Marchio Irfan Gorbiano, "'If it's good for the country, why not?': Jokowi justifies his Prabowo pick," *The Jakarta Post*, October 25, 2019, https://www.thejakartapost.com/news/2019/10/25/if-its-good-for-the-country-why-not-jokowi-justifies-his-prabowo-pick.html [accessed November 14, 2020].
[32] Ibid.

enter into the new arrangement? His official line was that he was motivated by patriotism and eager to make the greatest possible contribution to the advancement of his country.[33] Clearly, Prabowo and his party were tired of being in opposition, and for an ambitious and oft-disappointed politician the opportunity to be directly involved in the running of the country had great appeal. Prabowo and Gerindra were also probably looking to the future. A position within government would perhaps be a stronger starting point in the search for Indonesia's eighth president in 2024.

It is also important, as ever, to recognize that Indonesia's political culture at the party level does not typically involve the entrenched tribalism of the US, UK, or myriad other countries. Prabowo's own trajectory amply demonstrates this: in 1998, he had been a military man, engaged in the crumbling New Order's final rear-guard action against the forces of democratization. On the other side of the barricades, in the thick of the protesting students had been Amien Rais, leader of the Muhammadiyah Muslim organization and a hero of the reform movement. In the years that followed, Prabowo, now out of uniform, became a would-be Golkar presidential candidate, founder of Gerindra, running mate of Megawati, and committed backer of Jokowi's successful run for the Jakarta governorship. Then, two years later, he was standing against Jokowi for the presidency, and one of his most enthusiastic backers was none other than Amien Rais. And now, in 2019, Amien Rais's PAN was left behind in the opposition section of the DPR and Prabowo was in Jokowi's cabinet. Crucially, in an Indonesian context, none of this is particularly illogical or indeed unusual. Joe Biden's offering Donald Trump the commerce job in 2021 really *would* be unthinkable; but ultimately, Jokowi's giving Prabowo the defense portfolio in 2019 was not all that remarkable.

It does draw attention to one seldom-remarked fact, however: since the very start of his political career, Jokowi has been a member of just one party, PDI-P. What is more, he has never held a managerial role in that party. Despite the occasional urgings of his supporters, he has not broken away from his initial affiliation to form his own party, unlike both his predecessor SBY and his two-time challenger Prabowo. Jokowi has, in fact, proven remarkably constant by the usual standards of Indonesian party politics.

---

[33] Fardah, "Jokowi springs surprise with Prabowo's inclusion in new cabinet," *Antara*, October 23, 2019, https://en.antaranews.com/news/135216/jokowi-springs-surprise-with-prabowos-inclusion-in-new-cabinet [accessed November 14, 2020].

Bringing Prabowo into the fold also meant bringing his Gerindra Party, long-time pillar of the opposition, into the governing coalition. In October 2019, Jokowi was in a radically different position to that of five years earlier. His backers now controlled three-quarters of all DPR seats. All that was left of the opposition was PKS, the most distinctly Islamist of the mainstream Muslim parties, PAN, and the now politically isolated Partai Demokrat. None of these three sat particularly comfortably together, and there was no longer a Gerindra or a Golkar around which they could coalesce in opposition.

Some critics argued that a lack of a robust opposition was problematic in any democracy, and even outgoing vice president Jusuf Kalla stated that "An effective government needs checks and balances."[34] But, for the moment Jokowi had achieved something that had been seen as an ideal by Indonesian politicians for many decades, something espoused by Sukarno himself: political stability. It was something that had always appealed deeply to Jokowi, who, like Sukarno before him, places great value on the *gotong-royong* concept.[35] And in the specific context of his second presidential term, achieving that stability was a particularly attractive prospect. Jokowi's greatest motivation from the very outset of his political career, had always been to achieve tangible results, be they tidy Surakarta streets or island-spanning multilane highways, as quickly and effectively as possible. Political stability, he hoped, would help him succeed. Nobody, however, could have imagined what was coming just around the corner, far, far beyond any calculations of formulations.

---

[34] Fransiska N. Rahmad Nasution, "Effective opposition camp needed for Indonesia's next government," *Antara*, October 14, 2019, https://en.antaranews.com/news/134722/effective-opposition-camp-needed-for-indonesias-next-government [accessed 14 November 14, 2020].

[35] Sapiie and Gorbiano, "'If it's good for the country, why not?'"

Presidential practice in the age of Covid-19.

Chapter Twelve

A New Normal?: The Second Term and the Global Pandemic

T he electoral storms of early 2019 dissipated, and Jokowi moved towards his sixth full year in office and the first of his second term with a firm mandate and a solid position in relation to the legislature. But this was not entirely a period of calm. September 2019 saw significant student-led protests, the largest since the fall of Suharto, over a number of new laws which were then making their way through parliament. If there had been concerns twelve months earlier about the perceived political apathy of Indonesia's youth, here was a resounding rejoinder: thousands of young Indonesians, many of them born since the fall of the New Order, out on the streets with placards and banners. The key issues that had inflamed the demonstrators were a new law relating to Indonesia's powerful Corruption Eradication Commission, the KPK, and a long-overdue but controversial revision of the country's colonial-era criminal code.

The KPK, founded in 2002, was a flagship of the Reformasi period, tasked with investigating and prosecuting corruption and monitoring all levels of government. With its independence and significant powers, it had proven thoroughly effective and was one of the most admired and trusted institutions of state with the generally cynical Indonesian public. A popular perception of the KPK as a sort of band of Hollywood-style superheroes, conducting hi-tech surveillance and swooping dramatically on corrupt politicians without mercy, was encouraged by their record of complex sting operations. The Commission had, arguably, at times been injudicious in the use of its own powers, particularly when it came to publicly naming graft suspects without having strong enough a case to arrest them.[1] And some resentful politicians had, with a grain of justification, asked whether someone ought to be policing the policers. There were also claims, albeit with little evidence, that an all-powerful KPK might be putting off foreign investors and making officials too fearful to innovate.[2] The new law, which originated in the DPR rather than with Jokowi's executive, sought to create government-appointed oversight of KPK activities, including of its covert investigative methods.

The other major source of contention was a draft revision of Indonesia's cumbersome Criminal Code (KUHP). Significantly based on the Dutch colonial code, which dated all the way back to 1918, it has never been updated since Indonesia's independence in 1945. Some of the proposed amendments, particularly those around sexual relations, were seen by protesters as an attack on civil liberties and women's rights. Others, around the spreading of fake news and "insulting" the government and head of state, were read as erosions of free speech. A less dramatic criticism was that the revision was simply poorly drafted without the necessary clarity required for the definitions of crimes and their sanctions.[3]

The protests were represented in some international reports as being directly against the person of the president, and the controversial legislation was at times presented as further evidence of Jokowi's alleged "authoritarian turn." But, in fact, there was a widespread understanding amongst the student protesters that these were not measures originating with the president, and indeed that they needed to demonstrate that they would back him if he did as they wished and stepped in to halt the passage of the controversial bills through the DPR.[4] In the end, the KPK law passed, with protesters then going on to demand that Jokowi issue another Perppu blocking its implementation. But Jokowi did step in to delay the passage of the Criminal Code bill and several other contentious new laws, pushing their deliberation off into the future of the new parliamentary term.

---

[1] "Deadly Protests in Indonesia Cast a Pall Over Jokowi's Second Term," *World Politics Review*, October 2, 2019, https://www.worldpoliticsreview.com/trend-lines/28235/deadly-protests-in-indonesia-cast-a-pall-over-jokowi-s-second-term [accessed November 24, 2020].

[2] "KPK Soal Tudingan Hambat Investasi: Tak Berbasis Data," CNN Indonesia, September 24, 2019, https://www.cnnindonesia.com/nasional/20190924064836-12-433229/kpk-soal-tudingan-hambat-investasi-tak-berbasis-data [accessed November 24, 2020].

[3] "Deadly Protests in Indonesia Cast a Pall Over Jokowi's Second Term."

[4] Arya Dipa and Bambang Muryanto, "'We will keep fighting': Three days ahead of Jokowi's second term, protesters still rallying," *The Jakarta Post*, October 17, 2019, https://www.thejakartapost.com/news/2019/10/17/we-will-keep-fighting-three-days-ahead-of-jokowis-second-term-protesters-still-rallying.html [accessed November 24, 2020].

Unveiling Ambitious Second-term Plans

Outside of Indonesia, there was considerable political uncertainty. The United Sttes under Donald Trump was on the brink of a full-blown trade war with China, a situation which would threaten Indonesia and all other economies in the region. The headily ambitious annual growth targets of Jokowi's first term, targets which were seldom met, largely because of international conditions beyond the control of the Indonesian government, had been downgraded. From a goal of 7 percent growth coming into office in 2014, Jokowi was now aiming for 5.6–6.2 percent annually to 2024.[5] Given that there had actually been a minor slowdown in 2019, again largely due to external factors, these were still ambitious targets. But they seemed achievable.

On January 20, 2020, Jokowi signed a new National Medium-Term Development Plan (RPJMN). It was an ambitious document, building on the emphases of his first term and the five-point priority framework laid out after the election. It placed economic growth and development of human resources at the forefront, and although it could only directly determine the policies of the coming five years, it looked far beyond the end of Jokowi's presidency. The year 2045, the centenary of Indonesia's declaration of independence, had already emerged as a milestone in longer-term development aspirations for Indonesia, and now, at the start of his second term, Jokowi aimed to initiate a process that would place the country among the world's five largest economies by the time a quarter of a century had passed. If all went to plan, by 2045 poverty would have been entirely eradicated and per capita incomes would have increased fivefold.

In the more immediate future, the ferocious infrastructure drive of the first five years would continue, with forty-one projects given priority status, including high-speed railways linking more of Java's cities. There would also be a concerted effort towards "facilitating faster growth outside of Java and Sumatra," a reiteration of the Nawacita principle of development from the peripheries. More money would be pumped into tourism in the "Ten New Balis." And there were plans to facilitate massive development in four regional cities. Palembang in South Sumatra, Banjarmasin in South Kalimantan, Makassar in South Sulawesi, and Denpasar in Bali would all

---

[5] "Indonesia targets 5.6%-6.2% average GDP growth to 2024," Reuters, January 6, 2020, https://www.reuters.com/article/us-indonesia-economy-idUSKBN1Z516O [accessed November 23, 2020].

be turned from medium-sized provincial capitals to heavily-invested metropolises on par with the most sophisticated urban centers of Java.[6]

But the most dramatic element of the intended pivot away from the traditional centers of population and industry was Jokowi's plan to create a purpose-built new capital for Indonesia, more than 1,000 kilometers from Jakarta in East Kalimantan. The idea had been mooted during Jokowi's first term,[7] and then formally announced shortly after his second election victory. This was, with little doubt, the single most dramatic and ambitious example of the classic Jokowi approach, as seen over and over since the start of his career: presented with a problem, his tendency is always to identify the obvious solution, no matter how ambitious. Initial responses from bureaucrats to his broad-strokes suggestions have often been skeptical, even horrified. And the reactions from conservative economists and journalists have sometimes been similar. But throughout his first term the apparently impossible was achieved, and in double-quick time. Is the tourism potential of a particular region obviously underexploited? Build an airport! Is the connectivity between two neighboring population centers notably poor? Build a new bridge or toll road!

The problem that Jokowi was responding to with the plan for a new capital was one that few would deny. Jakarta's vast population and chronic infrastructure problems despite some dramatic advances over the last decade, come with all manner of attendant environmental issues, and some of the worst traffic jams on the planet. But there is more than that. Built on a coastal floodplain just a few meters above sea level, the city has always been susceptible to seasonal inundations; but in recent decades a combination of excessive groundwater extraction and massive building has seen the city actually begin to sink, with wet season floods becoming more extreme as a consequence. In the last few years, the idea has often been raised, without too much hyperbole, that Jakarta is not simply a city with problems, but that it might actually be doomed in the longer term. For Jokowi, the best solution was an obvious one: move the capital.

As with many of his other apparently radical developmental concepts,

---

[6] "Tourism, 'green fuel' top Jokowi development agenda," *The Jakarta Post*, February 12, 2020, https://www.thejakartapost.com/news/2020/02/12/tourism-green-fuel-top-jokowi-development-agenda.html [accessed November 23, 2020].

[7] Jewel Topsfield and Karuni Rompies, "Indonesia's capital Jakarta is so congested, government might move it to Borneo," *The Sydney Morning Herald*, April 13, 2017, https://www.smh.com.au/world/indonesias-capital-jakarta-is-so-congested-government-might-move-it-to-borneo-20170413-gvkj7y.html [accessed November 23, 2020].

this was not a wholly new idea on Jokowi's part. In the early years of Indonesia's independence, Sukarno had recognized the potential benefits, in terms of better binding together the new nation, of shifting the capital away from the traditional cultural and economic center of the archipelago. He, too, had focused on Kalimantan, and had identified Palangkaraya as the specific location for the new city. The project had never come to pass, but the concept had never really gone away. Just as with the Jakarta Metro, Jokowi was picking up on an idea that everyone knew about but that no one had ever been ambitious enough to take proper responsibility for.

Having considered Sukarno's favored site at Palangkaraya and a number of other locations, Jokowi's team eventually settled on a region in East Kalimantan close to the existing city of Balikpapan. On a visit to Abu Dhabi at the start of 2020, Jokowi invited investment in the new capital project from around the world and unveiled the sheer scale of the plan: "We do not want to just build a small-scale administrative capital, but a smart metropolis, since the population will be three times that of Paris, 10 times that of Washington DC; it will even equal the population of New York and London," he said.[8] The plan was to have the new city up and running, at least as a working center of administration, by the end of his presidency.

Inevitably, the plan was met with much skepticism and a good deal of derision, particularly from international journalists. Costs and logistics were the usual issues raised, with frequent comparisons to Myanmar's much derided purpose-built capital, Naypyidaw.[9] These criticisms often came from the same quarters that had been stressing the allegedly "doomed" nature of Jakarta for years. In fact, there was nothing unprecedented about the idea of shifting a major administrative capital of a large developing nation, and there were other, far more positive comparisons besides Naypyidaw. In the 1960s, the seat of the government of Pakistan shifted from the sprawling port city of Karachi to a purpose-built, more central, and in time very successful, new capital at Islamabad. And the Indian state of Andhra Pradesh has recently established an entirely new capital at Amaravati, with a carefully managed transition from the old administrative

[8]Budi Sutrisno, "City with population 'equal' to New York, London: Jokowi seeks investment for new capital," *The Jakarta Post*, January 13, 2020, https://www.thejakartapost.com/news/2020/01/13/city-with-population-equal-to-new-york-london-jokowi-seeks-investment-for-new-capital.html [accessed November 23, 2020].

[9]Ben Bland, "Dream state: Jokowi struggles to build his vision for Indonesia," *Nikkei Asia*, September 16, 2020, https://asia.nikkei.com/Spotlight/The-Big-Story/Dream-state-Jokowi-struggles-to-build-his-vision-for-Indonesia [accessed November 23, 2020].

hub. And one thing was certain: *something* radical would need to be done to ensure that the Indonesian capital, wherever it was located, would be sustainable and functional by the time the 2045 horizon was reached.

But of course, by the time the National Medium-Term Development Plan was signed off in January 2020, a storm that would put paid to all manner of best-laid plans, not only in Indonesia, but around the world, was fast approaching.

Global Crisis and Personal Grief

Four days after Jokowi signed the National Medium-Term Development Plan, an article appeared in the leading medical journal *The Lancet*. Its title was "A novel coronavirus outbreak of global health concern."[10] The disease had emerged in Wuhan, China, some two months earlier, with symptoms reminiscent of SARS (Severe Acute Respiratory Syndrome). At first, news of the possible new virus was limited to doctors within Wuhan, but by the end of the year Chinese state media was reporting on official efforts to deal with an outbreak of mysterious pneumonia cases in Wuhan. Within the first weeks of 2020, Singapore, Hong Kong, and Taiwan began to report patients with SARS-like symptoms. Thailand confirmed its first case on January 13, and three days later a case was reported in Japan.

The Chinese government began taking dramatic steps to limit the internal spread of the virus. On January 23, Wuhan was locked down. Transportation was stopped and people were restricted from entering and leaving. The quarantine was extended to cities around Wuhan and eventually to all of Hubei Province: 60 million people in total were placed under the severest restrictions. By the end of the month, the World Health Organization had declared a global health emergency. The Philippines reported its first death on February 1, the first known fatality outside of China. A wave of Covid-19 infections was by now sweeping across Asia, and within a fortnight the first deaths were being reported in Europe, too. In Japan, meanwhile, more than 3,600 passengers aboard the *Diamond Princess* cruise ship were quarantined in an effort to prevent mass infections ashore. For many people in Indonesia, this gave them their first sense of direct connection to the crisis: there were sixty-eight Indonesian workers among the crew of the ship.

---

[10] Chen Wang, Peter W. Horby, Frederick G. Hayden, and George F. Gao, "A novel coronavirus outbreak of global health concern," *The Lancet* 395 (2020): 470–73.

Of course, Southeast Asia has had long experience of widespread novel respiratory infections, not least the SARS outbreak of 2002–3 and the H5N1 outbreak of 2005. Governments and the general public around the region were far better used to the concepts of mask-wearing, social distancing, and health checks at entry points than their European counterparts. But this, clearly, was something that went far beyond previous experiences. By the end of February, the first death had been reported in the USA. This was a truly global crisis, and on March 11 the WHO officially declared a global pandemic.

At the outset, Jokowi urged calm. At this stage, no one anywhere in the world could fully appreciate the scale of the crisis, though behind the scenes worst-case scenarios were plotted and presented to the relevant ministries in Indonesia. As an initial practical response, the government took steps to evacuate the Indonesian crew members from the *Diamond Princess* in Yokohama. Four of them later tested positive for Covid-19 and were treated in Japanese hospitals. Shortly afterwards, on March 2, came news that two Indonesians at home had tested positive for the virus, a 64-year-old mother and her 31-year-old daughter who had been in contact with Japanese citizens who later tested positive for the virus. Indonesia's Covid-19 journey had begun. It was as fast-moving and turbulent as the Kali Anyar river at the height of the rainy season.

As for every other government around the world, the great conundrum was how to strike a balance between limiting the spread of the disease and preserving the economy. Jokowi's administration was to come in for criticism, including from some of its own allies, for an alleged early failure to share enough information. The initial motivation had been to prevent excessive panic, to urge calm, as one would of a young swimmer caught in fast-flowing water. But with lurid rumors rapidly spreading on social media, Jokowi appointed an official spokesman, namely the secretary of the Ministry of Health's Directorate General of Disease Prevention and Control, Achmad Yurianto. A degree of control was still maintained on the flow of information. Again, this came in for much criticism, but officials were mindful of Indonesia's past record of street violence at times of political or economic instability, and fearful of triggering chaos and looting with rapid and dramatic policy decisions.[11] Nonetheless, it was clear that

---

[11] Ardi Priyatno Utomo, "Jeritan Pelaku Penjarahan Supermarket di Tengah Lockdown Italia: Kami Butuh Makan," *Kompas*, March 29, 2020, https://www.kompas.com/global/read/ 2020/03/29/193318270/jeritan-pelaku-penjarahan-supermarket-di-tengah-lockdown-italia-kami?page=all [accessed November 25, 2020].

provisions were needed for large-scale social restrictions.[12] Jokowi enacted Government Regulation No. 21 of 2020 concerning Large-Scale Social Restrictions in the Context of Accelerating Handling of Coronavirus Disease 2019 (Covid-19) at the end of March as a foundation for comprehensive actions to be carried out by ministries and local governments to slow the spread of the virus.

In the midst of this period of crisis came sad news from Surakarta. The president's mother, Sujiatmi, had passed away after four years of treatment for cancer. She was seventy-seven.

Jokowi's relationship with his mother went beyond the usual affection of a child for its parent, beyond even the Javanese emphasis on honor and respect for one's elders. Sujiatmi had been, since his youth, Jokowi's great moral and spiritual guide. While it had been his father who impressed upon him the importance of education, it had been Sujiatmi who guided and reassured him through the frustrations and disappointments of his educational career as a teenager. It had been she who had given him both practical backing and emotional guidance in his attempts to launch his own business career. And as he moved into politics he had often turned to her. Her blessings carried a particular weight, and her well-known prayerful religiosity provided a calming spiritual anchor for the whole family. Her death was by no means unexpected, but it came at a particularly difficult moment for Jokowi, the moment in his presidency during which the way ahead was least clear, the waters most turbulent, and a time when virtually all plans and aspirations had been rendered uncertain by external factors. If there was ever a moment during which he might have relied on Sujiatmi's guiding light, then this was it.

She passed away at the Slamet Riyadi Army Hospital in Surakarta on the afternoon of Wednesday, March 25. She was buried at her family's plot in Selokaton, Gondangrejo, Karanganyar, the following day, close to the hamlet where she had grown up, and where she had first met Jokowi's father as a schoolgirl, more than six decades earlier.[13]

Speaking to the press, an obviously emotional Jokowi said, "We treated

---

[12] Lenny Tristia Tambun, "Jokowi Teken PP PSBB dan Keppres Kedaruratan Kesehatan Masyarakat," *Berita Satu*, March 31, 2020, https://www.beritasatu.com/nasional/615035-jokowi-teken-pppsbb-dan-keppres-kedaruratan-kesehatan-masyarakat [accessed November 25, 2020].

[13] Rakhmat Nur Hakim, "Ibunda Presiden Jokowi Meninggal Dunia," *Kompas*, March 25, 2020, https://nasional.kompas.com/read/2020/03/25/17290241/ibunda-presiden-jokowi-meninggal-dunia [accessed November 25, 2020].

her, we tried every treatment, at the Gatot Subroto Army Hospital. But indeed, Allah Subhanahu wa ta'ala has willed it. On behalf of my extended family, I would like to ask for prayers that all sins be forgiven by Allah Subhanahu wa ta'ala and for *Khusnul Khotimah* [a good end]."

In Surakarta, Jokowi's first political partner and successor as mayor, F. X. Hadi Rudyatmo, paid his own respects to the woman who had become well-known in the city.

"She was a figure who nurtured, and showed respect. And the most important thing is that she was *njawani* [thoroughly Javanese in her philosophy and behavior], because whoever she was with, she never saw or looked at ethnicity, religion, qualification, or rank," he said. Rudy also praised Sujiatmi's particular approach to hierarchical Javanese customs. She always spoke the refined form of the Javanese language, even when talking to younger people (in Javanese custom, a younger person should always speak to their elders using the refined version of the language, while the elder may reply using the coarser *ngoko* version). Her social attitude, forged in the mixed community and cheek-by-jowl circumstances of the Kali Anyar riverbank in the early 1960s, was very much an inheritance that she had passed on to her son, and that had carried him to the presidency.

Sujiatmi's funeral was without the large crowds of government officials that would normally be expected after the death of a family member of so senior a politician. A few cabinet members who had known Sujiatmi personally, including coordinating minister for maritime affairs Luhut Binsar Panjaitan, joined the ceremony. But others were asked to pray for the deceased at home and in private.[14] And in another stark reminder of the circumstances, all mourners visiting the funeral home ahead of the burial went through temperature checks and hand-sanitizing stations, and all members of the funeral procession itself, led by Jokowi and his son Gibran, carrying a formal portrait of Sujiatmi—were wearing facemasks.[15]

A Period of Adversity

For Jokowi, there was little chance for a period of private mourning and personal introspection following the death of his mother. As captain of the national ship, he was now tasked with steering Indonesia in the stormiest

---

[14] "Ritual 'brobosan' antar jenazah ibunda Presiden Jokowi ke peristirahatan terakhir," BBC, March 25, 2020, https://www.bbc.com/indonesia/52033001 [accessed November 23, 2020].
[15] Ibid.

of waters. On the final day of March, he made use of the Perppu mechanism in a further move to tackle the pandemic.[16]

"Because we are currently facing a compelling situation, I have just signed a Government Regulation in Lieu of Law (Perppu) on State Financial Policy and Financial System Stability," he said, announcing the move. By this stage, 136 people were known to have died of the virus in Indonesia and Covid-19 had been identified in all but two of the country's provinces. This rate of spread was in line with the predictions prepared by government health advisors at the start of the pandemic, but it was still a frightening situation for Jokowi and his ministers, and for all Indonesians.

The new Perppu provided a foundation for the government and financial authorities to take extraordinary steps to protect public health while also attempting to shield the economy and stabilize the financial system. Although Perppus can be contentious, and can be seen as presidential overreach when deployed too readily, these, surely, were precisely the sort of extraordinary circumstances for which the mechanism was designed. When it was brought before the DPR, it was passed into formal law without resistance.

Jokowi moved to enhance the 2020 State Budget expenditure by Rp405.1 trillion to tackle the crisis. Rp75 trillion was allocated to the health sector and the social protection budget was increased by Rp10 trillion. Other expenditure targeted an economy that was already clearly starting to falter: tax incentives worth Rp70.1 trillion, business credit and recovery programs, especially for micro, small, and medium enterprises, worth a total Rp150 trillion. Credit relief was mandated for individuals and small businesses.

In terms of practical measures to slow the virus, Indonesia opted for "Large-scale Social Restrictions," known by the Indonesian-language acronym PSBB, rather than full nationwide lockdown measures. This was in part down to recognition of the sheer scale of the country, its diverse population and social conditions, and the complex and often informal nature of its economy. But PSBB measures were still stringent. They were to be implemented by regional governments but had to be approved by the national Ministry of Health, the idea being that central coordination should be maintained without individual governors, regents, or mayors attempting their own containment measures without oversight.

---

[16] Mohammad Ridwan, "Perppu diteken! Presiden Jokowi tambah Rp405,1 triliun atasi pandemi Corona," *Lensa Indonesia*, March 31, 2020, https://www.lensaindonesia.com/2020/03/31/perppu-diteken-presiden-jokowi-tambah-rp4051-triliun-atasi-pandemi-corona.html [accessed November 25, 2020].

Jakarta, inevitably, was the first place to request, and receive, permission to enforce PSBB measures in early April. Schools and restaurants were closed, public transport was put on limited capacity, and the city's iconic hordes of Grab and Gojek motorbike taxi drivers were forbidden to carry passengers. Other regions of Java requested PSBB measures soon afterwards, as did provinces in Sumatra, Sulawesi, and Kalimantan, with restrictions alternately easing and tightening as the caseload fluctuated across the year.

Meanwhile, Jokowi's government continued to formulate means of protecting the economy and providing some kind of safety net for the vast Indonesian population. In the first instance, the president ordered all ministers, governors, and mayors to cut spending plans that were not prioritized in the State Revenue and Expenditure and Regional Revenue and Expenditure budgets. The businessman's mindset that he had first brought to the mayor's office in Surakarta had always made him mindful of the waste in the body of government. The pandemic now gave new impetus to the elimination of needless spending.

Speaking at the presidential palace in a limited cabinet meeting by teleconference, a mode of official communication which had rapidly become normalized, on instructions to regional governments, Jokowi ordered officials to tighten their belts.

"The budget for official travel, unnecessary meetings and other purchases that are not directly for the public must be trimmed," he said.[17]

Meanwhile, Presidential Instruction (Inpres) No. 4 of 2020 concerning Refocusing Activity, Budget Reallocation and Procurement of Goods and Services in the context of the Acceleration of Handling Coronavirus Disease 2019, ordered national and regional governments to overhaul existing budgets, with a renewed focus on healthcare and economic measures. Jokowi also tasked central and local governments with guaranteeing the availability of basic commodities. Mindful, as ever, of the *wong cilik*, the "little people," he also sought means to maintain some kind of purchasing power for the poorer classes.

"Help laborers, daily workers, farmers, fishermen, and micro and small businesses to maintain their purchasing power," he told officials. One means of doing this was a prioritizing of cash-labor programs on projects under the Ministry of Public Works and Public Housing, the Ministry of

---

[17] Dhifa Setiawan, "Penanganan COVID-19 di Indonesia Mendesak, Ini Imbauan Jokowi untuk Menteri dan Kepala Daerah," *Pikiran Rakyat*, March 25, 2020, https://www.pikiran-rakyat.com/nasional/pr-01356114/penanganan-COVID-19-di-indonesia-mendesak-ini-imbauan-jokowi-untuk-menteri-dan-kepala-daerah [accessed November 23, 2020].

Transportation, the Ministry of Agriculture, and the Ministry of Maritime Affairs and Fisheries to provide an income for casual workers. The central government also provided an additional Rp50,000 per month to existing recipients of the Cheap Staple Food Card, which provides cash to meet essential needs for poor families, bringing the monthly allocation to Rp200,000 per family. This amounted to an increased budget allocation of Rp4.56 trillion nationwide. Another card-based welfare scheme, the Pre-Work Card, was also rushed to implementation ahead of schedule. Originally announced during the election campaign the previous year, this card would provide funding for vocational training for school leavers and the unemployed, including micro entrepreneurs who lose their market, of which there were many during the pandemic. The government allocated Rp10 trillion to the scheme for 2020.

The government also launched a scheme to cover excess interest for people with subsidized housing loans, and to help providing initial down-payments for subsidized houses, with a budget allocation of Rp1.5 trillion. There were tax breaks for workers in the manufacturing industry, and a relaxation of credit requirements for micro, small, and medium enterprises, with a lowering of interest rates and a year-long postponement of repayments. There was also a year-long suspension of credit repayments applied to the operators of taxis, motorbike taxis, and fishing boats.

"The banking sector and non-bank financial industry are prohibited from chasing up installment payments, especially using debt collectors. It is prohibited and I ask the police to record this," Jokowi said.

All this required enormous public expenditure. But it was notable that Jokowi's government was taking concrete steps for the benefit of poorer Indonesians, the people who relied on the daily sales of street food, or the fares of motorbike taxi passengers, to meet the essential cost of living, the sort of people the president had grown up among on the banks of the Kali Anyar.

Jokowi himself attempted to strike an optimistic pose. "Believe that we are a great nation, we are a fighting nation, a warrior nation, God willing, we can do it; God willing, we will be able to face these tough global challenges today," he said in a live-streamed address at the end of March 2020. And the heavy focus on economic mitigation did appear to have an impact: Indonesia's economy did not suffer as severe as slowdown as that of many other countries in the region. But, as was the case for every political leader and every country around the world, the foe here defied simple battlefield tactics and allowed no clear vision for the ultimate victory. And no amount of financial mitigation could truly alleviate its impacts. From the street vendors of Surakarta to the owners of tourism businesses in Labuan Bajo, millions upon millions of livelihoods had been drastically impacted more suddenly and unexpectedly than by any of the political upheavals or natural disasters of Indonesia's past. And the virus itself was still spreading at an alarming rate.

Seeking Coexistence with Covid-19?

Though it initially fared relatively well on the economic front, clearly Indonesia was not among the Southeast Asian countries that achieved dramatic successes in early control of the virus itself. Vietnam, Thailand, and Singapore were all notable for effectively stemming the outbreak during 2020. As is so often the case, direct comparisons are unfair to Indonesia, which is far larger in area and population and more diverse and complicated in geography than any of its neighbors. And Indonesia, like the European countries which were particularly badly hit, does not have the same coercive political culture of some other countries in the region. But there is no doubt that its handling of the pandemic, in public health terms, could have been better. There was particular criticism for a lack of extensive testing in the early stages, inadequate contact tracing, and an overreliance on the less accurate rapid blood testing system, instead of polymerase chain reaction (PCR). It was July before the Indonesian authorities were properly applying WHO contact tracing guidelines and shifting away from the rapid tests.[18]

From relatively early in the pandemic, the Indonesian government began looking to a long-term future in which Covid-19 might be a constant presence. This was born in part of Jokowi's own desire to continue his ambitious project for Indonesia. Work, progress, transformation had been his aims, and the measure of his own success, since entering politics. During the early years of his first term, he had at times been frustrated by the slow rate of progress of the many developmental projects, still rapid by any previous Indonesian standards but sluggish compared to his fleet-footed action in Surakarta and Jakarta. By the end of his first term, however, he had achieved formidable momentum, which should

---

[18] Tom Allard and Kate Lamb, "Endless first wave: how Indonesia failed to control coronavirus," Reuters, August 20, 2020, https://www.reuters.com/article/us-health-coronavirus-indonesia-insight/endless-first-wave-how-indonesia-failed-to-control-coronavirus-idUSKCN25G02J [accessed November 24, 2020].

have carried him easily into a second term. But with Covid-19 impacting every aspect of governance, and every aspect of daily life, there was a serious threat of the one thing that Jokowi had abhorred since his earliest days in business: stasis. For the president, then, the concept of a "new normal" was seductive: the possibility of somehow making peace with Covid-19 instead of adopting a siege mentality until an effective medical solution materialized.

Within the presidential palace, Jokowi and his staff had rapidly gotten used to masks, social distancing, and habitual sanitization. Meetings switched online, and the video conference became the standard mode of operation. Jokowi had always been an early adopter of technology in government, and he had used social media platforms to increase transparency by publicly broadcasting meetings during his time as governor of Jakarta, for example. And his enthusiasm for Indonesia's online and tech sectors was well known. So this simple practical shift came easily, and indeed appealed to his interests. He even managed to create a limited sort of virtual *blusukan*, arranging video calls with teachers to get insights into how they were managing to facilitate home schooling, for example.

But the practicalities of daily work within the highest tier of the government were far removed from the realities of a vast nation of more than quarter of a billion people, and what a "new normal" might look like on the streets of Jakarta, in the villages of Central Java, in the resorts of Bali and beyond, was not immediately obvious. With rates of infection fluctuating in different regions across the country, Jokowi attempted to steer a middle way. Where the R-rate appeared to be falling, a move to some kind of openness, with well-socialized promotion of mitigation methods and testing regimes, was encouraged, while PSBB (Large-scale Social Restrictions) remained in place where the virus was clearly still at a high level.

In Indonesia, there was no clearly identifiable first and second wave of the virus across 2020 as there was in the badly hit European countries. Instead, there was a continuous rise in cases, with the curve likely somewhat exaggerated as the testing regime moved up a gear in the later part of the year, though rates did, finally, begin to show some sign of reaching a plateau from September.[19] Still though, with grim inevitability, by November 23 the total number of known Covid-19 cases in Indonesia since

---

[19] Heru Andriyantu, "Indonesia Coronavirus Cases Set New Record," *Jakarta Globe*, November 13, 2020, https://jakartaglobe.id/news/indonesia-coronavirus-cases-set-new-record [accessed November 24, 2020].

the start of the pandemic had passed half a million, with more than 16,000 confirmed deaths, including at least 282 healthcare workers.[20]

But, by this stage there was a glimmer of light on the horizon. In quick succession came announcements from labs across the world of promising results in vaccine trails. Indonesia's state-owned Bio Farma pharmaceutical company was already collaborating with China's Sinovac, one of the front-runners in the vaccine race, to run a major trial in West Java. The arrangement included a role for Bio Farma to produce some 17 million doses when a successful vaccine came online.[21] But as news of other successful trials emerged, Jokowi revealed that the government was already pushing for a fast-tracked vaccine approval process with the National Agency of Drug and Food Control (BPOM), which would potentially allow for the first inoculations to take place by the end of the year.

2021: Another Year of Uncertainty

Jokowi marked the end of a torrid year, the first of a new decade and the first full year of his second term, with a cabinet reshuffle. He had warned back in June 2020 that, given the unprecedented crisis, there would be no tolerance for ineptitude at the top and there were a number of notable changes. Social affairs minister Juliari Batubari had been caught up in a corruption scandal and was replaced by Surabaya's widely respected mayor, Tri Rismaharini. Popularly known as Bu Risma, she had been the sprawling East Java capital's first democratically elected mayor and its first female leader. Her transformational approach to city governance, and in particular her dramatic and much-lauded "cleaning and greening" approach, had often invited comparisons with Jokowi's own mayorship of Surakarta, and her appointment to the cabinet was a popular one. She had even been mentioned in some circles in early speculation about the 2024 presidential election, though perhaps more likely as a running mate than as the principal candidate. Health minister Terawan Agus Putranto, who had inevitably been a focus of criticism over the pandemic response,

---

[20] Rizki Fachriansyah, "Indonesia surpasses half a million coronavirus cases," *The Jakarta Post*, November 23, 2020, https://www.thejakartapost.com/news/2020/11/23/indonesia-surpasses-half-a-million-coronavirus-cases.html [accessed November 24, 2020].

[21] Resty Woro Yuniar, "Indonesia's Sinovac COVID-19 vaccine trial to continue, as Brazil halts theirs," *The South China Morning Post*, November 10, 2020, https://www.scmp.com/week-asia/health-environment/article/3109265/indonesias-sinovac-COVID-19-vaccine-trial-to-continue [accessed November 24, 2020].

was replaced by Budi Gunadi Sadikin. And to complete the post-2019 *gotong-royong* reconciliation process, former opposition vice presidential candidate Sandiaga Uno was brought in as the new tourism and creative economy minister.[22] Stylish, youthful, and generally seen as highly competent, Sandiaga is a broadly popular figure even amongst voters wary of Prabowo, and inevitably his is another name often mentioned in premature discussions of the 2024 election. His appointment to the tourism job was widely seen as a smart one and far less controversial than the earlier cabinet appointment of his former senior running mate, who had, it should be said, settled into his own role in defense smoothly. Most of the people who mattered, it seemed, were now batting for Team Jokowi, which, given the Covid-19 crisis and the need for unified action, was really Team Indonesia at this stage.

As 2021 got underway, and with the entire world in a state of near-paralysis due to the pandemic, confirmed Covid-19 cases in Indonesia approached 1 million, with confirmed deaths edging rapidly towards 30,000.[23] But, at the same time, the vaccination program got swiftly underway. From the get-go, a two-track system was in place. The main government funded program, initially using both the massive pre-ordered Sinovac supply, and stocks of the AstraZeneca vaccine, obtained under the World Health Organization's COVAX scheme, prioritized health workers, public servants, and the elderly. Those not in those categories were encouraged to sign up for a parallel, paid scheme. Although this inevitably attracted some criticism about the neglect of those not in the priority groups but without the wherewithal to pay for private vaccination, it did allow for a speedy start to the roll-out. Unfortunately, this was later hampered by a global shortfall of AstraZeneca supply, and in April Jokowi's government approved alternatives and placed orders for the Russian Sputnik vaccine and other Chinese-manufactured jabs.

By mid-year, a third facet had been added to the national vaccination program. A scheme had been unveiled in which private companies were encouraged to fund vaccination for workers and their families. Some 22,000 companies, accounting for around 10 million people, quickly

[22] Marchio Irfan Gorbiano, "Jokowi announces end-of-year Cabinet reshuffle," *The Jakarta Post*, December 22, 2020, https://www.thejakartapost.com/news/2020/12/22/jokowi-announces-end-of-year-cabinet-reshuffle.html [accessed June 4, 2021].

[23] Rebecca Ratcliffe, "Covid patients turned away as hospitals in Indonesia face collapse," *The Guardian*, January 26, 2021, https://www.theguardian.com/world/2021/jan/26/covid-patients-turned-away-as-hospitals-in-indonesia-face-collapse [accessed June 4, 2021].

signed up for the scheme, which would use the Sinopharm vaccine to avoid having any impact on the main government-funded roll-out. The program was named for that classic principle of mutual cooperation on which Jokowi places so much value: *Vaksinasi Gotong-Royong*.[24] By late May 2021, around 28 million individual doses had been given and around 11 million people, about 4 percent of the Indonesian population, had been fully vaccinated. This may seem like a low proportion, but it actually compared very favorably to neighboring countries, including Malaysia, Australia, and Japan, all of which have far smaller populations and ostensibly much more robust healthcare systems.[25] Nonetheless, Jokowi's goal of achieving herd immunity by March 2022, requiring full vaccination of more than 180 million people, would require ferocious determination, an uninterrupted supply, and a great deal of *gotong-royong*.

The annual temporary mass-migration of workers back to hometowns and villages at the end of Ramadan in May was another challenge in slowing the spread of the virus. In neighboring Malaysia, where a similar phenomenon takes place annually, it prompted a dramatic spike and a consequent lockdown, and by the middle of 2021 there were signs that it had had a negative impact in Indonesia, too. By early June, there had been 1.8 million recorded cases and 50,000 deaths since the start of the pandemic, though some evidence suggested the actual rates could be markedly higher.[26] And by July a devastating new surge was underway, with daily recorded deaths topping 1,000 for the first time, and oxygen supplies running low in hospitals across the country. The route out of the pandemic remained unclear.

---

[24] A'an Suryana, "Commentary: Indonesia's company-funded vaccination drive boosts the national rate but has limitations," CNA, May 27, 2021, https://www.channelnewsasia.com/news/commentary/indonesia-vaccination-programme-rate-covid-19-challenges-gotong-14881924 [accessed June 4, 2021].

[25] Tim Lindsey and Max Walden, "Indonesia may be on the cusp of a major COVID spike. Unlike its neighbours, though, there is no lockdown yet," *The Conversation*, June 2, 2021, https://theconversation.com/indonesia-may-be-on-the-cusp-of-a-major-covid-spike-unlike-its-neighbours-though-there-is-no-lockdown-yet-158955?utm_source=twitter&utm_medium=bylinetwitterbutton [accessed June 4, 2021].

[26] Tom Allard, "EXCLUSIVE COVID-19 far more widespread in Indonesia than official data show: studies," Reuters, June 3, 2021, https://www.reuters.com/world/asia-pacific/exclusive-covid-19-far-more-widespread-in-indonesia-than-official-data-show-studies-2021-06-03/ [accessed June 4, 2021].

Into Recession

Within a few months of the start of the pandemic in early 2020, even the more restrained economic growth targets that Jokowi's government had set for its second term had begun to look wildly optimistic. The tourism sector, in particular, had been devastated, with virtually all international travel halted and the huge domestic tourism market heavily curtailed. And the vast informal economy that keeps cash circulating in towns and cities across the country, the food stall operators and market vendors and motorbike taxi drivers, was severely stifled.

In April that year, the Asian Development Bank (ADB) was still projecting 2.5 percent growth for Indonesia in 2020, which allowed some sense of comfort. The projections for other major Asian economies, including India and China, from the World Bank and ADB were also still showing modest growth. Still more hearteningly for Jokowi, at that point the Moody's rating agency was projecting Indonesia's economic growth in 2020 to reach 3 percent, rising to 4.3 percent for 2021. If these projections were accurate, they would mean Indonesia bucking the heavily forecast international trend for negative growth in 2020, a vindication of the extensive stimuluses to maintain public purchasing power. But the slowdown was still shocking in its scale: the Economist Intelligence Unit had downgraded its growth forecast for Indonesia from 5.1 percent to just 1 percent.

But as the pandemic went on, it became clear that even these modest hopes might have been unwarranted. The second quarter of 2020 saw a grim 5.32 percent contraction of the Indonesian economy. From the middle of the year, as PSBB measures were eased in some cities and regions, there were signs of a modest uptick in economic activity. But the pandemic was by no means over, and by September Jakarta had reinstated full PSBB measures, with infections rising rapidly once more, and the city's hospitals struggling to cope. At the same time, the capital saw another round of protests, this time with the students joined by trade union representatives. They were demonstrating against a huge package of job-creation and investment-boosting measures, combined as a single "Omnibus Law." It featured no fewer than 79 modifications to existing laws, and it was conceived very much with Jokowi's stated electoral promise to improve Indonesia's investment climate and cut red tape. It was also meant to provide a serious shot in the arm for the national economy as a whole at a time of record unemployment. But for detractors, all this came at an unacceptable price: the Omnibus Law would, they said, erode the various significant benefits and protections of workers' rights accrued over the years. In the end, the protests petered out and the bill was passed, pending a judicial review.

Across the third quarter, government expenditure was up by a dramatic 9.76 percent. But everything else, from household spending to imports and exports was down. At the start of November came the inevitable confirmation: Indonesia's economy had contracted again in the third quarter, by 3.49 percent.[27] For the first time in twenty-two years, for the first time since the financial chaos of 1998 that heralded the end of the New Order and the start of Reformasi, Indonesia had officially entered recession. It was, to be sure, by no means as bad as it could have been and by no means as bad as the economic situation in many other countries around the world. And by mid-2021, international economists would be forecasting a modest, and fragile and Covid-19-dependent, return to growth for Indonesia in the second half of the year.[28] But for Jokowi, a businessman first and foremost, for whom progress, productivity, and growth were the ultimate measures of success, it was a bleak moment. It was also a moment that changed the tone of the plans for the rest of his presidency: his paramount task now would be to ensure a fulsome recovery.

---

[27] Adrian Wail Akhlas, "Breaking: Indonesia enters first recession since 1998 on 3.49% Q3 contraction," *The Jakarta Post*, November 5, 2020, https://www.thejakartapost.com/news/2020/11/05/breaking-indonesia-enters-first-recession-since-1998-on-3-49-q3-contraction.html [accessed November 24, 2020].

[28] Grace Sihombing and Claire Jiao, "Indonesia Aims for V-Shaped Recovery After Disappointing GDP," Bloomberg, May 5, 2021, https://www.bloomberg.com/news/articles/2021-05-05/indonesia-economy-struggles-to-bounce-back-as-demand-drags [accessed June 4, 2021].

Looking to the future.

Epilogue

Zaman Jokowi?
Looking towards a Legacy

B y the time Jokowi completed his first term as president, he already
had a tangible legacy. It came in the form of thousands of kilometers of fresh tarmac, stretching east to west across Java and running
through the forests of Sumatra and Papua. It came, too, in new harbors for
isolated fishing communities; new irrigation reservoirs for farming villages
from Central Java to East Nusa Tenggara; and new or expanded airports
serving emerging tourist destinations. But there was much more to his
nascent legacy than concrete infrastructure projects. There had also been
a greater shift from a Java-centric development dynamic to a whole country approach than had been achieved under any of his predecessors. And
a committed pursuit of social justice was demonstrably underway in the
provision of new economic opportunities for those Indonesians living in
long-neglected outlying regions, and in the strengthening of the networks
of universal healthcare and education and the establishment of social welfare provisions for economically marginalized families across the country.
These successes will surely endure long beyond the end of his second term.

Realizing Dreams, Executing Plans

Jokowi's heavy developmental focus, and in particular the concerted
emphasis on infrastructure, has at times been belittled or even derided by
his critics. Within the country, the "people can't eat infrastructure" line
has been heavily deployed, albeit generally by those who have never had
difficulty finding enough to eat. Hostile foreign commentaries, meanwhile,

sometimes take a patronizing line, with the idea that Jokowi "loves infra-structure," as if his sustained focus on infrastructure development were a mere foible or indulgence.

But a new bridge connecting communities separated by a river or bay is not built for decorative purposes, it is a practical intervention which may provide local people with vastly improved access to markets, services, job opportunities. On a national level, a vastly expanded network of modern roads, ports, and airports has the same effect on a vast scale. It has long been recognized that Indonesia's vast economic potential is hampered by poor connectivity and the heavy developmental imbalance towards Java, and an ambitious infrastructure drive in a county of this scale can hardly be considered a gimmick. After all, China, the emerging superpower of the twenty-first century, has been engaged in a massive infrastructure expansion for several decades, building a web of multilane highways and high-speed railways stretching to the furthest reaches of the country. Indonesia is a country with comparable scale, and even more challenging geography; here it is not simply deserts or mountain ranges that have to be considered, but large intervening stretches of seawater and some of the most unstable geology on the planet. Nonetheless, progress on this front, even during Jokowi's first term alone, has been undeniably dramatic. To have made such progress in transforming the physical infrastructure in the space of five years, not least in a democratic country dominated by complex coalition politics, and with a reputation for sluggishness and bureaucracy, is no mean feat.

Crucially, Jokowi has always seen infrastructure development not as an end in itself but as an essential means to create an economically advanced Indonesia. This is hardly a surprise given his business background. A successful entrepreneur does not build a new hi-tech workshop or install a piece of state-of-the-art machinery for reasons of vanity or prestige; he does it for one reason only: to improve his bottom line. Jokowi's infra-structure projects are likewise intended to improve the bottom line of national development, the concrete component of his greater ambitions for structural reform.

Physical infrastructure is a permanent contribution to the matter of the nation, and one that often has a catalytic effect on wider development. This has been the underpinning principle of Jokowi's approach. His spend-ing on road building, for example, has been prodigious. But he was, and remains, a businessman who created his own company from scratch. He brought to politics that businessman's understanding of the use of capital as a means of investment intended to generate a return. He has also brought a businessman's creative approach to the financing of projects, leading to breakthroughs in government development funding beyond the limited state budget, through public–private partnerships and the involvement of investment schemes.

What has set Jokowi apart, however, has been his confidence in the certainty of returns beyond the immediately projectable, and his readiness at times to conceive of those returns in terms beyond the bluntly monetary, particularly when it comes to "developing Indonesia from the peripheries," turning the border regions from a national "back porch" to a national "front porch" and pushing hard for a shift from entrenched Java-centric development to an all-Indonesia-centric approach. This, surely, is the mindset not only of a small-town businessman but of the boy who grew up on the banks of the Kali Anyar river in close proximity to real poverty. Jokowi's father had turned away from the relatively secure but stiflingly limited life in a village *priyayi* family with the aim of establishing a business of his own, putting his young family through considerable precarity in the process. Jokowi, in turn, was able to envisage a solidly comfortable middle-class future for himself, a goal which remained abstract as he took the first youthful steps to achieve it. What Jokowi possesses, and what he has had since childhood, is the mentality of a dreamer. This, however, is a dreamer who does not merely dream but who identifies the vital steps required to realize those dreams no matter how big, and who is prepared to take the necessary risks in their execution. This is the mentality that carried him from the riverbank of his childhood to a prestigious university place, and from a humble start in the furniture industry to his successful business career. It is the mentality that won him every election he has ever contested. And it is the mentality that has driven the serious structural reforms that Indonesia has seen since 2014.

Infrastructure development does not end with the cutting of the ribbon and the movement of the first vehicles along the new road. When pursued as a philosophy, as it has been in Jokowi's Indonesia, it is intended as a door, a portal to the realization of potential. Industrial estates have been growing along the Trans-Java corridor,[1] and several districts, including Subang, Karawang, and Purwakarta, have shown increases in the collection of

---

[1] Peni Widarti, "Trans Jawa: Dampak Ekonomi Daerah Dirasakan 8 sampai 10 Tahun lagi," Bisnis.com, March 25, 2019, https://ekonomi.bisnis.com/read/20190325/9/904086/trans-jawa-dampak-ekonomi-daerah-dirasakan-8-sampai-10-tahun-lagi [accessed July 10, 2019].

regional tax revenues since the opening of the new toll roads. Some of these revenues come from large manufacturing operations, taking advantage of the eased logistics and setting up operations away from old industrial centers. But others have been raised by new or expanded tourism business and SMEs around the toll road exit points. Batik manufacturers in Cirebon have seen a marked uptick in revenues as motorists heading between Jakarta and Semarang or Surabaya pull off the highway in passing.[2] And visitor numbers at the Linggarjati Building Museum in Kuningan, West Java, have jumped from around 2,000 per month before the Trans-Java Toll Road opened to 5,000 to 6,000 a month since its inauguration.[3] These individual examples have been repeated, over and over, along the route of the road.

To the west, beyond the Sunda Strait, Sumatra is also seeing the impact of the infrastructure portal prised open during Jokowi's first term. The 2,889-kilometer Trans-Sumatra Toll Road is under construction, which will greatly reduce journey times and costs of transportation on this huge island. The new highway will provide access for various special economic zones and industrial areas under development, including Dumai, Bengkalis, Kemingking, Way Pisang, Tanggamus, and Tenayan.[4] It will also provide economic advances in less developed regions such as Bengkulu and Jambi, and will ease the path to market for Sumatra's natural resources and agricultural produce, while in the reverse it will reduce the cost of distribution for goods imported from other regions.[5]

But the patterns of knock-on development sometimes emerge more rapidly and more unexpectedly than anticipated. By the beginning of Jokowi's second term, state electricity company PLN was detecting marked upticks in electricity consumption in the southernmost regions of Sumatra where the new road was already in operation. On closer analysis, the increased demand was found to be concentrated in the vicinity of toll exits: the presence of the road was already, organically, generating increased economic activity, and thus increased use of electricity, as local MSMEs and larger manufacturers came into being where poor connectivity had previous stifled such enterprises. Property values around the toll road will obviously also increase as a consequence.

---

[2] Interview with Batik Trusmi, June 10, 2019.
[3] Ibid.
[4] Eko Sulistyo, *Konservatisme Politik Anti Jokowi* (Jakarta: Moka Media, 2019), 251.
[5] Basuki Hadimuljono, *Infrastruktur Meningkatkan Daya Saing* (Jakarta: Kementerian PUPR, 2017), 15.

The efficiency generated by the existing Trans-Sumatra Toll Road has already been valued at Rp2.23 trillion per year. Accumulatively, the toll benefits on a permanent basis are projected to reach Rp769.5 trillion, much greater than the cost of the entire project itself, which is Rp250.5 trillion.[6]

Although Sumatra is the immediate neighbor of Java, and although it has several large urban centers and a number of industrial regions, it has, more generally, much in common with underdeveloped regions of eastern Indonesia. The results already recorded in Sumatra bode well for the longer-term potential released by infrastructure development at the peripheries, not least the 4,385 kilometers of the Trans-Papua Highway and the 1,646 kilometers of roads being constructed in the Kalimantan border regions. Clearly, the outlays here are enormous and unlikely to produce rapid returns on a similar scale to those seen in Java and even Sumatra. But they do provide a solid foundation for later development in these long-neglected regions. This is the underpinning logic of Jokowi's supposed "love of infrastructure." It is also the logic behind the focus of the planned "Phase 2" of his presidency: human resources.

Building Workforce Capacity

To fully realize the potential opened up by the door of physical infrastructure, there is plainly a need to advance the capacity of the Indonesian workforce at all levels. A capable, educated workforce allows for more rapid responses within industry and attracts inward investment.

In Jokowi's own personal narrative, the dream of the boy on the riverbank was achieved not simply through the building of furniture workshop infrastructure and the availability of electricity and capital, but through the skills and intellectual wherewithal of the dreamer himself. The effort to gain entry to the best high school may have been frustrated, but the quest for a place at a prestigious university was a success. Then came the apprenticeship in a state-owned company and the risk of a journey to a distant peripheral region that it entailed, and in his uncle's business. Without these lessons, Jokowi would never have made a success of his own furniture company, would never have risen to prominence in the Surakarta business community, and would never have been noticed as a potential

---

[6]Achmad Dwi Afriyadi, "Sri Mulyani: Tol Sumatera Mampu Hemat Biaya Angkut Rp 23 Triliun," *Liputan6*, December 27, 2017, https://www.liputan6.com/bisnis/read/3207646/sri-mulyani-tol-sumatera-mampu-hemat-biaya-angkut-rp-23-triliun [accessed July 18, 2019].

mayoral candidate. This was a personal journey, of course, but the idea of taking Indonesian society as a whole through a similar process lay behind the priorities formulated for Jokowi's second term. The concept of improving national human resources spanned a gamut from facilitating the development of potential new "unicorns" at one end to efforts to eradicate poverty and childhood malnutrition at the other.

Prior to Jokowi's first term, the poverty reduction approach was typically carried out by sector, with funding for individual programs often coming from non-rupiah loans. Under Jokowi's policy, poverty reduction became a concern of all national development programs, with improved mechanisms for providing subsidies and better access to education and welfare.[7] The human resource development budget grew substantially. For education, a 2014 spend of Rp353.4 trillion had increased to Rp444.1 trillion by 2018. For health, Rp59.7 trillion in 2014 had become Rp111 trillion in 2018. The intention for the second term has been for the year-on-year increase to be maintained, with an ever heavier spending focus on human resource issues, as the major infrastructure projects are completed.

Moving into the 2019–24 period, the policy framework provided for a systemic approach to poverty reduction, with a synergized program and an integrated database, and further additions to the existing clutch of card-based social welfare schemes, namely the Pre-Employment Card, the Smart Indonesia College Card, and the Cheap Staple Food Card.

The idea of reducing and eventually eradicating poverty and improving education, and thus boosting human resources, is central to the 2045 vision for Indonesia to celebrate its centenary as a developed nation.[8] Even before that, with improved infrastructure and better investment conditions, there are predictions that Indonesia may be able to move from the lower ranks of the G20 to a place amongst the top five strongest economies in the world by as soon as 2030.[9] But Jokowi's priorities on the human development front are also closely intertwined with his own philosophical concerns for social justice, forged during his childhood amongst the marginalized yet mutually supportive community of the riverbank.

---

[7] Nursodik Gunarjo, *Nawacita Meretas Indonesia Maju* (Jakarta: Kominfo, 2016), 12–18.

[8] "'Indonesia Emas 2045' Pengertian & Visi [Lengkap]," Indonesiastudents.com, November 10, 2017, https://www.indonesiastudents.com/indonesia-emas-2045-pengertian-visi-lengkap/ [accessed July 16, 2019].

[9] Christine Novita Nababan, "RI jadi Negara dengan Ekonomi Terkuat Ke-5 Dunia di 2030," CNN Indonesia, February 23, 2018, https://www.cnnindonesia.com/ekonomi/20180223110749-532-278275/ri-jadi-negara-dengan-ekonomi-terkuat-ke-5-dunia-di-2030 [accessed July 20, 2019].

Searching for Simplicity

What has always typified Jokowi's approach to policy formulation and prob-lem solving is a search for simplicity, an avoidance of unnecessary compli-cations in both the conception and the implementation. And behind this characteristic is another, even more straightforward motivation, the desire for speed. Looking back at each of his three elected offices, mayor, gover-nor, and president, and comparing his developmental achievements in each with those of his predecessors, there can be little doubt that he is a very fast-moving leader. This has won him the approval of voters at each stage.

It is also the desire for simplicity and speed, for the greatest results in the shortest period of time, that has driven his habit of completing the work of others, never ditching well-laid plans just for the sake of putting his own unique stamp on things. The Bogor-Ciawi-Sukabumi and Bocimi toll roads; the Trans-Java Toll Road; various power plant projects; and the Jakarta MRT, these are all examples of projects that already existed but had stalled, either at the planning or implementation stage, but which Jokowi picked up and saw through. The Trans-Sumatra Toll Road, planned under Susilo Bambang Yudhoyono's administration, and West Java's Jatigede Reservoir, planned under Sukarno, also fall into this category, as does even the proposed capital relocation to Kalimantan. And the "finish-ing the job" approach applies not only to infrastructure projects: agrarian reform and the social forestry program that have been key in Jokowi's approach to rural affairs date all the way back in their conception to the Sukarno era. Jokowi's approach is simple: what has already been planned should be done, what has been started should be completed. Similarly, he has often sought to make use of existing legal mechanisms to tackle problems rather than attempting to legislate afresh, for example, using Law No. 2/2012 on Land to resolve land disputes during the provision of infrastructure for the public interest.

This is where a key but under-acknowledged aspect of his managerial style is to be seen: he is not always so much a "new broom" as a vigorous expeditor. Jokowi, as mayor, governor, and president, has often been a "Great Implementer," a trouble shooter who picks up the plans laid by those who have gone before and then sees them through.

The search for speed and simplicity is also to be noted as a driving factor in Jokowi's political decisions at the level of cabinet, parliament, and party. Coming into the presidency in 2014, he had been relaxed about dealing with an opposition majority in the DPR, an attitude partly born of his own customary easy-going optimism, but also based on his experiences in Surakarta and Jakarta, where he benefited from the assistance of tough deputies well able to wrangle the regional parliamentarians, whether the bulk of them were formal Jokowi affiliates or not. But the national DPR is a far fiercer beast than any city-level DPRD, and Jokowi quickly recognized that to move swiftly, simply, and with unfettered ambition in the areas that mattered to him, namely development and structural reform, having parliament on his side was essential. Likewise, as he moved into his second term, the greatest attraction of an overwhelmingly dominant ruling coalition was simply the leeway it allowed him to get things done. As he said at the time, because of Indonesia's two-term constitutional limit, he was no longer worried about the need to seek re-election; using his remaining time in office to achieve the maximum outcome was what mattered.

The discourse around a supposed "authoritarian turn" also needs to be critically reviewed in this context. Where apparent evidence for this is presented, it is typically either reactive to forces which are themselves anti-democratic, such as the sectarianism of the anti-Ahok movement or the fake news and black campaigning phenomena of the elections; or developmentally progressive in its intent, designed to foster a better investment climate, faster job creation, and so on. The same applies when it comes to choices of political personnel. And herein is revealed one of the most important things about Jokowi when it comes to understanding his approach to leadership and his vision for realizing Indonesia's dreams, and also to contextualizing the "disappointment" claimed by a relatively small number of his early enthusiasts and by a certain body of foreign commentators: he is not, at heart, a politician in the traditional sense.

Jokowi was in his forties when he was first elected to public office. But the preceding decades of adulthood had not been marked by long-standing party membership, grassroots canvassing, or even any particular interest in politics. They had been filled instead with education, work, entrepreneurship, love, and family life. Jokowi had come of age in the relatively politically stable, and indeed stagnant, 1980s, not in the heady fervor of the following decade. He had, like many Indonesians of his generation, a strong sense of Pancasila-rooted nationalism. But beyond that he was no political ideologue. He had no personal heritage in fervent youth-driven reform movements or democracy activism. His own student experience had involved hanging out in the canteen and planning the next mountain climbing expedition, or heading home to Surakarta by motorbike to help out in the family business.

Those who *did* have that particular activist political heritage certainly responded enthusiastically to Jokowi when he ran for the Jakarta governorship, and even more so when he went for the presidency in 2014. But some of that enthusiasm involved a projection of priorities that were not Jokowi's own. This, as is the case for virtually any fresh and distinctive politician upon whom great hopes are pinned, could only ever result in a degree of disillusionment. But it is vital to remember that when Jokowi won the 2005 Surakarta mayoral election, he did so as a political outsider, but not as a *political* outsider. Though he soon proved to be a canny operator in the day-to-day practicalities of political operation, he has changed little over the years.

If, for example, Jokowi sees fit to appoint a former general to a cabinet position based on qualifications and capacity for the role, it is not for him some violation of ideological purity; it is generally a decision based on his desire to keep moving, as swiftly as possible, towards his goal. And that goal, like his character, has been forged by his own life experience before he entered the political fray. His disinterest in politics as a game, as a discourse, is further demonstrated in his noteworthy constancy of affiliation, his evident lack of party-political ambition and willingness to be a mere PDI-P cadre with no internal leadership role, even while occupying the highest office in the land.

A 1960s childhood in the diverse but tightly bound community of the Kali Anyar riverbank and in the wider city of Surakarta beyond it; the proximity to poverty coupled with the achievable ambitions and upward mobility of his own immediate family; the close connection to the ancestral villages with their potholed roads, rutted tracks, and dry fields; and then his own elevation by way of education, work experience, and entrepreneurship to the ranks of the solidly prosperous middle class: all of this has given him a powerful sense of social justice, and of what both the *wong cilik* and moderately well-off Indonesians want, and what they need. This is not in any abstract ideological sense, but in the fabric and concrete detail of life, be it the ability to pay for a new school uniform or obtain treatment for an illness; or access to a reliable electricity supply for a new industrial unit and the chance to obtain a business permit without having to negotiate a morass of red tape and corruption. In a way, the entire first forty-four years of his life, up to his first election as mayor, was one long *blusukan*. It is with this in mind that the question of Jokowi's legacy should be considered.

Looking Forward to Looking Back on a "Zaman Jokowi"

In Indonesian popular imagination, as in most other countries around the world, the past is neatly blocked into "eras" (*jaman*, or *zaman*, in the Indonesian language). The three and a half centuries of European colonialism is conceived as a whole as the Zaman Belanda, the "Dutch Era." The brief but brutal occupation of World War II is the Zaman Jepang, the "Japanese Era." Politics too is, inevitably, retrospectively divided into themed eras. Of these, the most frequently discussed is inevitably the Zaman Suharto, whether it is viewed in baleful critique or through rose-tinted glasses. Even when no judgment is passed, the sheer longevity of the Suharto Era makes it an inevitable point of reference; certain things in every town, every community, the school, the clinic, the government office, date from the Zaman Suharto.

Subsequent Indonesian presidents do, of course, have their own eras. But they are somewhat nebulous, lacking clear distinction. It can be hard to identify an essence, or a crucial legacy of the decade-long Zaman SBY, for example. And when it comes to the quick succession of preceding presidents, they may all be blocked together in a Zaman Reformasi, a "Reform Era;" but it is relatively rare to hear talk of a Zaman Megawati or a Zaman Gus Dur.

So what is the likelihood that five, ten, or twenty-five years from now Indonesians will talk of a Zaman Jokowi and have a strong sense of its meaning? Predictions on this front are, of course, skewed by the Covid-19 pandemic. Without it, by this stage Jokowi would have been forging ahead, unhindered, with further massive projects. The capital relocation might have been well underway instead of stuck in a holding pattern like so much else. And international tourist arrivals could conceivably have been well on track to surpass those of high-profile neighboring destinations. How heavily defined by the pandemic Jokowi's second term will be remains to be seen and will be very much dependent on the Covid-19 endgame. The virus has certainly slowed progress, and the inevitable economic impact means that a return to full speed will take time. The loss of lives, and the loss of livelihoods, is the principle tragedy. But the crisis has also brought a faint suggestion of frustration to the presidency itself given the momentum and very long to-do list with which Jokowi began his second term, and given that speed and simplicity are always his aspirations. The Covid-19 pandemic is compatible with neither. Tourism, in particular, very much a success story of Jokowi's first term, has been decimated and will likely be slow to recover, even as other aspects of the economy get back on track. The vast, and ever-growing, domestic tourism sector will likely prove more resilient, and businesses in Labuan Bajo, Lake Toba, and all the other "New Balis" will likely see a resurgence of visitors from Jakarta, Surabaya, and other big Indonesian cities long before international travelers return in any great number. Indeed, a concerted pivot towards domestic tourism, as more stable and more sustainable in an uncertain world, may be one medium-term consequence of the pandemic, and not only in Indonesia.

However, even in worst-case scenarios, even if much of the energy of Jokowi's remaining years in office must be given over to crafting a recovery, there seems a very real chance that in decades to come the term "Zaman Jokowi" will have meaning to Indonesians. Individual policies; furious debates over new laws; controversies over particular appointments; the divisive rhetoric of an election campaign: such things tend to be revealed as ephemera as any given presidency passes its endpoint. It is the concrete changes that typically retain their weight in the longer term, and in that Jokowi already has a legacy. Just as was the case on a much smaller scale in Surakarta, residents and frequent visitors to Indonesia readily attest the physical transformations in the country over the last half decade. And crucially, these transformations are not restricted to the capital, nor even to Java. In places deep in Kalimantan, for example, there is now smooth tarmac where in 2014 there was only mud and potholes.

Principles of universal healthcare coverage and extensive social welfare programs, and concepts of village funding, may become so embedded that no one will actually remember which president it was that initiated or implemented them. But where development has a robust physicality memories tend to be longer. Today, Indonesia has a solid foundation of improved infrastructure, fostering greater connectivity, upon which to build a more advanced and less Java-centric economy. Decades from now, perhaps even at the horizon of 2045, it seems reasonable to believe that an Indonesian working in an industrial hub that developed at the exit from a major toll road, or living on a small island with its own micro power plant, will, if asked about that particular manifestation of structural development, point back to the Zaman Jokowi.

There is another, less immediately tangible aspect of a likely Jokowi legacy, and that is its narrative. The story of a boy who grew up fishing and hunting for duck eggs on the banks of the Kali Anyar in Surakarta and went on to become the president of Indonesia is a simple one that cuts through sharply in the popular imagination. There have already been movies, cartoons, and myriad books about it presented to the Indonesian public. What gives it its traction is not merely that the child of the river-bank was able to become president; it is the entirety of his trajectory. There is the educational success through diligence and parental encouragement, leading to a place at a prestigious university, not one in the United States accessible only to the sons and daughters of a tiny Jakarta-based elite, but one conceivably accessible to any Indonesian. There is the simple love story, leading to a happy and stable family life. There is the establishment of a thriving business, leading to a life of considerable comfort, but not inconceivably rarefied, and still firmly embedded within the local com-munity. All of this seems eminently achievable to millions of Indonesians given the necessary focus and energy, given the capacity to dream. And so what comes afterwards in the final chapter of the Jokowi narrative, the presidency, seems achievable too.

As with Barack Obama in the USA, it will not matter, ultimately, if who-ever succeeds Jokowi in 2024 is a reversion to the old elite, a retrograde step. A certain threshold has been passed, and it is perfectly possibly that a future president of Indonesia is right now growing up in a working-class or lower-middle-class household, the son or daughter of parents who run a small enterprise, the very existence of which was made possible by the concrete developments of the Zaman Jokowi, and who will grow up with better access to education and healthcare, with greater expectations, and with bigger dreams.

Glossary and Acronyms

A Note on Currencies

The value of the Indonesian rupiah against the US dollar has fluctuated significantly over the decades. During Jokowi's childhood, it traded at around Rp500 to US$1, falling to Rp16,800 to the dollar during the economic crisis in 1998. In mid-2021, US$1 was equivalent to approximately Rp14,000; thus a million rupiah was around US$70.

A Note on Personal Names

People from many of Indonesia's regional cultures, not least the Javanese, do not customarily use family names. A two-part name like Joko Widodo does not represent a given name and a family name, and international media formulations such as "Mr Widodo" are neither accurate nor appropriate. In this book, we have generally referred to individuals with the name most commonly used by the Indonesian media and public. Prabowo Subianto, therefore, is referred to as "Prabowo" and Joko Widodo himself as "Jokowi."

3T – Term used for the characteristics of the most remote and underdeveloped regions of Indonesia (*terdepan, terluar, tertinggal*; frontier, outermost, and underdeveloped).

ASEAN – Association of Southeast Asian Nations; Southeast Asia's ten-member regional grouping.

Asmindo – Indonesian Furniture and Handicraft Industry Association; Jokowi founded and chaired Asmindo's Surakarta branch in 2002.

Bappenas – Kementerian Perencanaan Pembangunan Nasional Republik Indonesia (National Development Planning Agency).

BAWASLU – Badan Pengawas Pemilihan Umun (General Election Supervisory Agency).

Bebas-Aktif – "Free and Active," the long-established defining principle of Indonesia's foreign policy.

Bhinneka Tunggal Ika – Indonesia's national motto, typically translated as "Unity in Diversity."

Blusukan – Jokowi's trademark practice of "site visits," checking on the progress of projects or gauging the situation on the ground and connecting with members of the public.

BPJS Kesehatan – Badan Penyelengara Jaminan Sosial Kesehatan (Healthcare and Social Security Agency).

Carik – Village secretary.

DPD – Dewan Perwakilan Daerah (Regional Representative Council; sometimes also styled "Indonesian Senate" in English); Indonesia's second parliamentary chamber; makes up the MPR together with the DPR.

DPR – Dewan Perwakilan Rakyat (People's Representative Council; sometimes also styled "House of Representatives" in English); Indonesia's parliament and main legislative body, with 575 directly elected members.

DPRD – Dewan Perwakilan Rakyat Daerah (Regional People's Representative Council); regional equivalent of the national DPR at the provincial and regency/municipality levels.

Dwifungsi – "Dual Function," a key doctrine of the New Order era in which the military was expected to be directly involved in civil affairs as well as security and defense; formally ended in the Reformasi period.

FPI – Front Pembela Islam (Islamic Defenders Front); an Islamist pressure group, instrumental in the so-called 212 Movement.

Gerindra – Partai Gerakan Indonesia Raya (Great Indonesia Movement Party); a nationalist party formed as a vehicle for Prabowo Subianto; currently one of the larger parties in the DPR.

Golkar – Sekretariat Bersama Golongan Karya; one of the major Indonesian political parties, rivaled only by PDI-P for its national organizational capacity; with origins in the late Sukarno period, it became the electoral vehicle of Suharto's

New Order but transformed itself into a conventional nationalist party in the Reformasi period.

Golput – Deliberate abstention during an election (short for *golongan putih*, or "white group," referring to the practice of marking a blank part of the ballot paper).

Gotong-royong – Javanese term, usually translated as "mutual cooperation" or "working together"; much used in Indonesian political discourse and long considered an ideal of good governance.

Hanura – Partai Hati Nurani Rakyat (People's Conscience Party); a nationalist party formed and formerly led by Wiranto.

JKN – Jaminan Kesehatan Nasional (National Health Insurance Scheme).

Kabinet Indonesia Maju – "Forward Indonesia Cabinet" of Jokowi's second term.

Kabinet Kerja – "Working Cabinet"; Jokowi's first-term cabinet (the name had previously also been used for a Sukarno-era cabinet).

Kabupaten – Regency; the division of regional government below that of province (municipalities are the equivalent for urban areas).

Kartu Indonesia Pintar, KIP – "Smart Indonesia Card"; one of Jokowi's card-based welfare programs providing financial assistance for school-age children from disadvantaged backgrounds.

Kartu Indonesia Sehat, KIS – "Healthy Indonesia Card"; Jokowi's flagship card-based welfare scheme providing healthcare coverage for people from disadvantaged backgrounds.

Kecamatan – District; the regional subdivision below the level of regency/municipality.

Koalisi Indonesia Hebat, KHL – "Awesome Indonesia Coalition" of parties backing Jokowi's first presidential campaign.

Koalisi Indonesia Kerja, KIK – "Working Indonesia Coalition"; the coalition backing Jokowi's second presidential campaign.

Koalisi Merah Putih, KMP – "Red and White Coalition"; the coalition backing Prabowo Subianto's 2014 presidential run.

KPK – Komisi Pemberantasan Korupsi (Corruption Eradication Commission).

KPU – Komisi Pemilihan Umum (Electoral Commission).

Lurah – Village head, an official government appointment at one of the smallest subdivisions of regional administration; the post occupied by Jokowi's paternal grandfather in Kragan.

MPR – Majelis Permusyawaratan Rakyat (People's Consultative Assembly); the Indonesian legislature in its entirety, composed of the DRP and DPD together. The MPR was originally tasked with appointing the president; it now handles constitutional matters.

Muhammadiyah – Major Muslim organization (second in size to NU), founded in 1912; more modernist and internationalist than NU in its approach to Islam.

MUI – Majelis Ulama Indonesia (Indonesian Ulama Council); Indonesia's senior Muslim clerical body, formerly chaired by Vice President Ma'ruf Amin.

Nahdlatul Ulama, NU – Indonesia's largest Muslim organization; traditionalist and with strong culturally Javanese roots; Vice President Ma'ruf Amin was formerly NU supreme leader.

Nasdem – Nationalist party founded by media tycoon and former senior Golkar member, Surya Paloh.

Nawacita – Nine-point framework for Jokowi's first-term developmental approach.

New Order – The name used for Suharto's regime; Orde Baru in Indonesian.

PAN – Partai Amanat Nasional (National Mandate Party; a Muslim party with links to the Muhammadiyah organization and a broadly modernist Muslim base.

Pancasila – Five-point national philosophy created by Sukarno in 1945 and heavily emphasized during the New Order years; Pancasila remains the ultimate touchstone of Indonesian Nationalism.

PD – Partai Demokrat (Democratic Party); a centrist-nationalist party originally founded as a vehicle for Indonesia's sixth president, Susilo Bambang Yudhoyono.

PDI-P – Partai Demokrasi Indonesia Perjuangan (Indonesian Democratic Party of Struggle); one of the major nationalist parties, formed after a split in the original PDI engineered by Suharto's regime, and chaired by Megawati. PDI-P is Jokowi's party and has taken the largest share of votes in parliamentary elections in recent years.

Perppu – Peraturan Pemerintah Pengganti Undang-Undang (Government Regulation in Lieu of Law); a de facto law issued by the executive; must subsequently be debated and passed by the DPR to enter the statue book.

Pertamina – Indonesia's state-owned oil company.

PKB – Partai Kebangkitan Bangsa (National Awakening Party); founded in 1999 and closely linked to the Nahdlatul Ulama, PKB is described as a "nationalist Muslim party."

PKS – Partai Keadilan Sejahtera (Prosperous Justice Party); historically the most strongly Islamist of the mainstream Muslim parties; has moved to a somewhat more nationalist position in recent years.

PLN – Perusahaan Listrik Negara; Indonesia's state electricity provider.

PNI – Partai Nasional Indonesia (Indonesian National Party; sometimes also styled "Indonesian Nationalist Party" in English); a name used by a succession of nationalist parties, beginning with the original version founded by Sukarno in 1927.

PPATK – Pusat Pelaporan dan Analisis Transaksi Keuangan (Financial Transaction Reports and Analysis Center).

PPP – Partai Persatuan Pembangunan (United Development Party); originally a New Order-era umbrella group for Muslim parties; retains a Muslim ethos but has moved towards a more nationalist position.

Priyayi – Originally the Javanese nobility; associated in its lowest levels with semi-hereditary village administrative roles.

PSBB – Pembatasan Sosial Berskala Besar ("Large-Scale Social Restrictions"); the main measure adopted in outbreak management during the Covid-19 pandemic in Indonesia.

Reformasi – The Reform period that followed the end of Suharto's New Order period in 1998 as Indonesia moved to embrace democracy.

SBY – Commonly used abbreviation for the name of Jokowi's predecessor, Susilo Bambang Yudhoyono.

SEZ – Special Economic Zone.

SI – Sarekat Islam; one of the first Indonesian mass political organizations; key during the early nationalist movement.

Sumpah Pemuda – "Youth Pledge" of 1928; a key early formulation of Indonesian nationalism and national identity.

Trisakti – A Sukarno coinage meaning "Three Sacred Forces," referring to the idea of sovereignty, independence, and national character as key to Indonesian nationalism; cited by Jokowi and linked to the Nawacita framework.

UGM – Gadjah Mada University; a long-established public university in Yogyakarta; Jokowi's alma mater.

Wong cilik – "The little people," a Javanese term originally referring to the commoners of traditional society; today widely used in political discourse to refer to the working classes, or simply "average people."

Select Bibliography

Abdurakhman, Hasanudin. *Melawan Miskin Pikiran*. Bandung: Penerbit Nuansa, 2016.

Achroni, Keen. *Jokowi Memimpin dengan Hati*. Yogyakarta: Ar-Ruzz Media, 2018.

Adnan, Mubeen. "Foreign Policy and Domestic Constraints: A Conceptual Account." *A Research Journal of South Asian Studies* 29, no. 2 (2014).

Almuttaqi, Ahmad Ibrahim. *Jokowi's Indonesia and the World*. Singapore: World Scientific, 2020.

Ambarita, Domu D. *Jokowi Spirit Bantaran Kali Anyar*. Jakarta: Elex Media Komputindo, 2012.

Bojang, Alieu S. "The Study of Foreign Policy in International Relations." *Journal of Political Sciences & Public Affairs* 6, no. 4 (2018).

Bramantio et al. eds. *Urban dalam Wacana: Kesehatan, Budaya, dan Masyarakat*. Surabaya: Fakultas Ilmu Budaya Universitas Airlangga, 2013.

Buchori, Muchtar. *Indonesia Mencari Demokrasi*. Yogyakarta: Insist Press, 2005.

Bunnell, Tim, Rita Padawangi, and Eric C. Thompson. "The politics of learning from a small city: Solo as translocal model and political launch pad." *Regional Studies* 52, no. 8 (2018).

Cekdin, Cekmas and Taufik Barlian. *Transmisi Daya Listrik*. Yogyakarta: Andi Publisher, 2013.

Chng, Nancy and Richard Borsuk. *Liem Sioe Liong's Salim Group: The Business Pillar of Suharto's Indonesia*. Singapore: ISEAS Publishing, 2014.

Cribb, Robert and Colin Brown. *Modern Indonesia: A History Since 1945*. London: Longman, 1995.

de Soto, Hernando. *Masih Ada Jalan Lain: Revolusi Tersembunyi di Dunia Ketiga.* Jakarta: Yayasan Obor, 1991.

Elson, R. E. *Suharto: A Political Biography.* Cambridge: Cambridge University Press, 2001.

Endah, Alberthiene. *Jokowi Memimpin Kota Menyentuh Jakarta.* Solo: Metagraf, 2012.

———. *Jokowi Perjalanan Karya bagi Bangsa Menuju Cahaya.* Solo: Tiga Serangkai, 2018.

Evans, Kevin. *Guide to the 2019 Indonesia Elections.* Melbourne: The Australia-Indonesia Centre, 2019.

Gamble, Andrew. *Politics: Why It Matters.* Cambridge: Polity Press, 2019.

Gunarjo, Nursodik. *Nawacita Meretas Indonesia Maju.* Jakarta: Kominfo, 2016.

Hadimuljono, Basuki. *Infrastruktur Meningkatkan Daya Saing.* Jakarta: Kementerian PUPR, 2017.

Hamid, Abdul. "Jokowi's Populism in the 2012 Jakarta Gubernatorial Election." *Journal of Current Southeast Asian Affairs* 33, no. 1 (2014).

Haryatmoko. *Etika Politik dan Kekuasaan.* Jakarta: Penerbit Buku Kompas, 2003.

Hidayat, Arif. *Keajaiban Doa Ibu.* Jakarta: Penerbit Al-Maghfirah, 2013.

Holsti, Kalevi. *International Politics: A Framework for Analysis.* 3rd edn. Englewood Cliffs, NJ: Prentice Hall, 1997.

Ihsan, A. Bakir. *Etika dan Logika Berpolitik.* Bandung: Remaja Rosdakarya, 2009.

Irawanto, Budi. "Young and Faithless: Wooing Millennials in Indonesia's 2019 Presidential Election." *ISEAS Perspective 2019*, no. 1 (2019).

Judisseno, Rimsky K. *Aktivitas dan Kompleksitas Kepariwisataan.* Jakarta: Gramedia Pustaka Utama, 2017.

Junef, Muhar. "Sengketa Wilayah Maritim di Laut Tiongkok Selatan." *Jurnal Penelitian Hukum De Jure* 18 (2018).

Kementerian Pariwisata. *Kebijakan Pengembangan Destinasi Pariwisata Indonesia 2016–2019.* Jakarta: Kementerian Pariwisata, 2016.

King, Dwight Y. trans. *The White Book on the 1992 General Election in Indonesia.* Singapore: Equinox Publishing, 2010.

Kumolo, Tjahjo. *Nawa Cita untuk Kesejahteraan Rakyat Indonesia.* Jakarta: Penerbit Buku Kompas, 2017.

Mahardi, Dedi. *Indonesia Butuh Jokowi.* Jakarta: Buana Ilmu Populer, 2018.

Majeed, Rushda. "Defusing a Volatile City, Igniting Reforms: Joko Widodo and Surakarta, Indonesia, 2005–2011." Princeton University, 2012.

Marham, Idrus. *Keutamaan Jokowi: Studi Kepemimpinan Nasional dalam Perspektif Kesinambungan Pembangunan*. Bekasi: Penjuru Ilmu, 2017.

Mas'udi, Wawan and Akhmad Ramdhon. *Jokowi: dari Bantaran Kalianyar ke Istana*. Jakarta: Gramedia Pustaka Utama, 2018.

McCormick James M. ed. *The Domestic Sources of American Foreign Policy: Insights and Evidence*. Maryland: Rowman & Littlefield, 2012.

Mulder, Niels. *Ruang Batin Masyarakat Indonesia*. Yogyakarta: LKiS, 2000.

Nawacita Institute. *Wujud Kerja Nyata*. Jakarta: Republika, 2017.

Nugrahanto, Asita D. K. Anton. *Sekelumit Kisah Si Tukang Blusukan*. Yogyakarta: Kana Media, 2014.

Nurulloh. *Presiden Jokowi Harapan Baru Indonesia*. Jakarta: Elex Media Komputindo, 2004.

Panduwinata, Fitrianidan Vido Chandra. *Analisis Kinerja Kemen-terian Luar Negeri Indonesia (2015–2018)*. CSIS Working Paper Series: WPSINT-3/2018.

Penders, C. L. M. *The West New Guinea Debacle: Dutch Decolonisation and Indonesia, 1945–1962*. Adelaide: Crawford House, 2002.

Power, Thomas P. "Jokowi's Authoritarian Turn and Indonesia's Democratic Decline." *Bulletin of Indonesian Economic Studies* 54, no. 3 (2018).

Prasodjo, Darmawan. *Jokowi Mewujudkan Mimpi Indonesia*. Edited by Trias Kuncahyono. Jakarta: Gramedia Pustaka Utama, 2020.

Qusyairi, Mukti Ali. *Jalinan Keislaman, Keumatan, & Kebangsaan: Ulama Bertutur tentang Jokowi*. Jakarta: Republika, 2018.

Ricklefs, M. C. *A History of Modern Indonesia since c.1200*. 3rd edn. Basingstoke: Palgrave, 2012.

Risse-Kappen, Thomas. "Public Opinion, Domestic Structure, and Foreign Policy in Liberal Democracies." *World Politics* 43, no. 4 (1991).

Rusdianti, Summa Riella and Cahyo Pamungkas. eds. *Updating Papua Road Map, Proses Perdamaian, Politik Kaum Muda, dan Diaspora Papua*. Jakarta: Yayasan Pustaka Obor Indonesia, 2017.

Safitri, Myrna A. *Menuju Kepastian dan Keadilan Tenurial*. Jakarta: Epistima Institute, 2011.

Setneg. *Laporan 4 Tahun Pemerintahan Jokowi-JK*. Jakarta: Setneg, 2018.

Solossa, Jacobus Perviddya. *Otonomi Khusus Papua Mengangkat Martabat Rakyat Papua di Dalam NKRI*. Jakarta: Pustaka Sinar Harapan, 2006.

Spillane, James J. ed. *Pariwisata Indonesia: Siasat Ekonomi dan Rekayasa Kebudayaan*. Yogyakarta: Kanisius, 1994.

Sujadi, Akhmad. *Tol Laut Jokowi Denyut Ekonomi NKRI*. Jakarta: Balai Pustaka, 2019.

Sukma, Rizal. *Islam in Indonesian Foreign Policy: Domestic Weakness and the Dilemma of Dual Identity*. London: Taylor and Francis, 2003.

Sulistyo, Eko. *Konservatisme Politik Anti Jokowi*. Jakarta: Moka Media, 2019.

Sunarya, Wahyudin and Giri Ahmad Taufik. *Pengantar Hukum Minyak dan Gas Indonesia*. Jakarta: Indorecht Publishing, 2018.

Suparno, Erman. *Grand Strategy Manajemen Pembangunan Negara Bangsa*. Jakarta: Empowering Society Institute, 2009.

Susantono, Bambang. *Revolusi Transportasi*. Jakarta: Gramedia Pustaka Utama, 2016.

Syafi'ie, Inu Kencana. *Sistem Administrasi Negara Republik Indonesia*. Jakarta: Bumi Aksara, 2011.

Syuropati, Mohammad A. *1800++ Peribahasa Jawa Lengkap dengan Arti dan Tafsirannya*. Yogyakarta: Kauna Pustaka, 2015.

Tanjung, Flores, et al. *Sejarah Pariwisata*. Jakarta: Yayasan Pustaka Obor Indonesia, 2017.

Thayrun, Yon. *Jokowi Pemimpin Rakyat Berjiwa Rocker*. Jakarta: Noura Books, 2012.

Tjiptoherijanto, Prijono and Yumiko M. Prijono. *Demokrasi di Perdesaan Jawa*. Jakarta: Pustaka Sinar Harapan, 1983.

Tri Sambodo, Maxensius. *Akses Listrik & Kesejahteraan Masyarakat*. Jakarta: LIPI Press, 2016.

Tyson, Adam and Budi Purnomo. "President Jokowi and the 2014 *Obor Rakyat* controversy in Indonesia." *Critical Asian Studies* 49, no. 1 (2017).

Ulfatin, Nurul and Teguh Triwiyanto. *Manajemen Sumber Daya Manusia Bidang Pendidikan*. Depok: Rajawali Pers, 2016.

Wahanani, Ipho Adhita. *Program Perilaku Hidup Bersih dan Sehat (PHBS) Menuju Solo Sehat 2010*. Surakarta: Universitas Sebelas Maret (UNS), 2010.

Waluyo, Dwitri and Endra S. Atmawidjaja. *Infrastruktur Meningkatkan Daya Saing*. Jakarta: Kementerian PUPR RI, 2017.

Wang, Chen, Peter W. Horby, Frederick G. Hayden, and George F. Gao. "A novel coronavirus outbreak of global health concern." *The Lancet* 395 (2020).

Widjojo, Muridan S., et al. *Papua Road Map: Negotiating the Past, Improving the Present and Securing the Future*. Jakarta: Obor Indonesia, 2009.

Wuryanto, Budhi, *Sukarno Muda*. Yogyakarta: Lokomotif, 2010.

Zaenuddin, H. M. *Jokowi Dari Jualan Kursi Hingga Dua Kali Mendapatkan Kursi*. Jakarta: Ufuk Press, 2012.

Index

39; and Independence, 30, 31, 34; and Pancasila, 34, 39, 45

Sukarnoputri, Megawati, 41, 81, 82, 166, 236; and PDI, 38, 41, 46; and PDI-P, 41, 42, 46, 84, 126; president, 42; vice president, 41

Sumatra: airports, 115–16, 134; electrification, 138, 141, 262; forest fires, 180; infrastructure drive, 241; road construction, 101, 132, 259; oilfields, 198; seaports, 195–96; tourism, 111, 114, 118, 120, 121; Trans-Sumatra Toll Road, 101, 132, 259, 262–63, 265

Surabaya, 79, 129, 130, 131, 132, 134, 269; bombings, 164–65

Surakarta (Solo), 13, 19–20, 79. *See also* Jokowi as mayor of Surakarta

terrorism: attacks, 164; counterterrorism, 165; laws, 165

Thohir, Erick, 203, 225, 234

toll road networks, 10, 101, 116, 128, 129–31, 132, 135, 169, 174, 219, 232, 242, 262, 265, 269; Jagorawi Toll Road, 130; Jakarta-Cikampek Toll Road, 101, 130; Trans-Java Toll Road, 130, 131, 132, 262, 265; Trans-Sumatra Toll Road, 101, 132, 259, 262–63, 265

tourism: advertising campaigns, 113; arrivals, 110–11, 118, 122, 268; development, 102, 105, 108–11, 112–13; "Four Pillars of Tourism," 111–12; halal tourism, 118; "New Balis" program, 115, 269 ; new destinations, 112, 113–15; "Ten New Balis" program, 111, 114–15, 118, 119, 121, 241; "Wonderful Indonesia" brand, 112–13

Trans-Pacific Trade Partnership, 143

Trisakti ("Three Sacred Forces"), 92, 95–96, 133; and Sukarno, 92, 95, 96, 133

Trump, Donald, 143, 234, 236, 241

tsunami: Aceh, 63, 168, 184

United Nations, 43, 186, 188, 214, 215–16

"Unity in Diversity." *See* Bhinneka Tunggal Ika

Universitas Gadjah Mada (UGM), 59–60; and Jokowi, 60, 109, 172

Uno, Sandiaga, 167, 203, 220, 225, 229, 254

village development, 128–29, 170, 171; electricity, 136; funds for, 170–74; reservoirs, 174–75; Village Forest program, 178–79, 269; Village Fund projects, 170–74

Wahid, Abdurrahman (Gus Dur), 41, 43, 74, 164; and NU, 41; president, 41

Widoyo, Joko. *See* Jokowi

Wiranto 164, 234; and Hanura, 164

Wiroredjo (Jokowi's maternal grandfather), 53

wong cilik ("the little people"), 23–24, 97; and Jokowi, 23–24, 73, 75, 77–78, 98, 149, 155, 249, 267

Yogyakarta, 33, 38, 57, 58, 133

youth: and Jokowi, 225, 226, 239

"Youth Pledge" (1928), 33, 226

Yudhoyono, Agus Harimurti, 145

Yudhoyono, Susilo Bambang (SBY), 13, 42, 203, 204, 207; and PD, 42; president, 89, 90, 101, 106, 107, 115, 126, 150, 151, 165, 207, 209, 265

Photo Credits

All photos not listed on this page are deemed to be the author's.

INTERIORS:

p14 wikipedia: https://id.wikipedia.org/wiki/Berkas:
Joko-FX.jpg; pp18, 124 Indonesian Ministry of Public
Works and Housing; p30 Public domain - available
Wikipedia: https://en.wikipedia.org/wiki/Proclamation_
of_Indonesian_Independence#/media/File:Indonesia_
declaration_of_independence_17_August_1945.
jpg; pp86, 104, 162, 182, 202, 238 Before Index: Press,
Media and Information Bureau, Indonesian Presidential
Secretariat; p142 Cabinet Secretariat of the Republic of
Indonesia

4 COLOR INSERT 1

pp4/5 Top https://commons.wikimedia.org/wiki/
File:Surakarta_Day_View.jpg / Bottom Indonesian
Ministry of Public Works and Housing; p8 Top Wikipedia:
https://commons.wikimedia.org/wiki/File:Bur_Gayo_
atau_Gunung_Dataran_Tinggi_Gayo.jpg; p15 Top
Wikipedia: https://commons.wikimedia.org/wiki/
File:FX_Hadi_Rudyatmo.jpg / Bottom Wikipedia: https://
commons.wikimedia.org/wiki/File:Gubernur_DKI_Bas
uki_P_%E9%90%98%E8%90%AC%E5%AD%B8.jpg;
p16 Bottom Solo Pos/Agoes Rudianto (as credited in
original book); p17 Top Wikipedia: https://commons.
wikimedia.org/wiki/File:Mayor_of_Surakarta_and_Vice_
Mayor_of_Surakarta_in_wayang_costumes.jpg / Bottom
International Institute for Sustainable Development; p18
Bottom Wikipedia: https://commons.wikimedia.org/
wiki/File:BatikSoloTrans.jpg; p19 Top Jakarta Regional
Government / Bottom Wikipedia: https://commons.
wikimedia.org/wiki/File:Jokowi_blusukan.jpg; pp20/21
Indonesian Ministry of Public Works and Housing; p22
Top Wikipedia: https://commons.wikimedia.org/wiki/
File:Prabowo_and_Indonesian_Pencak_Silat_Association.
jpg; p23 Top Indonesian Ministry of Agrarian Affairs and
Spatial Planning / Bottom Press, Media and Information
Bureau, Indonesian Presidential Secretariat; p24 Top Press,
Media and Information Bureau, Indonesian Presidential
Secretariat / Bottom Ministry of Education and Culture;
p25 Bottom Indonesian Ministry of Villages, Development
of Disadvantaged Regions, and Transmigration; p26 Top
Wiki: https://en.wikipedia.org/wiki/File:Sukarno_and_
council_in_front_of_Bandung_Court,_Bung_Karno_
Penjambung_Lidah_Rakjat_227.jpg / Bottom Wiki:
https://en.wikipedia.org/wiki/File:1955_Indonesian_
Election_Sukarno.png; p27 Top Left Wiki: https://
en.wikipedia.org/wiki/Sukarno#/media/File:Presiden_
Sukarno.jpg / Top Right Wiki: https://en.wikipedia.org/
wiki/File:President_Suharto,_1993.jpg / Bottom Wiki:
https://en.wikipedia.org/wiki/File:Suharto_resigns.jpg;
p28 Top Wiki: https://en.wikipedia.org/wiki/File:B.J._
Habibie_with_presidential_decorations.jpg / Bottom
Wiki: https://en.wikipedia.org/wiki/File:Golongan_
Karya_rally_1997.jpg; p29 Top Wiki: https://en.wikipedia.
org/wiki/File:Indonesian_Democratic_Party_of_
Struggle,_1999.jpg / Bottom Wiki: https://commons.
wikimedia.org/wiki/File:Abdurrahman_Wahid_World_
Economic_Forum_Annual_Meeting_Davos_2000.
jpg; p30 Top Wiki: https://indonesia.go.id/assets/img/
president/1544063001_mega.jpg / Bottom Wiki: https://
en.wikipedia.org/wiki/File:Susilo_Bambang_Yudhoyono.

jpg; p31 Top Wiki: https://commons.wikimedia.org/wiki/
File:Jusuf_Kalla_Vice_President_Portrait_2014.jpg /
Bottom Wiki: https://commons.wikimedia.org/wiki/
File:Ma%27ruf_Amin_2019_official_portrait.jpg; p32
Top Press, Media and Information Bureau, Indonesian
Presidential Secretariat / Bottom Press, Media and
Information Bureau, Indonesian Presidential Secretariat

4 COLOR INSERT 2:

p1 Ministry of Environment and Forestry; p2 Bottom Press,
Media and Information Bureau, Indonesian Presidential
Secretariat; p3 Top Press, Media and Information Bureau,
Indonesian Presidential Secretariat / Bottom Wiki: https://
commons.wikimedia.org/wiki/File:Jokowi-SBY.jpg; pp4/5
Wiki: https://commons.wikimedia.org/wiki/File:Kabinet_
Kerja_Jokowi-JK_2014.jpg; p6 Top Wiki: https://
commons.wikimedia.org/wiki/File:Finance_Ministry_
Sri_Mulyani_Indrawati_2016.jpg / Bottom Wiki: https://
commons.wikimedia.org/wiki/File:SD_meets_with_
Indonesia%E2%80%99s_Coordinating_Minister_for_
Maritime_Affairs_170607-D-SV709-107_(34355864283).
jpg; p7 Top Wiki: https://commons.wikimedia.org/
wiki/File:Secretary_Tillerson_Shakes_Hands_With_
Indonesian_Foreign_Minister_Marsudi_Before_Their_
Meeting_in_Washington_(34290251502)_(cropped).
jpg / Bottom Wiki: https://en.wikipedia.org/wiki/
File:PelantikanDjokoSetiadi2016.jpg; pp8/9 Indonesian
Ministry of Public Works and Housing; pp10/11
Directorate General of Human Settlements/Pambudi
Yoga Perdana; pp12/13 Antara/Ahmad Subaidi; p14/15
Ministry of Energy and Mineral Resources; pp16/17 Agus
Suparto; p18 Top Indonesian Ministry of Public Works
and Housing / Bottom Antara/Indrianto Eko Suwarso; p19
Top Indonesian Ministry of Public Works and Housing /
Bottom Indonesian Ministry of Tourism and the Creative
Economy; p20 Top Press, Media and Information
Bureau, Indonesian Presidential Secretariat / Bottom
Wiki: https://commons.wikimedia.org/wiki/File:Joko_
Widodo_and_Malcolm_Turnbull_in_Sydney_2017_13.
jpg; p23 Top Wiki: https://commons.wikimedia.org/wiki/
File:Joko_Widodo_and_Ma%27ruf_Amin,_Buku_Pintar_
Pemilu_2019_(Seri_Pertama,_2019),_p20_(cropped).jpg
/ Bottom Wiki: https://commons.wikimedia.org/wiki/
File:Prabowo_Subianto_and_Sandiaga_Uno,_Buku_
Pintar_Pemilu_2019_(Seri_Pertama,_2019),_p21_
(cropped).jpeg; p24 Top https://commons.wikimedia.
org/wiki/File:2019_Indonesian_presidential_ballot.
jpg; p25 Top Wiki: https://en.wikipedia.org/wiki/2019_
Indonesian_general_election#/media/File:Pemilihan_
Umum_Indonesia_2019_170419002.JPG / Bottom Press,
Media and Information Bureau, Indonesian Presidential
Secretariat; p26 Wiki: https://commons.wikimedia.org/
wiki/File:Mark_Esper_and_Prabowo_Subianto_in_
Bangkok.jpg; p27 Top Wiki: https://en.wikipedia.org/
wiki/People%27s_Representative_Council#/media/
File:MPRDPRDPDBuilding.jpg / Bottom Wiki: https://
commons.wikimedia.org/wiki/File:Indonesia_DPR_
session.jpg; p28 Top Press, Media and Information
Bureau, Indonesian Presidential Secretariat / Bottom
Press, Media and Information Bureau, Indonesian
Presidential Secretariat; p29 Top Indonesian Ministry
of State Secretariat / Bottom Cabinet Secretariat of the
Republic of Indonesia; pp30/31 Wiki: https://commons.
wikimedia.org/wiki/File:Kabinet_Indonesia_Maju_1.jpg